Legerdemain

The President's Secret Plan
The Bomb
And What the French Never Knew

James J. Heaphey

History Publishing Company, LLC
PO Box 700
Palisades, New York 10964-0700

Published in the United States by
History Publishing Company, LLC
Palisades, New York

Library of Congress Cataloging-in-Publication Data
Heaphey, James J., 1930-
    Legerdemain: the president's secret plan, the bomb, and
what the French never knew / James J. Heaphey. — 1st ed.
    p.cm.
    Includes index.
    LCCN 2007934056
    ISBN-13: 978-1-933909-35-6 (hardcover)
    ISBN-10: 1-933909-35-8 (hardcover)
    ISBN-13: 978-1-933909-36-3 (softcover)
    ISBN-10: 1-933909-36-6 (softcover)

    1. Morocco—History—1912-1956. 2. Morocco—Politics and
government. 3. Espionage, American—Morocco. 4. United
States—Military relations—Morocco. 5. United States—
Foreign relations—1945-1989. 6. France—Foreign relations—
1945-1958.   I. Title.

DT317.H43 2007   964'.04
                    QBI07-600214

Printed in the United States of America on acid-free paper

9 8 7 6 5 4 3 2 1

First Edition

For Pam

Drawings by Don Reiman
Map by Pam Heaphey
Photographs by Jilly Hopper
and
James Heaphey

Contents

Acknowledgments

Without Don Bracken, Publisher, History Publishing Company, and Pam Heaphey, my wife, this book would probably not have been completed. And, if completed without them, it would have been of considerable less quality.

Don and I began looking at this project when it was about two chapters old. His confidence in the story and his constructive criticism were invaluable. Our frequent email correspondence—often daily—kept me motivated and focused.

Pam encouraged me to tell the story. Over the years, I have told her parts of it, and she has said "write it!" When I decided the time had come to follow her advice, she helped me with research and descriptions, read and critiqued drafts, and was always there with me.

Dr. Satrio Joedono, Lin Gall, and Glenn Gall carefully reviewed the manuscript. Their attention to detail in checking spellings of place names, suggesting changes in syntax, and bringing style considerations to my attention helped greatly in improving the manuscript. They also suggested changes in phrasing and ways to make the manuscript more understandable.

Tom Cameron, Senior Editor at History Publishing Company, designed the layout, selected the typeface, and gave me excellent editorial advice. All readers will appreciate his artistic touches, as do I. Jennifer Johanson was the final proof reader. Marcia Carlson was the indexer. Thanks to both for putting the final touches and polish necessary to turn my manuscript into a book.

James J. Heaphey
Williamsburg, VA
October, 2007

Author's Note

Legerdemain is a story of deceit involving once major powers fading from the geopolitical scene and two new powers emerging from World War II and now competing for global dominance in the balance of power. It is set in Morocco, North Africa, but extends into Cyprus and the Middle East. The political problems of the era are hauntingly similar to the problems the U.S faces today in that part of the world.

My mission, a secret role, placed me in difficult, and sometimes scary, situations where the U.S. practiced sleight of hand against the French in an attempt to extend its sphere of influence in the Mediterranean area.

We won. With a figurative sweep of the hand, Morocco disappeared from the French colonial system and reappeared in the U.S. sphere of influence.

Legerdemain is a classic title for this book because of the cunningly engineered transition in Morocco and because the term accurately depicts espionage as I experienced it—a morally ambiguous world of uncertain alliances and manipulated truth.

This is a creative nonfiction memoir. All of the public figures and organizations appearing in this book are real and their real names are used. All references to events, places, buildings, newspapers, and magazine articles are real. All descriptions of government security provisions are real. For their security, some characters appear here under pseudonyms.

This book could not have been written eight or so years ago because two major aspects of this memoir were highly classified secrets until the late 1990s.

If I say I went somewhere and interviewed someone, I really did. However, I might change the date on which this happened and some aspects of the context. I am unable to recreate the conversations word by word. I offer instead, realistic representations.

A few characters are composites of real people I knew and worked with. All of this creative nonfiction writing is employed to tell a story that is real and true in a manner appealing to the reader.

There is an apparent clash with the truth when I speak of live nuclear weapons at Nouasseur. I say they were there in 1953, maybe even 1952. In 1999 the *Bulletin of Atomic Scientists* published an article on where the atomic weapons were and when. The article was based on a Freedom of Information Act release. The report put in the hands of the *Bulletin's* editors was a pile of wrinkled paper with broad black markings throughout. In many cases the *Bulletin's* reviewing team just guessed at the locations and dates.

According to the *Bulletin's* article, full nuclear bombs arrived at Nouasseur in 1954. That, in itself, was shocking. Experts on nuclear weapons were in agreement that in 1954 we placed full nuclear bombs only at U.S. air bases in England. My belief is that full nuclear weapons were stored at Nouasseur in 1953.

No one disagrees that the storage places for atomic bombs, very specialized and highly unique buildings called Q areas, were in place on Nouasseur in 1952.

Medina.

Cast of Moroccan, Cypriot,

and

Egyptian Characters

Arafa, Moulay. Installed as Sultan of Morocco after Mohammed V was deposed.

Bey, Essad. Jewish Orientalist in Marrakech.

Didier, Pierre. (Pseudonym) Editor, *Le Petit Marocain*.

Didier, Mamouche. Pierre Didier's wife.

Dimitri (nom de guerre). Owner of Chez Dimitri in Ouarzazate.

Din, Mohi El. Former, now outcast, member of the military group that engineered the coup d'etat in Egypt.

Fulan, Si (pseudonym). The author's main contact in *Istiqlal*.

Glaoui, T'hami El. Berber leader.

Grivas, George. Greek army colonel, leader of EOKA.

Guillaume, Augustin-Leon. French Resident General in Morocco, 1951-1954.

Halima, Mina (pseudonym). Editorial staff, *Le Petit Marocain*.

Halima, Lalla. Mina's mother.

Isnard, Jacques (pseudonym). French intelligence agent operating undercover in Morocco.

Kittani, Abd El Hay. Respected religious scholar and leader of Zaouia Brotherhood in Morocco.

Krim, Abd El. Pioneer leader of resistance movements to colonial powers. Defeated Spanish and French forces in Morocco.

Lyautey, Hubert. First French Resident General in Morocco. 1912-1925.

Menasha, Moshe (pseudonym). Jewish businessman. Father of Mamouche Didier.

Menasha, Simcha (pseudonym). Daughter of *Moshe*.

Mohammed V. Sultan of Morocco until 1953 when deposed by French.

Sadat, Anwar. Minister of Public Relations, Egypt, after 1952 coup d'etat.

Zwina (pseudonym). Friend of Mina. Eventually joins *Istiqlal*. Is arrested by French authorities.

Groups and Organizations

Istiqlal (Freedom Party): The main political group struggling for the independence of Morocco.

EOKA: Greek-Cypriot nationalist organization that fought for expulsion of British Troops from Cyprus, for self-determination and for union with Greece.

Egyptian Free Officers Association: Clandestine group of Egyptian army officers who plotted and carried out the overthrow of King Farouk.

NATO: The North Atlantic Treaty Organization. Established a system of collective security whereby its member states agree to mutual defense in response to an attack by any external party on any one of the member nations.

MI6: British Secret Intelligence Service responsible for the United Kingdom's espionage activities overseas.

SAC: The Strategic Air Command, U.S.A.F., was in charge of America's bomber-based strategic nuclear arsenal.

Quai d'Orsay: The French Ministry of Foreign Affairs is located on the Quai d'Orsay, and thus the ministry is often called the Quai d'Orsay by metonymy.

UKUSA: An alliance of English-speaking countries led by the United Kingdom and the United States for the purpose of gathering intelligence via signals intelligence.

NSA: The National Security Agency is the U.S. government's cryptologic organization. It is believed to be the world's largest intelligence-gathering agency.

Q: One of the United State's highest security clearances, usually given for work with nuclear materials and for espionage on an enemy's electronic systems.

Medina: Native town and living quarters.

Hammam: Moroccan version of a Turkish bath.

Strategy Camelback: Secret strategy to forge an alliance with Istiqlal by providing assistance in their struggle against the French. Purpose: to be allowed to keep American air bases in Morocco after the French were forced out.

The Minaret:. Nouasseur Base newspaper.

Number Stations: send short wave transmissions of digits or letters intended for undercover spies in the field. Usually the transmission begins with a folk tune.

Zaouia: an Islamic religious school and army under the leadership of Abd El Hay Kittani.

Introduction

In 1952, the year in which this memoir begins, the United States and the Soviet Union confronted one another in a world-wide Cold War. I was a U.S. Air Force undercover agent in what was then French Morocco from 1952 to 1954.

The Mediterranean was a prime battleground. Economic and political disorder in Greece and Turkey after World War II were promising opportunities, if not dangling temptations. The Russians have long hungered for warm water ports. They backed a Communist Party attempt to take control in Greece and placed 300,000 troops on their common border with Turkey.

President Truman drew a line in the sand. He sent warships to the Dardanelles. The Russians backed off. He also sent economic and military aid to the Greeks and began a massive buildup of American military muscle in the Mediterranean.

The only way we could keep Russian troops out of the West German coffee houses and streets of Paris was with the threat of our nuclear power. The USSR conventional war machine far outmatched ours. It could count on huge reserves of its still young, combat-seasoned men under arms, pre-positioned war materiel still in good condition for combat, and relatively short lines of transport and communications. But we had the bomb and a delivery system that far outmatched what they had. In the late 1940s, Winston Churchill told the House of Commons that "Nothing stands between Europe today and complete subjugation to Communist tyranny but the atomic bomb in American possession."

Stalin, never known as a man who measured the ethical consequences of using a new weapon, called the atom bombing of Hiroshima "an act of superbarbarity." A few days later Stalin authorized a crash Soviet program to catch up. Trotsky famously said that Stalin's nightmare is that he might wake up one morning with less military power than his opponents. But Stalin had a way of making things happen if he was serious, because he had in his hands vast resources and in his heart pure ruthlessness.

When Truman made his commitment to keep Turkey and Greece out of Russian hands, the United States joined most of the European countries in a collective security plan called the North Atlantic Treaty Organization (NATO).

My home station was Nouasseur Air Base in what was then French Morocco. Nouasseur was legally a French Air Force Base that the U.S. Air Force used as a potential staging area for nuclear air strikes on the Soviet Union. There were no intercontinental nuclear-armed ballistic missiles in the early 1950s, not even on the drawing boards. The only way to strike the Soviets with our warfare trump card was from an airplane. At that time America and France were both members of the North Atlantic Treaty Organization.

The Cold War involved the world's impoverished countries as military sites and resource providers at the same time that most of these countries were undergoing surges of nationalism. French North Africa, a massive colonial block running 1,000 miles from Morocco in the west and through Algeria and Tunisia in the east, was one of the few remaining bastions of European rule, though each of these countries had nationalist forces armed and prepared to fight to the death for freedom from colonialism. If the nationalists in any or all of these countries were to gain control, they might forbid the presence of a NATO base on their terrain, or they might invite the Russians to establish a military base. Nationalist doctrine was considerably more socialist than capitalist.

A decision was reached in a highly-secure basement room of the White House—the kind of decision no one signs, stamps, or reads aloud, let alone releases to the media. Those gathered around the table nod. In this case, the nod established Strategy

Camelback. While official U.S. policy would be to work with the French as it always had, various American operations would be put in place to work secretly with Moroccan nationalist forces in order to win their favor and have their permission to maintain American bases after the French left. One of the operations would help nationalists organize strikes, another would train them in assembling and using explosive devices, and so it went. My operation was to provide information to the nationalists as they asked for it.

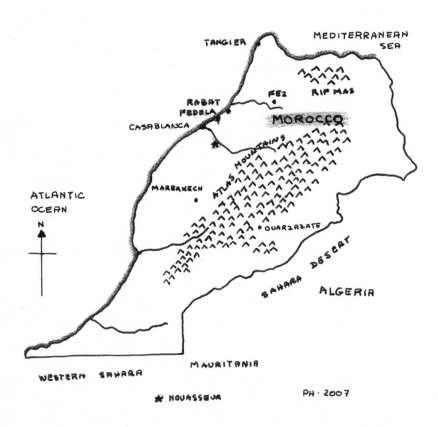

Chapter One

October 1952
Casablanca, French Morocco

We were surprised by one another. He by my youth. I by his size. The General had described him well, "he fills a doorway." But I was not really prepared to see that much bulk on a bar stool. The first thing he said to me was something like, "Tell me you're his messenger. Otherwise, this is absurd."

I tried to appear poised. "You're Bernard Hedgeworth, General Jackman's friend?"

He nodded and got off the stool. With a bottle of Chauvet red and a glass in one hand, he pointed to a corner table underneath an unraveling poster of a bare-breasted woman holding a bottle of *Apéritif Rossi*.

Hedgeworth had picked the meeting place, a café on *Boulevard de la Gare* in a mediocre Casablanca neighborhood. The kind of place where when you walk in you're overwhelmed by the stench of stale wine and pungent odors of hashish pipes. Nonetheless, you usually find, even in this kind of place, waiters gliding about with trays of glasses and bottles on upturned fingers as though they were serving four-star patrons.

I was uncomfortable. I had never met a Brit before and was a beginner in a field where this man was a master. The General told me he liked to drink, so I worked that angle.

After two bottles of Chauvet red, Hedgeworth was showing more tolerance, if not acceptance. My youth upset him, he said, because he worried about my capability to play, as he put it, "a seriously dangerous game in a Byzantine maze." But as we talked, mostly about the General, and drank, he seemed to gain some confidence in me; not a lot, just enough to keep him from throwing me back into the sea of normal life.

He had come to Casablanca that day from Cairo as a personal favor to my on-site boss, General Jackman. They knew one another from World War II when Jackman, as a young Captain in "Wild" Bill Donovan's newly-founded American spy organization, the Office of Strategic Services, was in London learning the ropes of spy craft. Hedgeworth was one of his instructors. They built a friendship from their mutual interest in, as Jackman had put it to me, "booze and girls."

"The British are still the best at this stuff," Jackman told me, shrugging his shoulders as a kind of regretful submission to fact, "and Hedgeworth has been one of their best for a long time."

There were two purposes for this meeting. One was to give me an opportunity to learn some things from an expert at undercover work with decades of experience in the Muslim world. The other was for him to give me a British secret service contact in French Morocco. It was not an official meeting. Jackman didn't even want me to tell my Air Force intelligence controllers about it.

"I'm here as a favor to Jacky," Hedgeworth said flatly. "Well," he added with a small grin, "there might be something in it for me . . . we'll have to wait and see. Tell me what you're doing and what you want and . . . how bloody old *are* you?"

"Twenty-two," I said. He frowned. My assignment, I told him, had to do with Truman's decision to secretly help the Moroccan nationalists. Our overt policy was to act in accordance with the alliance we had with the French as NATO partners. Our covert policy was to help the nationalists overthrow the French, hoping they would allow us to keep our Air Force bases in Morocco intact.

He shook his head, "You're operating out of a French Air Base, under NATO authority. Your cover is as editor of the base newspaper at Nouasseur. What happens to NATO if your game gets out? And how is an inexperienced kid going to keep it from getting out?"

"The General is hoping you'll help me keep that from happening . . . by talking with me about these things and providing me with a contact in Morocco, someone who can provide me with information that's not generally available. Another thing . . . we are not being entirely hypocritical. The U.S. State Department has been publicly critical of colonialism and privately having talks with the French about granting self-determination to Morocco."

"I'll try, kid," he said. "First, the overall picture. You guys have been passionately anti-colonialism since you booted us out. You're also passionately opposed to the Soviets. It's not just the nuclear stuff. You really don't like communism. It's anti-Christian and it's anti-capitalism. But . . . your best allies against the Russkies are European countries that are colonialists and are damned determined to hold on to their colonial possessions. The Russkies see opportunities in siding with the nationalist movements. It's consistent with their ideology . . . free the people. . . send the capitalists to hell. And, very conveniently, many of the countries where nationalism is on the go are strategically well-situated for their side of the cold war. The result? . . . A helluva challenging riddle for your policy guys. Kids like you can get chewed up being the trench soldiers in the short-lived policies those blokes dream up. If you do well, nothing you do will be recorded anyplace. Someone might remember and recommend you for an assignment. That's about as good as it gets for people like you. If you screw up, they'll either hide you or make an example of you to show how alert they are to incompetence in the ranks."

"That's cynical," I said.

"Bloody hell, kiddo, then tell me if you have an official document from your government or the Air Force or anyone assigning you this duty."

He had a point. Every job you held in the military was authorized by printed *Orders*. My *orders* placed me in Turkey doing communications tasks. "There are no orders that assign me here," I said. "I figured that was the way it had to be. How can they write *orders* assigning me here to this kind of job?"

"They could have written *orders* assigning you to Nouasseur as editor of the newspaper . . . No?" he said.

I nodded. I didn't really like what I was thinking.

"That's the way it is," said Hedgeworth. "You're not really here. If you screw up they say, "What's that name again, we don't have any records on him . . . or, I think that guy is AWOL from his assignment in Turkey.""

I started to ask him to elaborate because I was upset by his declaration that nothing I did well would become a line in a record. But I couldn't because he raised his non-drinking hand and said, "I'll tell you one about when Roosevelt and Churchill met with the Sultan here at the Casablanca Conference in forty-three."

"The American President and the Sultan made a markedly good impression on one another," Hedgeworth said. After they warmed up to one another, Roosevelt asked Mohammed V what he thought about the French Protectorate. The Sultan said it was no Protectorate. It was an oppressive colonialism. His major goal, he said, was to liberate his country. Roosevelt replied that the Sultan could have complete confidence in the independent future of his country and that in the meantime he should rigorously guard Moroccan mineral rights from exploitation by the occupying power.

Throughout this particular conversation, Churchill tried to interrupt Roosevelt. He coughed so fiercely that Roosevelt said, "Are you all right, Winston?"

"It's a new cigar brand. I'm not used to it yet," replied Winston. He continued to smoke it and cough violently.

Hedgeworth drained his wine glass and went on. "Do you ever think about the big similarities between you and the Soviets?"

"Well," I said, trying, "we're both born in revolution, intent upon spreading our values globally . . . huge land masses rich in resources. . . . Both of us got into World War II after surprise attacks . . . they were attacked by the Nazis and we got it from the Japanese . . . "

"And," he said, "you're both hopelessly idealistic."

"But our ideals are better than theirs," I said quickly.

He laughed. "Now to a contact for you. He's parading as Essad Bey, a Muslim prince these days. Ever heard of Jewish Orientalists?"

I shook my head.

"Jews who transform themselves into Arabs or Berbers," he said. "Bey's one of them. He knows everything that's going on, or he can find out. He's in Marrakech most of the time. Find Derb-el-Bir street." He took a blank card out of his pocket, wrote something in Arabic on it, then gave it to me. "Best way to get in touch with him is to get a coach and show this to the driver. It's the name of the street . . . Actually it's not much more than an alley. You'll find a small hotel of sorts there, but don't look for a sign; there isn't one. Ask for Abdelqadir. Tell him in French that you want to see Essad Bey and give him some money."

I looked at the squiggles on the card. "Be careful with these people," Hedgeworth said. "These are the guys you go to if you want a tank, or a virgin, or someone murdered. They'll do anything if the price is right. Abdelqadir works for Essad . . . and probably a lot of other people. Essad works for us now and then only because we pay him and because we threaten to expose him if he doesn't give us good information or do what we tell him to do. That's not a basis for trust."

"How will Essad know you recommended him to me?"

"Tell him you are the friend of a large British gentleman who enjoys roasted pigeons with pitchers of beer on the riverfront in Cairo. So your cover is as editor of a base newspaper. Not bad."

"I'm editor of the Nouasseur Air Base weekly newspaper *The Minaret*. There are no printing presses on the base that can handle it, so we have it printed in Casablanca."

Hedgeworth's smile was mildly approving. I was encouraged. "Not bad," he offered, "not bad at all. So you have to travel back and forth between the base and here, and you can go on all kinds of trips in Morocco and other places to write features and travel tips. You chaps are improving."

"It's even better," I said, feeling a fresh breeze of confidence. "I'm a correspondent for the European edition of *Stars and Stripes*, so I write feature pieces for them now and then."

He was grinning. I couldn't read it. Laughing at me? Impressed?

"What kind of difference do you think you can make?"

"I don't know," I said. "The General says that we're now superior at electronic intel gathering—you know, all our cabilities to spy from the sky—but we won't get far with just that. We must have human intel coming from ground."

"Yeh," he nodded, "Jacky learned that when he helped set up a network in the Mediterranean. That gave you chaps the ability to mess Rommel about with landings all along the coast. But the Air Force must have people with more experience . . . and other places to go, like the Army."

"We don't want to use Army people for two reasons. We're trying to show that we can work as a branch of the service separate from them, and the McCarthy Senate hearings on communists in American government positions make the Army look suspicious."

As for why I was picked, I told him I was in the Air Force Security Service. We listen to the Russians. I was in Turkey doing that when I was given this assignment in Morocco. In effect, Security Service was what the Air Force had by way of an intelligence division.

I was sent to Syracuse University for a year to study Russian. While there I was given an assignment to spy on two other people in my Security Service class. We all lived, learned, and ate in a section of dormitories and makeshift classrooms detached from the main campus. Our instructors were all former Russians.

All of us were undergoing security clearance by the FBI. Back at Brooks Air Force Base, where we had our headquarters, someone liked what I produced in my off-the-books job at Syracuse. When Security Service was told to produce a body for the job I now have, this person recommended me.

"Turf stuff with the Army," Hedgeworth said, rolling his eyes. "You guys still should have gone with their intelligence people. . . . Anyway how are you in contact with the Moroccan nationalists?"

"What do you know," I said, "about the *Istiqlal* Party?"

He grinned. "The only seriously organized group here. Work in three-person cells. Each member belongs to two cells . . . doesn't know anyone in *Istiqlal* other than those four people."

"I'm connected to two cell members," I said.

"Any idea of how high the cells are or what their function is?" he asked. "What you've done is good. But if you're on the inside of a cell that's a unit in the hierarchy dealing with propaganda, you can't make much of a difference with information about, say, French police operations. . . . Do you understand that?"

"I think so. If I've got the ear of a member of a cell that's low on the propaganda organization, he or she will have no way to cross the line and get my info to someone in the counter-police organization. But if I'm high up in the propaganda organization, there's a chance to cross the lines."

He nodded, indicating he was waiting to hear more.

"I don't know," I said, "I don't know how well placed my two cells are."

"Kid, that's good. Really good. You didn't try to shit me to impress me. That's a start. Now remember. To get the effect the Americans want, you've got to get bloody well high enough to be remembered as a swell ally when the French are gone and the new goons take over. The bloke you please in a minor propaganda or medical supplies cell won't be within miles of the ears of the new goons."

He laughed and waved to the waiter, threw some money on the table, and said, "Let's go. There's a show on tonight."

Outside he waved down a taxi. I wondered how he intended to get both of us in the back seat of an old VW Bug and found out that I would sit in front with the driver while he, almost entirely, occupied the back. I was surprised by how gracefully he moved his bulk around.

We went to *Hotel de Noailles,* where he was staying for the night, and took an elevator to the top floor. Hedgeworth led me to a door at the end of the hallway with an *Entrée Interdite* sign on it. He gave the lock a quick study, took out a tension tool and a pick, and unlocked the door with an ease that I envied. The first time I tried to pick a lock, I turned the tension tool too far and it stuck. An older member of the team I was with got it out, grinned at me and said, "Drinks on you tonight, kid."

After the door there was a metal stairway, another door at the top, and then we were on the roof. He led me over to a ledge, pointed down, and said, "You know you're in a French colonial city when there's this kind of difference in the lighting."

Below us was the tree-lined *Boulevard du Zouaves.* In both directions, there was a steady flow of amber headlights. The French considered amber a safer color than white for headlights though the overhead lighting was luminously white. On the other side of *Boulevard du Zouaves* was the *Bab el-Jedid* medina gate. It is actually a large open space in the walls named after a Berber Chief who attacked the medina with a Krupp assault cannon given to him by a German Count in the late nineteenth century. Explanations for the gift roamed from "a great and honorable Chief deserves a great weapon" to "thank you for the wonderful night in your harem."

A Frenchman driving down the *Boulevard* that night probably looked at the dim medina and thought, *There, but for the grace of a Christian God, go I.* The Arabs saw this contrast in another way. They believed the French were afraid of the dark, like children.

This is the way Hubert Lyautey, the first resident general of the protectorate, wanted it to be. His intent was to promote harmonious separation of social groups. The natives would be allowed to follow their traditions behind medina walls. The

French would live and follow their traditions in *nouveaux villes* built around medinas. Those natives who wanted to work in *nouveaux villes* could do so, provided they returned to their medina after work.

There were exceptions: wealthy Arabs shopped in the *grands magazines* and *boutiques*, dined in French restaurants, and drank mint tea at sidewalk cafés. Curious French walked the alleyways of medinas, bought souvenirs, ate foods prepared by street vendors, and enjoyed native music and girls. Moroccan Arab intellectuals were not intimidated by the French. They knew that Aristotle was being translated in the Moroccan Sultan's court when Oxford was still a muddy unlettered village.

"Before it begins down there, you should be told about a new chap in town," Hedgeworth said. "We think a top-drawer French secret service agent arrived in Morocco sometime during the past month or so. He'll be deep undercover."

"What do you mean by secret service," I said. "My training included a quick three hours on the French system, and my impression was that they had all kinds of secret service units; in the police, in different military branches, in various state agencies, and, the instructor threw in to lighten the load of making so many notes, 'maybe even at *Le Cordon Bleu.*' "

"The French are like the Americans," Hedgeworth answered, grinning broadly. "How's that Cole Porter song go, *Everybody's doin' it, doin' it, doin' it*. We're guessing he's military. Probably snooping around your air bases. The French are very suspicious of you chaps. They know you keep a lot from them. We think he's top-drawer. He'll be bloody good . . . and you'll never spot him if you see him."

He looked at me as though I, in particular, would not spot him. He seemed to be playing me like a yo-yo, showing me a little confidence and talking to me as a peer then treating me like the village idiot. I was getting angry. I wanted to tell him it's Berlin, not Porter, but instead asked, "How can you tell he's top-drawer?"

"His Numbers Station messages . . . Know what I'm talking about?"

I nodded. My trainers in San Antonio spent a day on how number stations send shortwave transmissions of digits or letters intended for undercover spies in the field. Usually the transmission begins with a folk tune. Anyone with a shortwave radio that can get upper side-band can listen. Knowledge of the encryption is needed to make sense of it. When you hear your folk tune, you get out your one-time pad.

"I know what a number station is," I said. "I don't know how his messages tell you that's he's elite."

"We've identified the person sending him the numbers. It's a Brit. The system being used is very sophisticated," said Hedgeworth.

"Where's the Brit located" I asked. He shook his head and changed the subject.

"What will you carry?" he asked abruptly. "Do they let you have a weapon?"

"I've practiced with a number of handguns, ended up with a Browning."

"Okay, but also hide a smaller piece in an ankle holster. Sometimes they'll find the chest or waistline handgun and stop because they think that's it. If you like the Browning, you might go for a Walther PPK." He gave me another derisory look and said in a slow and stern voice, not unlike the priests' tone in the confessionals of my boyhood, "But be sure to practice with it. The smaller the pistol . . . the bigger the recoil."

He looked down at *Boulevard du Zouaves* and said, "You've got yourself into a bloody stew here . . . I wonder if Jacky knows how bloody complex it is. In Egypt it's simple, us against the Egyptian Free Officers gang. In Cyprus it's simple, us against the Enosis gang. Here you've got the French trying to hold on while the politicians in Paris are debating the morality of colonialism . . . the French military is bleeding dry in Indo-China. The Sultan is loved by the Arab masses because he supports nationalism and is hated by the French Resident-General for the same reason. The *Istiqlal* chaps are mad at the Sultan because he wants to get the French government out without violence . . . he wants French businessmen to stay. The Sultan's influence—at best—extends to the foothills of the Atlas Mountains in the south and the Rif mountains in the north where the Berbers are. When the Berbers local chiefs are united, it's because T'hami El Glaoui pulls them together . . . and the only times El Glaoui pulls them together is to attempt over-throwing the Sultan. The House of Glaoua and the Sultan's family have been in a permanent state of animosity since the Arabs invaded Morocco . . . nine hundred or so years ago. It's a mess."

"I know some of this," I said. "Are there divisions within the Arabs of any consequence . . . other than between *Istiqlal* and the Sultan?"

"I said it's a Byzantine maze, and that's what it is. Ever heard of Abd El Hay Kittani?"

I shook my head.

"He's a *Chereef*, a descendent of the Prophet. Heads up the local *Zaouia* Brotherhood. The *Zaouia* are highly respected religious scholars . . . they run the best Muslim schools in the country, and they command tens of thousands of mountain warriors. Kittani doesn't accept the Sultan's claim to being the final word on Islam in Morocco and has a lot going for him because he's considered to be the greatest religious scholar in all of Morocco. That's a continuing threat to the Sultan's authority. And there's a personal vendetta, also. About forty years ago, Kittani's older brother was flogged to death on orders of the Sultan because he refused to bow when the Sultan passed by him on horseback. I think the Sultan was around sixteen years old at the time. Kittani has at least twenty-five thousand cavalry under his command, and he's made it clear that he wants to restore honor to his family by killing the Sultan."

Echos of air-bashing helicopter blades interrupted Hedgeworth, then I saw them, five Alouettes hovering over the medina.

"They'll drop tear gas and cluster bombs filled with nails." Hedgeworth said. "The point is to scare and wound more than to kill. They'll also drop incendiary devices to get fires going."

I knew that the French unleashed these *ratissages*, "rakings over," in retaliation and supposed this one was for something that happened the night before. Six Foreign Legionnaires, stationed at the French garrison in Casablanca, raped two Arab women in the middle of a medina street in plain view. Justice was swift. At sunrise the heads of the six Legionnaires were seen mounted on poles at *Bab el-Jedid* gate.

There were cracks of distant rifle shots, probably desperate attempts by some of those on the ground; but the helicopters whirled away, apparently unscathed. Then jeeps, motorcycles, and troop-carrier lorries streaked through the gate blasting their sirens.

"Psych Ops," said Hedgeworth. "Puts the fear of anybody's God into them."

Puffs of light gray smoke rose from the medina; here and there I saw flames that looked like fresh-lit matches.

"They're going through neighborhoods hammering anyone they see," said Hedgeworth. "There are special clubs they use to inflict a bloody lot of pain on the victim. It's hard as steel at the end that hits the victim and flexible at the wrist end of the holder, so the hitter feels almost no pain as opposed to the person he is hitting. It's also understood by everyone that any resistance is silenced with a bullet."

"You suggested," I said. "the French police will be on to me in no time. How will they handle it, and what should I do?" I looked at him.

Hedgeworth shook his head. "It all depends, son, on who catches you and what their ambitions are. The French rule in Morocco is formally hierarchical and uniformly legalized. But in practice, it is localized and departmentalized. That is, one deals with a matter of espionage in different ways depending on the locality of capture. If the head of that locality is interested in promotion, he would deal with it in one way; if he is interested in some profit, he would deal with it in another way. You're too small a fish for anyone to profit from having you in a jail cell, so you'd be tortured to see how much you can tell them about bigger fish in your pond. They would make you hurt in ways you cannot imagine until you could barely say another word. Then, of course, they'd leave you to die in some dungeon."

"What should I do," I said. "Is there a way out? Lying to them, maybe?"

He looked at me compassionately.

"That's why they gave me the cyanide pills," I said.

He nodded.

It lasted an hour or so. When it was over, I saw more flames and heard masses of female wailing voices. I was shaken and said something like "Bastards!"

"No place for that, son," said Hedgeworth. "Don't get judgmental or angry; don't go looking for good guys and bad guys. Just do your job, best you can, try to be more clever, more ruthless and trickier than the guy working against you. That's all you can do."

I thought I should tell him that I was raised in a Catholic school, that I still believed evil exists. But I didn't think that would go over well with him, so I said nothing.

"When I give little lectures back in London to the new recruits," he said, "I tell them that's lesson number one. Lesson number two is that you never imagine that what you don't know about a person is consistent with what you do know, or that what is kept secret from you is consistent with what has been revealed to you."

I didn't understand lesson number two, but pretended to.

As though he had read my mind, Hedgeworth added, "You will." And then he said, "Would you be surprised to hear I know the code name of your mission to win over the Moroccan nationalists?"

"I guess not," I said. "The General would want you to know, I think."

"True. But I didn't find out from him or you, and I know."

What I was doing was not the only operation in *Strategy Camelback,* so the leak could have come from any number of sources. I did not know all the other operations, but did know the CIA had some Arabic-speaking agents, undercover in Casablanca, Fez, and Rabat running their own operations. I also knew that one of those operations was helping *Istiqlal* organize strikes by Moroccan workers. And another was training *Istiqlal* on how to make inexpensive explosive devices.

I often wondered how it all came together. Supposing the nationalists were successful, how would the new Moroccan government know what we had done with all these operations? How could they appreciate our help enough to let us stay? I had once asked the General about that. He said, "You know, war is a crazy quilt no one fully comprehends. What you do, if you're you or me, is do what you're told and hope it works in your favor."

I spent the night in Hedgeworth's hotel room and left early to catch the bus back to the air base. The last thing he said to me was that he had thought of a way I could be useful to him and that he would let me know when he wanted me to do it.

There was a bus that left at six—American airmen called it "The Morning After Express"—enabling those who spent the night in Casablanca to be on time for work. You knew the bus was late if it had not arrived before you heard the Muezzin's first of five daily calls to prayer from *The Minaret* at *Bab el-Jedid* gate—*"Allah is Great. There is no God but Allah"*—repeated over and over for two minutes in a sing-song that penetrated every corner of the medina and beyond.

The bus route had been planned by diplomats. The stop was close to the medina so that it would be unlikely for a French person to see a drunken American airman waiting for the last-of-the-night runs at ten o'clock.

Arab vendors seized the opportunity, hawking their goods at the windows of the bus, offering anything from yesterday's newspaper to "Pictures of my virgin sister, naked!" Even when the motor coughed diesel fumes and rolled away, they ran along waving their commodities with the persistence of hungry dogs.

The medina wall opposite the bus stop was gunmetal gray at that time of the morning. Originally the walls were built to keep enemies out; the French used them to keep people in. Some of the best Arab poetry translated into English was about life in a medina. My favorite was,

> *Medina*
> *Each stone is a book*
> *as old as fables*
> *Each street is a story*
> *as intricate as night*
> *Each house is a novel*
> *with pages gnawed by rats.*

We nosed into the traffic of *Place de France* along with Arabs on foot, on bicycles, and in mule-drawn carts on their way to work for their French masters. *Place de France* was the first sight outside this exit from the medina. By colonial intention, it presented a grand view of the city's largest skyscrapers and widest boulevards, easily seen even though they were the required distance from the medina. In the middle of *Place de France,* there were remains of what had been a dominating clock tower. Resident General Lyautey had it built in 1910 to symbolize French order and organization. It had been destroyed by shells from American battleships in 1942. The French tried to rebuild the clock tower, but every effort was sabotaged by Arabs who didn't really want to know what French time it was.

Water vendors were positioning their large brass jugs on street corners while workers were whitewashing over anti-colonial graffiti that had been posted the night before. The French liked doing things in white—perhaps because Casablanca means "White City." The French steamship line, *Paquet,* and *Air France* travel brochures said "Come to the city of white and blue." I submitted an article to *Stars and Stripes* titled "White City or White Elephant?" The French were, I thought, inordinately proud of Casablanca. In their way of seeing things, they had brought stunning European architecture, cobblestone squares, and tree-lined *ronds points* to a land of backward people and savage customs. The article was rejected.

I could see why the French thought that way. Morocco was a feudal society similar to what Europe was like in medieval times. The Sultan was both king and spiritual leader. He had a court led by a Grand Vizier. Below that were pashas and caids who were the equivalent of European dukes and barons. They collected taxes and maintained order with private armies. But the Sultan's authority only extended to the foothills of the Atlas Mountains. Beyond that were tribes, mostly Berbers, who did not recognize the Sultan either as king or as spiritual leader.

When Morocco was a French Protectorate, the Sultan's power was contained by the French Resident General, who represented the French government. The extent to which the Resident General actually ruled Morocco depended on the personality and style of whoever held the post.

Medina.

Chapter Two

Nouasseur Air Base
French Morocco

"Sounds familiar," said General Jackman after I told him about my meeting with Hedgeworth. "He treated me like that when he was one of my MI6 trainers. Hedgie's 'bout as subtle as a camel shoved off a rooftop."

It was hard to imagine anyone treating the general like that. He was tall, athletically built, and stood with perfect posture even when he was relaxed. His eyes were steely blue. He had high cheek bones, and there was not a trace of slack under his jaw. We were drinking Stolichnaya pepper vodka from his private, mysterious stock. No one knew how he got his hands on it. No one ever saw it going into his office. I thought he enjoyed maintaining the mystery. Outside his office, he barely drank alcohol at all. A little champagne at certain ceremonies; otherwise, he drank mint tea or soda water.

There was nothing on his desk except a scarred RAF clock. The desk was more of a nice memory than anything else. I never saw him work at it. The top was a richly-glistening walnut burl with fluted square columns. The desk had been his father's.

In addition to pepper vodka, there was another uncustomary pleasure in the General's office, the sounds of World War II pop songs. Jackman had the best British hi-fi equipment available and hundreds of records, from the usual well-knowns like Glen Miller and Artie Shaw to rare recordings of unknowns like Dave Brubeck, an army corporal who entertained the troops with a GI jazz quartet. The General knew I was a jazz fan, so the hi-fi was on during our meetings.

Otherwise, it was just another typical office of a high-ranking American military official. There were the flags standing behind the desk chair: an American, a French *Tricolore,* and the new NATO Flag, a white and blue compass on a dark blue background. The U.S. military chain-of-command was depicted on a wall with solemn head-shot photographs starting at the top with the Commander-in-Chief and ending at the bottom with the base commander.

"I want to underscore what Hedgie said about those Marrakech contacts," the General said. "Careful. Be very careful."

The General and I related to one another in various roles. Right now he was playing my big brother, Tom, worrying about my getting into something over my head. At other times, we had a rapport distinctive to people sharing a secret. Then there was the normal hierarchical deference which was not easy for me. I'd been raised in Catholic schools, but never scored above a "D" in Conduct on my report cards. Sometimes we kidded around, which I think was not easy for him. For the world outside the two of us, the General projected an image of vanity, pretending that he wanted to have a direct relationship with me so that I would run a picture of him doing something on the front page of every issue of *The Minaret,* which I did, in addition to getting his picture and name into *Stars and Stripes* now and then. I think the ruse worked, that everyone thought I was his unofficial press agent and that our meetings, like this one, were related to publicity for him and the base.

"Hedgie's as fearless as anyone I've ever known," the General said, "so if he says something's dangerous, you can be damn sure it is."

"May I ask you to tell me more about him?"

The General pursed his lips. He did that when he was wavering on a decision. "I think you should know," he said.

Bernard Hedgeworth was born in Egypt in 1898. His father was Administrator of the Ismaili Head Office for the Suez Canal

Company. When he was five, he went off to school at Victoria College in Alexandria, the only non-Middle Easterner in a class of fifteen students. The other students were sons of Middle Eastern kings, princes, and businessmen. The British establish-ed the College in 1902 to provide a British Eton-type education.

The College was closed during World War I because the Ottoman Empire, which controlled Egypt as a colony, joined the Central Powers, declaring war on Britain, France, and Russia. At the age of seventeen, Hedgeworth joined the 10,000 Indian Army troops who had been sent to Ismailia to protect the Suez Canal against an expedition of 45,000 Turkish Marines march-ing on the Canal from Beersheba.

The Suez Canal links two oceans and two seas—the Atlantic and Mediterranean via Gibraltar to Port Said, and the Indian Ocean and the Red Sea via Bab Al Mandab, and the Gulf of Suez to the port of Suez. It penetrates Africa and India from Europe in one twentieth of the mileage necessary and one-hundredth of the danger and risks than are encountered by any other route. It is a priceless asset for all who have access to it.

Fortunately for the British, the march from Beersheba was across almost 200 miles of the Sinai Desert. When the Turks arrived they were tired and short of food and water. It was not difficult to meet and defeat them.

There was another reason why the Turks were not for-midable at Ismailia. Their plan depended upon surprise. Lon-don had sent an officer posing as a camel driver to keep an eye on the Turks. He maintained radio contact with Hedgeworth's father so that the Turks' locations were known by the defenders of the Canal.

After the battle, the MI6 officer came to know Bernard and realized he had come upon a rare resource for intelligence activ-ity in the Middle East—a young man who spoke Arabic fluently, who had befriended future Middle Eastern leaders as fellow schoolboys, and who had not only courage but fighting skills as well; for young Bernard had impressed everyone with his ability to handle weapons. With permission of the father, the MI6

Officer recruited this young talent and sent him undercover to Beersheba. Bernard posed as a sheep herder providing food for the Turkish troops as he mapped the Turkish trench positions. The map was one of the reasons the charge of the Australian light horsemen at Beersheba in 1917 succeeded.

"That's how he started," said the General. "He never went back to school."

"I'm older than he was when he did that," I said, wondering if Hedgeworth lacked confidence in me for reasons other than my age.

"Don't get sensitive about any of this stuff," he said. "Hedge's had some rough times in his career, and his personal life's been . . . When the war ended they brought him to London for training. He fell in love. Got married. She left him after a couple of years when she realized that he would always be a field man. There are no good desk jobs in MI6 for those who aren't recruited on the campuses of Oxford or Cambridge . . . Another subject. I had a call from *Stars and Stripes* about you and an airplane."

"They want a feature on the B-47 that came in here last week," I said. "Actually, they're hoping I can go along on a training flight. They cleared it with SAC Offutt, so it's up to you."

The B-47, the world's first swept-wing bomber, was an engineering marvel. American designers had teamed with German rocketry specialists to produce a sleek, rakish killing machine that combined fighter speed with bomber power. It had six jet engines plus solid fuel rocket engines mounted in the lower aft fuselage that gave it a spectacularly steep climb angle and produced a vast smoke cloud and ear-cracking explosive sound. It also had an outstanding range because it could be refueled in-flight with a flying boom lowered by a KC-97 Tanker. Without refueling, it had a four-thousand-mile range.

The Russians couldn't match it, nor had they mastered in-flight fueling. Though their nuclear bombers were formidable— a turboprop bomber called "The Bear" and a jet called "The Bison" could reach targets in Western Europe and Morocco—

they were determined to match our in-flight fueling advantage. So the B-47 was surrounded by secrecy because of the technology. And for another reason.

During the first few years of testing, there were far more than the usual crashes and accidents. The three-man crews confronted more than three hundred gauges, dials, switches, and levers. It was known as "The Crew-Killer." Always reluctant to announce flight accidents, the Air Force threw an exceptionally thick cloak of silence over the B-47's first few years.

"Seems that something's been done to lower the flight risks," said the General. "Otherwise Offutt would never give a green light to go that public."

I thought to myself that the SAC masters at Offutt knew I would not be able to say anything if there was an accident while I was up there in the B-47. I was a well-contained company man. So, I wasn't convinced that the plane's safety record had improved. I also knew that the General knew these things far better than I. He was trying to hold down my fears of flying in "The Crew Killer." Playing Tom, again.

"Oh," said the General, "then there's another thing. Offutt wants you to mislead readers. Tell them that the Caspian Sea is as far as we can get with the B-47 even with in-air refueling."

"Because . . . ?" I asked.

We want the Russkies to think that our primary target is the complex of oil wells, refineries, other industrial plants, storage facilities, and transport nets there at the Black Sea.

"Okay," I said. "May I ask how far into the USSR mainland we can go?"

"I have no real idea," he said. "This is all experimental, hypothetical stuff. If the guys you worked with in Turkey have reliable information on the Russkies defensive radar systems and we can break them down, we might get pretty deep into there. Maybe send a bomb up the ass of a ballet dancer in Moscow."

"I forgot to mention," I said. "Hedgeworth says there's a new high-level French spy under very deep cover in town."

"OK," he said, as though I'd told him the dining hall hours had changed. "Now two more assignments. First, what do you know about the Air Force Blue Book?"

"It's a record of unidentified flying object sightings," I said.

"We've had our first UFO reports here at Nouasseur," he said. "Both during the past week. A KC-97 crew say they saw a circular light making passes at them. A few days later an F-86 pilot—you might know him, Bob Johnson—says he chased an object at more than 530 miles an hour for 30 seconds but was unable to catch it. To him it appeared to be the size of a fighter plane, but he didn't see any tanks or trails."

"Where do I fit in?" I said.

He explained to me that the Air Force had an official explanation for UFO sightings. According to that policy, UFO sightings were one or a combination of the following: a mild form of mass hysteria, an attempt by an individual to gain publicity, a form of psychopathology, or a misidentification of various conventional objects.

"Your job," he said, "is to interview the witnesses—I have them all quarantined in the security barracks on the strip—and write a report for the Blue Book that conforms to Air Force explanations."

"What happens to the witnesses?" I said.

"None of your business," he said flatly.

Actually I could guess the answer. They would be sent to Project Blue Book Headquarters, Wright-Patterson Air Force Base in Dayton, Ohio, for debriefing. While there would be debriefing, the real purpose of bringing witnesses to Wright-Patterson was to brief them on Air Force policy and to warn them about publicizing their UFO sightings. What was most important for General Jackman was to keep it all as quiet as possible. Considering what we were up to at Nouasseur, the last thing he wanted was to be descended upon by UFO cults from around the world.

The other assignment was a story on what the Aircraft Control and Warning squads were doing in Morocco. "What do you know about them?" he asked me.

"Not much," I said. "They're mostly a Georgia National Guard group working out of radio and radar sites in the mountains and in the desert. They listen for Soviet bombers. If they hear any, they radio early warning signals to the five SAC bases in country."

"I want you to do a story on the calibration teams," he said. They work in conjunction with a B-50 that flies routes likely to be taken by the Bears and the Bisons. The B-50 flies around the Atlas and Sahara, keeping records of their altitudes and azimuths. Those records are compared to what was picked up during the times of the flights by the AC&W units. Calibration involves identifying blind spots and finding where to place new AC&W units to fill the gaps."

"I would have thought this would be too classified for publication," I said.

The general grinned. "Hell, we want the Russians to know what we're doing—or to think they do. I'll tell you what to write."

Teueir to Erfoud.

Heaphey and typesetters working on *The Minaret*.

Nouasseur Air Base Dallas Hut (living quarters). Quonset Huts (offices).

Chapter Three

Ain Diab
A Neighborhood in Casablanca

"My wife and family, they only know about my printing business," said Pierre. "It's probably not necessary to mention . . . but you might otherwise be surprised by some of the things you hear from my wife's sister."

Pierre Didier was driving me to his home for dinner and to stay overnight. He was the owner of *Imprimerie Maroprint*, a printing establishment, and editor of *Le Petit Marocain, Maroprint's* major publication; he was a small, trim man who wore his hair swept dramatically straight back from his temples. It would not be an exaggeration to say he resembled Rudolph Valentino, except he walked with a pronounced limp, and often used a cane.

Le Petit Marocain, a pro-French daily newspaper, was published in French and Arabic. The French version had a circulation of around 150,000. The Arabic version had a circulation of around 20,000. My newspaper, *The Minaret,* was typeset and printed at Didier's facilities. Typesetting involved placing individual letter-faces next to one another with tweezers. When a page had been laid out, letter by letter, word by word, the typeface was inked and a sheet of newsprint rolled against it, producing a proof that was read and edited. The corrected proof was given to the typesetters who did their best to follow the suggestions. The second proof was then edited—sometimes it was necessary to go on to third and fourth proofs before the typeset was ready to be run against the paper that would end up in readers' hands.

None of the typesetters at *Imprimerie Maroprint* spoke or read English, so proofreading for spelling was not easy. It was done by reading the text backwards so that your concentration was on the individual word rather than its context. I proofread for content. A young Berber woman, Mina Halima, fluent in Arabic, French, and English, proofread for spelling. She was a granddaughter, probably one of hundreds, of the legendary Berber Chief, T'hami El Glaoui, who ruled, as much as anyone could, the Berber tribes in the High Atlas Mountains.

Pierre had not told me he married into a wealthy Jewish family, so I wasn't prepared for his house in the luxurious beach suburb of *Ain Diab*, where residences were surrounded by walls draped in hedges of bougainvillea, jasmine, honeysuckle, and roses. Pierre's home was a large, brown-stucco building surrounded by grandly spreading palm trees and flower gardens. I didn't know that beyond the trees behind his house was a mansion belonging to his wife's family. There was a haunting flowery and saltwater scent when I opened the car door.

We entered Pierre's home by one of several side doors into a closely-beamed, high-ceilinged room with an opening to a vestibule at one end and a fireplace at the other. Simple white walls were decorated with geometrically designed Moroccan rugs, elaborately etched brass trays, and large mirrors that reflected lighting from candles on brass candlesticks of varying heights.

I had not seen the woman wearing a red caftan standing by the fireplace until Pierre said, "Mamouche," and she approached us, "may I present my colleague, Monsieur James. James," he said to me, "here is my wife, Mamouche."

She was a small, rather thickly built woman whose large nose imposed ungenerously on what was otherwise a pleasant face. Her perfume was too sweet for me, probably perfect for Pierre. She smiled warmly and spoke English, although it appeared difficult for her. "Monsieur James," she said, extending her hand for me to kiss, "we are so pleasured to welcome you in our home."

Seeing Pierre standing next to her, one arm around her waist, the other leaning heavily on his cane, I was more aware of his being lame than I'd been at *Imprimerie Maroprint* where he moved in confident strides between typesetting desks and offset presses, usually with a glass of mint tea in his hand.

Mamouche took my right hand in both of hers and led me to a hassock covered in jewel-like silks. A problem for me. My body is well over six feet three, most of which is taken by stubbornly inflexible legs. Sitting almost on the floor Moroccan style was uncomfortable and embarrassing. How can one look good when his knees are inches from his ears?

I was temporarily saved from humiliation by the entrance of a tall black man dressed impeccably in turban, dark band collar shirt, and white suit. Pierre said, "Here is Hajji who takes good care of us. He wonders what he can bring you to drink, James."

Hajji was the first Harratine, pitch-black skinned descendants of slaves from West Africa and the Sudan, I had ever seen. Their intense color is both a disadvantage and an advantage. Arabs and Berbers shun them because of it, but also are intimidated by them because pitch-black skin is associated with evil spirits called jinn. Harratines predominate in mystical professions such as conjurer, spiritual healer, and seller of secret potions.

I was tempted to make a joke like "Oh, bring me one of your special concoctions, Hajji," but wisely bypassed that sparkle of boyish humor.

Pierre misunderstood the reason for my pause. "We have alcohol here, James, if that would be your choice. Jews have much in common with Muslims, but not the avoidance of alcohol."

I wondered if he had any idea of how overwhelmed I was by all of this. "Scotch on the rocks, *s'il vous plait*," I said. Hajji backed away in long strides, bowing, but really in command of the room. He had what talent scouts search for: presence.

To avoid sitting down, I pretended to have an interest in the ornate wood molding on the opening that led to the vestibule. I walked over to it. I saw a circular staircase. And then I saw *her*.

She was descending the staircase in denims and a light blue diaphanous caftan buttoned only in the middle of her firm upraising breasts. Her navel was exposed, as was much of the rest of her. She wore her long dark hair parted in the middle so that it fell forward framing a small brown face with full lips and high cheekbones. Her nose was also Semitic; but with her, it was an enhancement. She came down the stairs and entered the room with an air of easy nonchalance, as though she might just keep on going right past us.

"James," said Pierre, "here is Simcha, Mamouche's sister."

Her eyes swept over my body, giving the impression that it was the first time she'd been made aware there was anyone in the room other than herself. She held out her hand and said softly, *"Enchanté, monsieur."* I kissed her hand lightly while searching for judgments in her eyes and mouth, both of which were inscrutable. I silently vowed to improve my French and hated the thought of exposing my gracelessness at sitting almost on the floor.

"Monsieur James, do you know *tagine?*" Mamouche asked at the dinner table. It is . . . Pierre . . . *quoi?*"

"It is stew," Simcha volunteered playfully. "Very Moroccan. Very spicy. Along with couscous, it is one of the few things rich and poor Moroccans share."

Mamouche frowned.

We were sitting on low divans at a carved cedar table. Candles on floor stands provided soft lighting. The first dish was already on the table; it looked like steamed eggplant in sauce. I didn't like it but tried to sound sincere in my praise, which was a problem because I couldn't remember if the right word was *délicieux* or *délicieuse, bon* or *bonne,* and I knew I would mispronounce whatever I tried, so I said, "Very good."

A short and round Harratine woman . . . wearing a granny-style dress with a yoked bodice, removed the eggplant dishes. Hajji placed in front of Pierre a large earthenware pot that was shaped like a volcano. Pierre removed the lid, releasing spicy and steamy aromas of lamb and vegetables. *"Voilà,* James," he said, *"tagine."* Hajji did no more than take the lid from Pierre and snap himself into a standing position, but he stole the scene.

While we were eating the eggplant, Simcha had talked about French colonialism, mocking the claim that they were carrying out *"la mission civilatrice."* The real mission, she said, is to make sure no one interferes with French businessmen stealing Morocco's resources and dumping fabrics, china, and furniture here that they can't sell in France or Europe, as the British did in your country when you were a colony."

As Pierre allotted *tagine* on our plates, he said, "I should have given you a warning. Simcha studied at the American University of Beirut where she discovered that the Lebanese are better off without the French there."

"What are they stealing?" I asked Simcha.

"The *they* is CFAO, a French conglomerate," she said, "They take phosphates, lots of phosphates, because this country is phosphate rich. Also iron, lead, zinc, manganese, cobalt. They own livestock farms, fisheries . . . they have dozens of fish canning shops ten miles from here . . . they take anything they can get their hands on . . . they pay slave wages to the Moroccans who do all the work. The *they* is also the French government. They force Moroccans to enlist in their armies, to march and die but never get promoted. If they come home alive, they come home to nothing. No benefits . . . unless working like a slave is a benefit. And all of this gets praised in newspapers like Pierre's."

There was an awkward silence.

"What was your major at AUB?" I asked.

"Political science, economics" she said, "and freedom."

Mamouche laughed uncomfortably, "Simcha thinks Morocco is . . . like *grande* women's prison."

"And you?" I asked.

"Maybe . . . but it's not the French who do this, it's the Muslims. For example, a Moroccan man can marry any woman of the Book, which includes Jews and Christians. Muslim women are not allowed to marry a non-Muslim man."

"Simcha," Pierre said, "is not telling you that the French offer Arab women and children something better than they have ever had. For example, real education. The Muslims' idea of education is to confine children in tiny windowless rooms where they sit swaying back and forth endlessly repeating verses from the Koran while the preceptor flicks at them with his twig to hold their attention. And . . . what about the roads? The French have connected many parts of the country with roads built at great expense."

Simcha laughed. "Now the French are playing the British . . . the white man's burden? Pierre does not tell you that the road signs on these new *routes* are in French. Not one in Arabic."

Pierre went on, "When the French came in 1912, they identified this country's major cultural and architectural treasures—shrines, monuments, cities. Then they brought in art historians and urban planners who wrote out preservation strategies. No new buildings were to be built in the historic medinas. And all repairs had to be done according to standards that preserved the architectural integrity of the original structures. The new cities were separated from the native quarters by building-free zones. Modern things, like gasoline stations, could be built only in the new cities."

"So." I said, "the French showed respect for the Moroccan culture and history . . . ?" I was somewhat surprised by Pierre's enthusiasm for the Protectorate.

"Oh yes," said Simcha, "by cunning colonial design. The French believed that Morocco would be easier to colonize if Moroccans did not really notice that they were being colonized.

They learned from their experience in Algeria and Tunisia that the more obtrusive the colonial interventions in indigenous daily life, the greater the resistance to colonization from the local people."

Mamouche passed on to me the plate of *tagine* Pierre had handed to her. He was serving slowly, torn between his defense of the Protectorate and his role as host. "I hope you enjoy our food," she said. And then added, "Simcha, she sees *ruse* in everything. She has belief that the Protectorate keeps *les Arabes* in their Medinas *parce que*. Pierre . . . *parce que . . . ?*"

"Because," Pierre said, "it is easier to control them there. When they want to, according to Simcha, they can surround a medina with guns."

It seemed obvious to me that Simcha was right. But I didn't fully understand what was going on over the heady *tagine* aromas, so I said nothing. The *tagine* itself was unambiguously delicious.

Simcha was unwilling to let it go. "How can you be so blind, Pierre. This French respect for Moroccan culture is a mask for keeping the Moroccans powerless. *Mon Dieu!* They didn't allow Moroccans to use advertisements or glass windows; they restrict the use of electricity in the medinas. Why? To keep the locals from being anything but dependent upon their French lords. The only way the Moroccans can compete with the French is by developing their own industries. Without electricity . . . ? *C'est impossible!* It's French diabolical cleverness."

I looked at Mamouche and said, "May I ask, are you with Pierre or in between him and your sister?"

She stirred her fork and said, "I believe things are not as bad as Simcha tells you. And not as good as the French say they are."

We returned to the previous room for dessert and brandy. My legs were numb. I was glad to make the move. Two men were standing by the fireplace. Pierre introduced them as "My father-in-law Moshe Menasha and *Chereef* Abd El Hay Kittani."

Moshe Menasha was short and large-bodied with a full beard. He wore a blue silk robe and a skullcap. Chereef Kittani had the white-bearded, blue-eyed head of an old Norse patriarch and wore a burnoose with white and black stripes. Was he the Chereef that Hedgeworth had described to me as a rival to the Sultan?

I had hoped to stay there on my feet talking with them for a while; but Hajji placed the dessert dishes on floor-hugging trays, and we were invited by Pierre to sit and enjoy. "Pastry crescents filled with almond paste," Pierre said to me. "with only a dash of hashish . . . very high quality."

Moshe Menasha grunted getting down to a hassock, but once there crossed his legs and appeared to be at ease. Overall, I thought he looked like a man who was quite comfortable with himself, in the best of ways. Kittani folded his long thin body effortlessly and sat in a lotus position as though born in it.

"James," Pierre said, "I have asked my father-in-law to tell you a little about his father and himself because I think you will enjoy seeing Morocco through his eyes, and you might find a place for it in your writing some day. Simcha is the best one to do the translating."

I wondered if this was his way of keeping Simcha editorially quiet.

Moshe Menashe's story began with his father Shlomo, who left Morocco by steamship for Brazil in the late nineteenth century, at the age of nineteen, along with fourteen other Sephardic Jews. Jews were making money trading on the Amazon River, and there was no work in Morocco. The fifteen young men had been schoolmates. Each of them took a book for Yom Kippur with them and they agreed to gather every year to celebrate it."

Eventually Shlomo Menashe and his friends were scattered up and down the Amazon, trading with one another. Some, who like Shlomo hired natives to work the rubber trees in the area, traded rubber collected as milky white fluid from the trees with others who had pots, pans, and other utensils. They stayed true to their agreement. Every year at Yom Kippur, they gathered someplace on the Amazon for three days. Local tribesmen who handled their boats would clear a place in the jungle and build a hut there. The Jews stayed in the hut for three days, saying their Yom Kippur prayers while the natives stood guard. During the nights, the natives lit bonfires and fed them until dawn to keep away wild animals and snakes.

Shlomo did well. He bought a rubber plantation and was joined by a woman, Massetta, who had been recommended by his Rabbi in Casablanca. It was an unsuccessful marriage. Massetta tolerated nothing about life in the Brazilian jungle and died of malaria a year after her arrival. However, she had born a child, Moshe.

One day Shlomo received a letter from his Rabbi about the French rubber plantations in Southeast Asia. Someone had smuggled Brazilian rubber tree seeds out of Brazil and gotten them to Asia, where the environment provided efficiencies impossible in the Amazon jungle.

Shlomo let the word get around that he was too despondent over the death of his wife to remain in Brazil. He would be willing to sell his plantation at a bargain price in order to take himself and his son back to Morocco.

A Portuguese trader from Rio de Janeiro took advantage of Moshe's predicament. Shlomo and Moshe sailed to New York city, visited with a cousin's family, and heard George M. Cohan sing "I'm a Yankee Doodle Dandy" on a Broadway stage.

Shlomo died when Moshe was nineteen, the same age his father had been when he left for Brazil. However, Moshe was anything but poor. His father had not reinvested what the shrewd Portuguese trader paid him.

The French were very capable engineers and reasonably effective in running mining companies, so they took full advantage of Morocco's mineral resources. They were talented as small fishermen, but going out to sea and making big catches was not their thing. So they were perfectly satisfied to let people like Moshe take that over.

Moshe went into sardine fishing. He bought a Danish fish factory ship—the first fish factory ship ever seen in a Moroccan port. Over the years he bought more ships, and his business flourished.

Simcha had minded her role. There were no side comments throughout her father's presentation. She had, as far as I could tell, translated his words and inflections accurately. When he was finished, she whispered in my ear, "I'll tell you something if you promise me that if you ever write about this, you'll include it in your piece. . . . There's more than a little hashish going into Europe with the sardines."

When Moshe finished, Abd El Hay Kittani asked Pierre in Arabic to ask me a question. "The *Chereef*," Pierre said to me, "hears that your new President Eisenhower has rejected the idea of limited nuclear war, that he will use nuclear weapons fully. No compromise."

"Yes," I said, "the President has ordered the country to prepare for nothing short of all-out nuclear war."

"Excuse me, please," said Pierre, "I think what the *Chereef* and perhaps all of us wonder is how such a completely terrifying war strategy could be even suggested. It's a scorched earth policy. All that is left of the world is scorched earth. Don't most American foreign policy experts advocate limited nuclear warfare?"

"They do," I said, "they recommend that we respond to any Soviet ground attacks, particularly in Europe, with as much nuclear weaponry as is needed to make up for the difference in conventional firepower between them and us, but no more than that. It's believed by many that this would be a sufficient deterrent to the Soviets. Mr. Eisenhower has rejected that approach. If we or our allies are attacked, we will respond with our full nuclear power."

"Wonderful," said Simcha. "The Russians can't reach the U.S. yet with their nuclear weapons, but can reach Morocco where you've got these deadly threats pointed at them. You're making Moroccans . . . *je voudrais dire* . . . seated ducks."

I lied. "We have the delivery systems in Morocco, but not the live bomb itself. It takes a lot of clearances by a lot of bureaucratic offices to send the components that make the bomb operable. Then there's delivery time and all the time it takes to rig a B-36 or B-47 with a deadly live bomb. The Russians know all this. They know that our Moroccan bombers are not a threat unless they provoke us. And, even then, they know it will take us three or four days to be prepared to respond from Morocco. I don't think that attacking Morocco is high on the Soviets' priority target lists."

The *Chereef* said something to Pierre, who then said to me, "What about this idea of massive retaliation to everything? Is it true what we hear, that the United States will respond to any provocation with a full-scale nuclear attack?"

"That's our policy," I said. "It sounds grotesquely brutal, even barbarian, but let me try to explain the situation as our President sees it. Given the Soviet intention to take over more and more territory, we can do one of two things. We can return our non-nuclear military strength to World War Two levels. This would cripple our economy and perhaps turn us into a military state. Or we can rely on nuclear weapons, which would be much less expensive. The President has chosen the nuclear strategy. But that is not effective unless the Soviets believe we will use the nuclear weapons, and use them massively. If they think we will give them a chance to retaliate to our attack, they are more likely to try a provocation, such as taking over West Berlin, as a risk worth taking. And a place like Morocco is more likely to be hit by them if they have a chance to retaliate."

I watched Kittani's face as Pierre translated. His blue eyes were fixed in a stare at me. He said something to Pierre.

"The *Chereef*," Pierre translated, "says that is very interesting, that your massive retaliation policy is good for Morocco. He also says something that I am not sure I can translate accurately. It is something like . . . Americans are much more clever with power than I thought."

Simcha said, "Everyone knows Americans have the best of everything it takes to build a very powerful military force. We grant that, and then point out that you are not cunning enough to know how to use all that power to your advantage."

As Pierre walked with me up the stairs toward the bedroom I would use, he said, "The *Chereef* hopes that he said nothing tonight to insult you. We all think of Americans as being very open people who enjoy a good argument. However, we do make mistakes, insulting without meaning to do so."

"I enjoyed the discussion," I said, "and was not insulted at all."

"*Mais oui,*" he said, "and that is one of the reasons we admire Americans."

I thought I'd like to hear sometime from him the reasons why they dislike us.

Lying in bed that night in one of the Didier guestrooms, I had to stretch my legs a lot to get relief from cramps. When my legs quieted down and I gave up hope that Simcha would come sneaking into the room, I went to sleep.

Chapter Four

The Road to Nouasseur

Simcha did reappear—the next morning—sitting in a sleek, very shiny, very red MGTD Midget roadster. The chrome gleamed. The top was down revealing glove leather upholstery . . . and Simcha. She wore white slacks with a peach open-collared shirt. It was a beautiful day. Pierre had told me at breakfast that she had offered to drive me to the base. *"D'accord?"* he said, barely concealing a grin.

"First," she said, as we backed out of the driveway, "I should have added something to my comment about the hashish traveling with the sardines."

I thought, *yes . . . I was waiting.*

"My father is a very decent man. He does a lot for people who need help. You've met Mina? At Pierre's office?"

"Sure," I said.

"Her mother Lalla would be destitute if it were not for my father," Simcha said. "Lalla helps him with the hashish. It's very simple . . . what she does. And my father pays her very well for it. He could get anyone to do what she does for half the price. He's doing this to help her live with some dignity. She can't do anything of any value in the market place."

"I understand," I said. "I was raised in a Catholic theology that doesn't put much stock in following conventional morality as though there's nothing else in the world. For example, I was taught that it is not a sin when a man who can't buy food for his children steals it. It was that sort of attitude that got us in disfavor with the rich Protestants . . . Tell me, was the Kittani man with your father *the* Kittani?"

"Yes. He does business with my father, and my father employs a large number of Kittani's followers."

Simcha then told me why she was driving me to the base. She wanted a job with *The Minaret*. "My father will be moving to Israel soon, and he expects me to go with him or marry a rich Jewish boy here. But I have another plan."

In Beirut she'd worked on the school newspaper. "I did everything from copy reading and layout to writing bylined news and feature stories. In my junior and senior years, I was a stringer for AP and UPI. I've got clips. There was an American on the paper. She's now with *TIME* magazine in New York . . . Ruth says that if I get a little more experience on English language newspapers or magazines, she can get me a job in New York. . . . You don't have to pay me anything. I can help you with the non-English speaking typesetters. I can typeset myself . . . I can type. I know layout. I'll do whatever helps."

She was talking fast and driving faster, gesturing with quick hand movements to emphasize her points. Fortunately the road from Casablanca to Nouasseur is a perfectly straight road because about a hundred yards ahead of us, a sheep herder was casually coaxing his flock across it.

Simcha's reaction time was rather good. She braked without ejecting us through the front window. Both of us took it in stride. That's the way it was with driving in French Morocco. Everyone drove at the highest speed possible in their cars, on their bicycles, or on their horses, camels, or donkeys. All of these modes of transportation—including walking, also—jumbled together, each person contesting for the straightest line between himself and his destination. One of the things discouraging automobile ownership in French Morocco was the accident insurance rates—the highest in the world.

As we waited for the herd to pass there were sounds of the engine purring, tiny bells clanking, and the distant shouting of four French Navy guys playing volleyball in front of an ancient Moroccan fortress that was used as a French Navy transmission station. They stopped shouting when they caught sight of us. I knew what they were thinking. The French military had still not risen materially or spiritually from the disgrace they had suffered when the Nazis—almost effortlessly—plowed them under and took whatever they wanted from them. Those four guys saw a trophy in the hands of an American airman—an unpleasant reminder.

The rank smell of sheep mixed curiously with Simcha's pleasant perfume and the car's exhaust fumes. I wished we weren't stuck there. I thought about her working on the paper. There was no question I could use her. If she were willing to work without pay, there was no doubt I wanted to jump at the offer. I was understaffed as things were. I needed more time to work undercover, and I wanted to add pages to *The Minaret*. What I didn't know was what the security problems might be.

"Simcha," I said. "I'd like to work this out with you. I need help on production—editing, layout and proofreading. You probably know all that stuff better than I do. I need a managing editor to see to getting the paper out so that I can have more time to pursue stories, especially those that take me out of town. In exchange I'll give you a continuing number of feature stories and a column. OK, so far?"

She said, "More than OK."

"I work in a bureaucracy," I said, "which is a place where people sitting at the top exist to give people like me approvals. I'll do two things to give them a sense of having a job. First, I'll get the Base Commander's approval. Then I'll get approval from the people in Washington who are in charge of all military base newspapers."

"That's a long time," she said, "*n'est-ce pas?*"

"No, if the Commander approves and gives me a high TWIX priority, I can get an answer in less than forty-eight hours."

"A . . . tweex?"

"That's shorthand for teletypewriter exchange service. It involves teletypewriters, transmission channels, and switchboards."

"I adore Americans," she said.

The sheep were clear of the road, except for one that dashed back and forth between the departing herd and the roadster until the herd was far enough away to make the game too exhausting. Simcha shifted gears, and we were off in a roar.

"Would it be all right to tell you how I feel about Pierre?" she said.

"Considering that you're coming to work on *The Minaret* and Pierre is the printer, I think I *should* know more."

"I live with Mamouche and Pierre because I cannot live with my parents' conservative Jewish traditions—I respect my parents, I respect conservative Jewish traditions, but I cannot live by them. Mamouche and Pierre do not live by them. I appreciate their letting me stay in their home. But what Pierre does . . . it is despicable. You can't publish a newspaper in this country unless it's pro-colonialism. Pierre used to be a man of respect, a war hero. I do not mind if one is not engaged in the nationalist movement; I am not . . . but to publish a newspaper that supports the protectorate. *Merde*."

Just ahead on our right, we were coming to a village where Arabs who worked on base lived in cone-shaped straw homes.

"Is this," Simcha asked, "what the French teenagers call *Petits USA?*" I nodded. She was referring to the village *souk*. It specialized in second-hand American goods, particularly magazines and shopping catalogs, like *LIFE* and *SEARS*, old calendars with American scenes, and secondhand T-shirts. French teenagers in the area were entranced by American popular culture. They listened to the base station's DJs, sang American hit tunes at their parties, jitterbugged awkwardly, and shopped at *Petits USA*.

Some parents came to *Petits USA* with their children on Sunday. On Sunday afternoons slabs of freshly slaughtered wild boar were sold at the *souk*. The boars were captured in the Atlas

Mountains and kept alive in pens until very early Sunday morning when they were killed by a swift sword thrust in the neck and roasted.

"Even if I'm told you can't work with me on base, you can submit articles to me," I said. "I have an idea for your first one. There's a French movie crew shooting on base and in that village. Find the person in charge and try to get an interview."

She smiled at me the way a man likes to think a woman smiles only for him.

We were approaching the Nouasseur gate. To the right were the bleak French *Armée de l'Air* hangers and Quonset Huts. The usual aircraft—Alouette helicopters and Breguet twin-engine ground-attack planes—were on aprons. The Breguets were feared by Arab cavalry. Men on horse and camel backs, wielding swords that could behead an enemy with a deft flick of the wrist, were more than outmatched by low-flying demons from the sky, dropping bombs and spraying machine-gun bullets. During the past few weeks, there was a new presence— Canadian Royal Air Force North Star transport planes. They came from Canada via Newfoundland and the Azores, stayed overnight, then went on to Nairobi where they picked up Canadians fleeing the long knives of the *Mau Mau*.

"I know why the Canadian planes are here," said Simcha. "rescuing rich Canadian plantation lords from the uprisings in Kenya. It's not right."

"Why?" I said.

"They're the usual *colons*," she said. "They come to the country, ravage it, exploit the natives, seize the fertile land for themselves, grab the pretty girls, bring them into their homes to, as they say, provide them with the niceties of decent housing and food. Then the fathers and brothers take the girls as unwilling lovers. . . . Do you not see the shame? And are you not sickened by the mantle of justice in which this is wrapped . . . the *colons* are beneficiaries; the natives are reborn by the *colons* beneficence. I wish I had some vomit."

"No," I said, "what I see is that wild-eyed Mau Mau, with long knives dripping of blood, are frightening ordinary families living ordinary lives. I don't have any trouble dividing good from evil here. Do you have any idea of how the Mau Mau stalk those families, scare them to death before they cut them to pieces. Simcha, I hate to admit this. I know I should be more worldly, sophisticated, but it reminds me of movies about American Indians massacring settlers I saw when I was a boy. I remember one in particular. It was called 'Drums Along The Mohawk.' It haunted my dreams for nights."

"*Mais,*" she said, angrily, "think of what drove the Mohawks to do such terrible things. *Ce n'est pas juste* to paint them *sauvage et brutale.*"

We couldn't continue the conversation. We had arrived at Nouasseur.

All four of the French and American Air Police who manned the gate came out to greet Simcha and her bright red roadster. She was laughing at the mural leaning against a wall of the front gate. It was a large painting depicting a North African town with three haggard Arabs dressed in djellabas, the long, loose garments with full sleeves and a hood that are the traditional dress in North Africa. They were sitting on a rug, beating a drum while an American standing under a palm tree shielded his eyes with his hand as he looked out away from them over an arid landscape. On top of the painting was a banner with the words "Welcome to Morocco."

Chapter Five

Nouasseur Air Base
Front Gate

While Simcha bantered with the air policemen in French and English, I phoned the base photographic unit hoping Jilly Hopper, the main photographer for *The Minaret,* was available to pick me up. She was. I hung up and watched Simcha bewitching the guards. A Russian army could have walked casually through the gate area.

Though I recognized the jeep, "Jilly's Jeep" was printed in large white letters on the hood, the sun obscured the front window. So I made my usual mistake of going to the wrong door. Jilly's Jeep was a right-side drive, one of a thousand made by Toyota in 1950 for U.S. military forces in Japan. For reasons explainable only in bureaucratic closets, this one was sent accidentally to the Nouasseur motor pool. None of the American or Moroccan drivers wanted to drive it because the steering wheel was on the right-hand side, so Jilly, born and raised in England, owned it. According to her she had nothing to do with the printing on the hood. "I just went over to get it at the motor pool one day," she said, "and what do you know. Guess the lads had themselves some fun."

"Hullo," Jilly said, in a way that always made me feel as though seeing me was a joy. "Where to, *mon* editor?"

"Know where the General is?"

"I saw his car parked in front of the high school auditorium. Is it true that he's directing the school play this year?" There was a gossipy curiosity in her voice, as there often was.

"Yes," I said, "Let's go there."

Sergeant Jilly Hopper was sandy-haired and fair-skinned; a typical British type of young woman who is almost good-looking. Even though I usually saw her dressed in drab uniforms and klutzy shoes, I found her attractive.

The tar road from the gate into the Nouasseur area was not a scenic route. Almost all the buildings were either Quonset or Dallas huts. Quonsets are prefab metal buildings with semi-cylindrical corrugated roofs. They were used as mess halls, shower-toilet rooms, and offices. Dallas huts were living quarters. They were built of prefabricated plywood, usually consisting of 400 square feet of living space, with a pot belly oil stove in the middle and a light bulb hanging from a wire at each end of the hut. There were four screen windows that were shuttered during sandstorms, many of which lasted three or four days. How many other people lived in your hut depended on your rank.

The huts were separated by arid, dusty patches of sand and dirt. Here and there you would see an unsuccessful attempt to grow something green. Even Jilly, whose creative photographic abilities were remarkable, could not render Nouasseur as anything but desolate. That, for her, was not a negative. She intended to stay in Morocco after she served out her enlistment term to capture contrasting Moroccan landscapes in a book of black-and-white photographs. For her barrenness and verdancy were equals as photographic art forms. She had an unpublished manuscript written by Edith Wharton when she visited Morocco in 1920 from which she hoped to draw excerpts to accompany her pictures.

Nouasseur was part of a string of American military bases in the Mediterranean, stretching from Spain to Turkey and Pakistan. In French Morocco, there were three other U.S. Air Force bases, at Sidi Slimane, Ben Guerir, Rabat-Sale, and a large deployment of land-based sailors in Port Lyautey.

The Sixth Fleet was on the water with aircraft carriers, aircraft, submarines, and escort vessels with marines. In case the cold war turned hot, the Sixth would, according to the plan, turn back any Soviet naval thrust westward through the Mediterranean at six choke points, beginning with the Strait of Gibraltar and stretching 2,300 miles eastward to the Dardanelles. In between were the sea south of Sardinia and Sicily, the water between Crete and Greece, Crete and North Africa, and Crete and Turkey.

Four U.S.A.F. bases were in Spain in addition to a home port for the Sixth Fleet at Rota. In Italy, Naples was a naval supply complex; Gaeta another Sixth fleet home port. There was an attack sub base at Sardinia. San Vito Dei Normanni was an intelligence base. Wheelus Air Force Base in Libya was a transport and training base. We had listening posts in Cyprus and Malta to gather electronic data from northern Africa and the Soviet Union's southern borders. In northern Turkey, we gathered electronic data from deep within the U.S.S.R. Most of our presence and activities were stamped TOP SECRET.

"Jilly," I said on the way, "I'd like to ask the General to assign you to *The Minaret* on permanent duty, but I don't want to do that until I know how you feel about it. I don't know your security clearance level, so we might have to raise it, which means more snooping around your old neighbors and workplaces by the FBI."

"I'd bloody love to do it," she replied quickly. "What's the clearance about?"

"Two concerns. First, do you know what ELINT is?"

"Electronic intelligence. Thank you very much." Jilly didn't like being talked down to.

"Sometimes I do stories that touch upon it. I never know how far I can go, so I focus on writing a good piece, then let the General's boys play with their red pencils. Sometimes I don't get a censored version back. They just tell me to forget I was there.

The Air Force needs to have some trust in your ability to erase your memory when you're asked to."

"Don't get barking mad on me." Jilly did the British thing with her "k" and "t" sounds. You really heard them. Her "k" never sounded mushy. Her "t" never sounded like a "d." Especially when she was angry. "Of course I can be trusted. I gossip about the little things. I don't go babblin' about big things. What's the second concern?"

"Politics. We can't publish things that will insult the French or the Arabs or the Berbers. I published a story on Berrechid Mental Institution . . . "

"The town down the road from here?" She said.

"Yes. They have around a thousand patients there, one general physician and one qualified nurse. I printed that, and General Jackman read me the riot act. Since then I have to get clearance by our Public Information Office for anything I want to print that has anything to do with local affairs."

"Right . . . ? I didn't know we cared about anyone's feelings."

I smiled thinly. "If a story or any part of it is censored, we forget it existed."

"Righto," she said. "When do I start?"

"As soon as the General agrees. I'll ask him to give you temporary clearance until we get an interim from the FBI."

"Do you mind," she asked, as she often did before going ahead and asking something that one might well have not wanted to hear, "everyone says the General will do anything you ask because he likes the publicity you give him."

"Is that what they say?"

"Not that I mind at all. I think they're all jealous of you."

I rolled my eyes.

Jilly stopped the jeep next to the front door of the Quonset, as close as possible if I was going to be able to open the jeep door. She called it her VIP treatment.

"So he's directing the play," she said. "Do you mind, everyone wonders about that?"

"I thought everyone was wondering about my secret powers over him. Why don't they stick to one thing at a time about any one person. Aren't there rules? Tell everyone you and I are going to take pictures of the General as he directs and get him a job in Hollywood."

She laughed. One of the things I liked about Jilly was that she seemed to find my humor funny—and she had a nice laugh. I could have explained how Jackman got to like acting when he did undercover work in World War II, how he stayed with it as an amateur, acting and directing when he could. There was no need for Jilly to get her head into that.

As I was getting out of the jeep, Jilly whispered, "Tell me, guv, do the censors pick the cheesecakes you run? Do you give them pics of Debra Paget in a bathing suit, say, and some of Betty Grable in one of those tight-fitting tap-dancing outfits?"

"OK," I said, "this is your first secret to keep. The General himself provides all the cheesecakes."

"Smashing," she said, "absolutely smashing. I love this job."

As I walked in the Quonset hut, a bugle blare almost drove me back out. Quonset huts were even worse on the inside than they looked from outside. This one was one of the worst because it pretended to house an auditorium. Listening to the high school band struggle with Souza was like being trapped in a tin can that mercilessly echoed shrill blasts.

General Jackman, in a brown T-shirt and fatigue trousers, stood in a corner of the stage as the kid playing "Uncle Teddy" bounded absurdly down the prop stairs. I saw "Arsenic and Old Lace" each of the four years I was in High School in Cleveland, Ohio, so I knew it well. I seldom thought about my high school years because I spent them learning that I would not succeed as a jazz pianist.

"Randolph," the General said, "there's enough humor in the fact that this man thinks he's Theodore Roosevelt, blows a bugle, and yells '*Charge*' as he runs down the stairs. If you go down the stairs like a clown, you spoil the scene."

After the rehearsal, I sat alone with the General on folding chairs. He used three of them, one for his upper body and one for each foot. I told him about the evening at Didier's and that I wanted Simcha and Jilly on my staff.

"Does this Simcha know about Didier?" he asked.

"No, she hates him because she only sees him putting out the paper. I don't think his wife knows either."

"He's something," said Jackman.

"What can you tell me about him, General?"

"Very interesting man" said Jackman.

And he was, indeed. Beginning in the fifteenth century, Didier males were French Jewish businessmen in Spain. Their major activity was financial investment—they provided some of the capital for Christopher Columbus in 1492. When the Spanish Inquisition threatened their survival, they and the other members of their families became *conversos*—Jews who pretended conversion to Catholicism.

By the time Pierre was born, the family had dropped the pretense. Some of them returned to Judaism; others, like Pierre's parents, dropped religion altogether. Pierre graduated from the University of Orleans in France and went to Casablanca as a tax official in 1939. He volunteered for the Free French Forces in 1940 right after the Germans invaded France. He was assigned as an officer in charge of Arab troops in the Fourth Moroccan Mountain Division. Native troops from Morocco, Algeria, Senegal, and Tunisia were the major source of manpower for the Free French Forces because few Frenchmen volunteered. The colonial native could be simply drafted into service.

Didier, his fellow officers, and the troops became decorated heroes in Italy when they broke the German's Gustav Line in 1944. Between that line and Rome, there was no German opposition left. Pierre took shrapnel in the leg and was permanently crippled.

When the Fourth Division returned to Casablanca, they were given nothing as veterans. Even the wounded were left to take care of themselves. Pierre could take care of himself because he was French and well-educated. His former Arab troops suffered because there were no medical benefits and also no recognition of what they had done for France. The French expected them to just go back to bowing and scraping. Pierre persuaded his father-in-law to hire a number of them: some in the sardine business and some in the hashish business. Pierre became a Moroccan nationalist. He joined and worked with the *Istiqlal* Party while maintaining the front of being editor of an anti-nationalist newspaper.

When he finished his short bio on Pierre, the General said abruptly, "Sergeant Hopper. Can you trust her?"

"I think so," I said. "She asks a lot of personal questions, but I've noticed she doesn't pass things on. She's a passive gossiper, if there is such a term. She likes to pretend she likes mischief, but I think she's reliable if she's told to be so. Also, I told her there would be a security clearance issue for the job to focus her on being discreet."

"I hope you know what you're doing," he said, going into the big brother Tom role. "OK, I'll ask them to rush the clearance. But if you suspect she's catching on to what you're up to . . . or if she gets nosy about the bird cage . . . tell me immediately. I'll ship her out the same day."

"You thinking about Siberia or something like that?" I asked. I felt guilty, getting Jilly into something that could become a problem for her.

He looked at me and gave a half-smile. "Yeh, San Antonio to be exact. With a note from me and another by a reviewing board about her lack of psychological and patriotic stability."

The General was not essentially hard-hearted, though he certainly appeared to qualify for it at times. There were just some things that for him could not be compromised. Even if he believed Jilly to have been no more than silly in gabbing about the secrets of the Q area, he would punish her as a highly potential enemy of the state. "Enough on that. I have a word from Washington to pass on."

I said, "Yes, sir," wondering about Jilly.

"Your controller wants you in Cyprus on December twenty-third. You should plan on being there three, maybe four, days."

It would have been difficult for me to think of anyone I would less like to be with on Christmas holidays than Gil Tompkins. He was a political appointment to Security Service. I was working under General Jackman; but he was not a member of Security Service, so I had to be under the supervision of someone in Security Service. No military permanent member of the Service wanted to have anything to do with my assignment because it was not really a Security Service operation. So they put my file on the desk of a civilian political appointment.

Cyprus was the Mediterranean Security Service headquarters for two reasons. The best technology available to NATO for electronic surveillance was located in the Cypriot Troodos Mountains, and Security Service used Cypriot airstrips for surveillance missions. Most of the members of NATO who used electronic surveillance seriously had a headquarters on the island, so meetings of their staffs were easy to arrange and secure. My purpose in going to Cyprus would be to attend some of the meetings and to find out the latest my controller had cooked up for me.

"How much do you know about UKUSA?" asked the General.

"We've agreed to share intelligence with the British, Canadians, Australians, and New Zealanders. Right?"

"It's been moving along," He said. "There's an established division of territory by geographical areas for each partner, and each country has set up a specific organization to coordinate all intelligence that's gathered electronically in its assigned area. In our case, a new outfit, the National Security Agency, takes point."

I'd heard that an agency so clandestine that the public would not even know it exists had been set up. So this was its name.

"Do you think that will work?" I asked him. "I mean, can any agency coordinate all of the army, air force, and navy electronic spy units?"

He laughed and said, "Hell no. Anyway, I was told that the jingle bells meeting—that's what they're calling it—will be about that stuff."

"You know, sir," I said, "I don't have a world of confidence in Tompkins. And I don't really understand why I'm being summoned to this meeting."

"I know. I know," he agreed, "there are times when I wonder if the Washington offices are still in friendly hands. But we work with what we're told to work with. Who knows why you're, as you put it, summoned. Even someone like Tompkins can find opportunities in a bogus assignment. In fact, men like him get good at it because it's how they survive. They learn how to use the details of a bogus assignment to do something which enables them to move on to the next political appointment, the next bogus assignment."

"So," I said, "I play it by ear, try to keep the damage level down."

He shrugged his shoulders. "Another thing," I said, "Last night at the Didiers I was put on the spot about the President's statement on planning only for all-out nuclear war."

"I can certainly understand that," he said. "We've made this country a priority target for the Soviets. We're all wondering why Eisenhower is taking such a radical position."

"I think," I said, "it could create even more problems keeping the SAC bases here after the French leave. If the Moroccans see our presence as a magnet for Soviet bombers . . . .?"

I excused myself and started walking away when the General threw out some more bad news.

"Another thing. Mrs. Jackman expects you to be at my final rehearsal party. Bring your book . . . OK?"

He was referring to the fake book I used when I played piano. Fake books contain hundreds of songs because they print only the melody notes, lyrics and chords. Mrs. Jackman preferred Major Albright's playing, but he didn't always show up.

I wanted to object, but the coward in me took control. "Yes, of course. I'm looking forward to it."

Amelia Jackman might have been the most misplaced person at Nouasseur. Wives of base commanders stationed overseas shoulder considerable responsibility for the base's social life. They bring to this role a variety of enthusiasms. Mrs. Jackman was born, perhaps addicted to, the part. Whether it was cocktails or dinner or whatever, Amelia Jackman was compelled to give the sort of party that her guests talk about at least through the next day or so. She was probably the first to give a Sirocco Party, in tribute to the blistering sandstorms that torment Morocco. When she asked me to do a story on the party—"It might even be something for *Stars and Stripes*," she said. I nodded but never went to my typewriter about it.

Nouasseur presented a considerable challenge to her. She confided in me more than once that parties "are difficult here because there is so little outside talent." Not like at Langley, for example, where "I had a solid list of notables to bring to the O Club from off-base: Congressmen, civic leaders, distinguished professors, well-known musicians, controversial newspaper editors, vivacious women and so many more. Oh, corporal, you should have seen the conga lines I led at the end of my champagne parties."

She addressed me with the old army rank of corporal rather than the Air Force rank of airman second-class. I don't know if she was aware that the Air Force had become a separate service, though she must have noticed her husband was wearing blue rather than khaki. She was one of the few people to whom I wanted to say that I was not simply a "corporal," that my job required different ranks at different times. My youthful appearance required me to limit the masquerades to lower enlisted and officers' ranks.

I could have told Mrs. Jackman that there were many interesting people in Casablanca, but I knew she would ask, "Do they speak English?" Amelia had served as her husband's hostess in Germany, France, and Japan. Always in English. I suspected she didn't want to risk the ever-lurking embarrassment of mispronunciations. I understood that.

Driving from the school auditorium to *The Minaret* office, I
told Jilly that the General wanted assurance "that you won't
talk about the places we go, especially when a story is censored."

"I'm on board," she said, "stories that are censored are
places I've never been."

"Jilly, I want to go further than that. I want you to tell anyone who asks you any questions about where we go that you
can't talk about it. If you get in the habit of discussing where we
go, there are possibilities that you'll arouse suspicion when you
don't talk about a particular day or night. If you tell a friend
you're going to Rabat, they probably would ask you later about
how it went in Rabat. If we tell you after you've been there that
you weren't there, what do you tell your friend? Keep it simple.
You're not allowed to talk about what you do when you're gone
from this base with me."

"I really don't need the extra flap," she said. She was angry.
"Don't talk to me like I'm the first person you've ever given an
order . . . I've been taking orders longer than you've been giving
them."

We were both quiet for awhile.

There was yet another reason—other than the reasons I'd
given her and my undercover work—why I wanted to impress
upon Jilly the need to be discrete, a secret of colossal pro-
portions. Nouasseur was a nuclear weapons storage area, and
very few people knew that. Not even the French government
had been told.

In the early 1950s, most nuclear weapons were stored at
National Storage Sites under the civilian Atomic Energy Commission. However, effective military uses required that some be
kept at Operational Storage and Assembly Sites near or on military bases in the states and overseas. These were called Q sites
because a Q Clearance was required for any person who worked
at them.

Theoretically, the national security Q clearance was an assurance of trust. It involved a year of thorough investigation by FBI agents, military criminal investigators, psychologists, and military security officials. If you made it through all that and received the Q, you could be trusted to protect the country's highest crypto secrets. I was given one when I worked in a branch of security service that spied electronically on the Russians. Even when you were doing something that didn't involve cryptanalysis, holding a Q gave people confidence that you would keep your mouth shut about highly classified matters, especially when you have coffee with KGB agents.

I didn't have complete confidence in Qs, especially after working two weeks as a reviewer reading investigation reports on subjects studying Russian either at the Navy's language school in Monterey, California, or at Syracuse University. After reading a report, I would meet with four other reviewers who had read the same report. We discussed our views and gave the individual a security-risk grade on a one-to-ten scale. A "one" indicated the person was low risk. A "ten" indicated the person was high risk. I can't recall one instance in which the five of us were even close to being in agreement on the number, so we used the average.

The work was done in a Quonset hut surrounded by double barbed-wire fencing and well-armed military police at Brooks AFB Security Compound, just outside of San Antonio. Everything that happened in that compound was classified as top secret.

Though I was told to be completely objective in my rankings, I realized after reading a few files that objectivity was impossible. FBI investigators followed a standard procedure, but each report conveyed the investigator's individual style and attitude, particularly in the section where neighbors, teachers, and former employers were interviewed. There were no limitations in the procedures on how far back the investigator should search. In some reports, neighbors and teachers who knew the subject when he was a child, were quoted. In others, the subject's personal history went no further back than high school.

In addition to that obstacle to objectivity, I had two bosses who disagreed with one another on standards. My military boss was a Russian-American who insisted on keeping the best linguists. My civilian boss was obsessed with a fear of homosexuals because the British had recently discovered a network of homosexuals who were passing on secrets to the KGB while they worked at high levels in MI6. If there was a hint of homosexuality in a file, my civilian boss expected me to nail it and lower my ranking. My military boss expected me to be lenient with anyone who showed unusual skills in learning Russian. Each of them considered his position to be absolutely essential for national security and the other's position to be self-serving.

The Nouasseur Q area was about a hundred yards or so from the main runway. You could see it clearly from the runway because a smooth highway was required for delivery of atomic weapons from the Q area to the B-36s. In 1946, after vigorous national debate about the merits of leaving the atom bomb project in the hands of the military, it had been a U.S. Army Corps of Engineers' project, Congress legislated control over the atomic bomb to a group of civilians called the Atomic Energy Commission (AEC). The military was the only government agency that could use the atomic bomb; but there was fear the military might misuse the bomb if it owned it, so the compromise was, as the wording of the first AEC issuance put it, "Q areas will be geographically dispersed, but always associated with an abutting military reservation."

Congress selected the Sandia Corporation of Albuquerque to be in complete control of construction and management of Q areas. They were to be similar to the point of being reproductions of one another. Each would consist of forty buildings, including a solid reinforced concrete bunker with walls seventeen-feet thick. Bands of paired false fenestration and a projecting entrance offset gave the structures an appearance of having windows and doors like an office building. Inside some of the structures, there were igloo nuclear weapons storage buildings.

Those who knew what was inside the igloos called them "bird cages" because each capsule, or pit, was housed in a cage. Keeping each capsule inside a cage kept it from touching another capsule. If two capsules were to actually touch one another, a chain reaction would be set off that would devastate Nouasseur, Casablanca, and miles beyond.

The Q area was surrounded by a chain-link double-fence line, one of which was electrified and topped with strands of barbed wire. Six armed guards and two jeeps with more heavily-armed Air Policemen patrolled the perimeter. An HH-43B Huskie helicopter hovered overhead at night with spotlights spread out on the Q area, making it appear to be in daylight.

Mina told me the Arabs who worked on base and lived in *Petits USA* noticed the nightly Huskie sound and spotlights. They had their own interpretation of what was going on. "According to them," said Mina, "Barbary pirates stashed gold and other treasures all along the western Moroccan coast. The Americans, according to this interpretation, believe they have found one of the burial places and are digging down at night to find it. You don't see the actual digging, because it takes place deep underground."

The air strip was 12,000 feet of asphalt-concrete. Nearby was a B-36 hangar that was a major engineering breakthrough. Until this one was built, B-36 hangars were inflexible concrete blocks. This one, built of steel, was double-cantilevered. It was expandable to accommodate up to six B-36s at once.

We told the French we stored the bombs' bodies, called nonnuclear assemblies, in the Q area. Actually we stored both the bodies and the pits, the plutonium and/or uranium cores. This was done as a test case. American bombers needed ready and quick access to live nuclear weapons. It was decided to secretly try out the idea of storing bodies and pits at one installation overseas.

Nouasseur was selected because it had the best runway and infrastructure already in place. Also, those who made the selection were sure that if the French were told a secret—we're storing bombs' bodies—they would concentrate on keeping the secret rather than wondering "is that all?"

No one at Nouasseur who did not have a Q clearance was to know anything about the Q area. They were told that the Q area was an ordnance facility with office buildings. They were also told, "Don't ask questions about it. Ignore it."

Storage of atomic weapons, even at national storage sites in the U.S. under the Atomic Energy Commission, was highly controversial. Having them at operational storage and assembly sites near or on military bases in the states was more controversial. Having them at overseas military bases was so controversial that it was kept top secret.

There had been accidents involving the movement of atom bombs, all of which the Air Force covered up. The worst happened in 1950 when a B-29 carrying a non-nuclear assembly crashed in Guam, killing twelve of the twenty passengers and crew, damaging or destroying forty-eight house trailers and twenty automobiles. Nineteen people on the ground were killed, and fifty-eight required hospitalization. All of the fire-fighting crews and equipment that had been rushed to the burning plane were disabled. Burning gasoline and wreckage were strewn over an area of two square miles.

The explosion of nearly five thousand pounds of high explosive was felt thirty miles away. The Air Force cover story was that ten 500-pound conventional bombs had exploded.

As risky as it was, the bomb was America's trump card. There was no other way we could counter the Russian advantages in all other military resources. Truman said in 1949 that had it not been for the bomb, "the Russians would have taken over Europe any time they wanted to." Liberal voices raged about the immorality of threatening to use such a weapon. But Truman was a follower of Clausewitz—though we have no way of knowing if he ever read him—war is an instrument of politics rather than the other way around. Therefore, you lead with and never relinquish your best weapon. Ethics fade in relevance when survival is at stake.

My work as the base newspaper editor put me in frequent contact with crews of aircraft that carried atomic bombs; all of them had Q clearances. Though they kept secrets well, they had insider jokes about "the bird cage." Being with me as much as she would be, Jilly would get curious. There was no chance of getting Jilly a Q. If she had an interim top-secret level clearance, I could tell her that jokes about "the bird cage" involved a security matter so important that she should not be curious about it and never talk about it. Perhaps that was like my nuns telling me that I was old enough to know that storks don't bring the babies and that where the babies come from is something I should not be curious about. But it was the only plan I had for having Jilly work with me and keeping us both from being shipped out to San Antonio with career death certificates tucked away in our personnel files.

"We're here, guv," said Jilly, "At least I am."

"Oh, sorry," I said, "Got to thinking about something."

"I noticed," she said. We were parked on the side of the Quonset hut office for *The Minaret.* It and the street shone with the peculiar radiance that precedes a storm. A cleaning woman was going out the front door with a duffel bag slung over her shoulder. She moved quickly when she saw us. We knew that the bag was filled with wastebasket treasures—things like copies of *LIFE*, Sears Catalogues, pictures, and candy and gum wrappers. She was taking them to be displayed on sandy dirt and sold to French teen-age girls at *Petits USA.* We looked away and gave her time to make her getaway before we entered the Quonset.

I was in love with *The Minaret.* It was not the setting. The office was a lackluster collection of steel desks, rigid-back steel chairs, office typewriters, brown file cabinets, and sluggish fans claustrophobically contained within semi-circular, corrugated metal walls. It was like living in half of a tin can with a small walled room with cot. We called it "the sick room."

I thoroughly enjoyed getting the paper out, every step of the way. Even the smell of ink in typewriter ribbons was appealing to me. On the day we distributed it, you saw people reading it in offices, as they walked down the street, in their jeeps as they waited for whomever, in cafeterias, at the clubs, in hospital beds, sitting on their cots in Dallas huts, wherever.

"*Bonjour, mon ami et mon capitaine,*" Alain yelled out. He was not the yelling type, but a sudden downpour of heavy rain was echoing harshly inside the hut. Alain was my makeshift tutor in French, so he felt obliged to get me into the language in as many situations as he could.

"Not right now, Alain," I said, "I want to tell you that Sargeant Hopper has been assigned to *The Minaret.*" I was always embarrassed by my pronunciation of French. Generally, I could live with that, but not when I was in an *I am in charge of this newspaper* situation. "Also, I think we'll have another new staff member, a young local woman."

As usual, Alain gave me a quick nod of understanding. He was probably more interested in congratulating Jilly, anyway. He always flirted with her, as he did with most of the women he met. Alain gave every impression of being a charming French gigolo, which, I thought, he probably was.

He was also the husband of Major Courchene, who ran the Nouasseur Public Information Office. She was my nominal boss. At our first meeting she said, "I know you're the General's pet because you publicize him on base, in *Stars and Stripes,* et cetera, et cetera. I intend to leave you alone, but I want one thing from you—a job on the paper for my husband." Then she went to the door and brought him in. They had married in France a month earlier. The major was a nice-looking woman who was probably attractive to many men; but Alain, I thought, was outside her net, the effortlessly handsome type that young French boys dream of becoming.

He asked her if he could speak with me alone for awhile.

"I know this is difficult for you," he said after she left. "Permit me, please, to make it easier. I need the feeling that I'm giving something. I'll do anything you ask."

"Your English is excellent," I said. "Would you be willing to help me with my French? And would you like to do a column for the paper on something like useful French phrases and cultural tips for the troops when they're off base?"

He said, *"D'accord!"* and gave me a "Shall we begin?" look.

A few days after I left Simcha in the hands of the Nouasseur gate guards, or was it the other way around, I received a call from her. "I have the story on the film you asked me to do," she said. "In fact I'm here at the gate with the film's producer. We want to come see you but . . . "

"You need me to get you in," I said. "Stay there. Someone will pick you up and have passes for you."

Thirty minutes later Jilly brought Simcha and Jacques Isnard to *The Minaret* office. Isnard was an entirely different Frenchman from Alain. Whereas Alain was dark and lithe, Isnard was fair and bulky. Not fat, but large-bodied. Alain had a warm and lyrical tone, a Maurice Chevalier voice. Isnard was Edith Piaf. Husky. Uncompromising.

Simcha appeared to be captivated by him. I told myself it was the movie thing. Guys who make movies get a lot of girls. She introduced him as though it was a special privilege to do so.

Alain was unimpressed and didn't try to conceal it. Uncharacteristically, he openly challenged Isnard. "You are the first *Centre Cinématographique Marocain* person I have met. My first encounter with a propagandist who pretends to be an artist. Did we learn this technique from the Nazis?"

Centre Cinématographique Marocain was created to encourage the development of an Arab-language cinema that would show favorable views of the French. Egyptian movies, the only Arab-language movies available prior to the *Centre* productions, promoted Arab independence from Western authority and culture.

The presence of Jacques Isnard suggested that I might not have the chance to get to know Simcha well enough to figure her out. She told me he had asked her to go back to Paris with him when he was done at Nouasseur. He had lots of contacts in journalism as well as in the movie industry.

Simcha's dislike of the French caused her to hesitate, and the fact she'd been around womanizers also helped her resist the offer; but she was tempted. Who isn't by Paris?

Isnard said something in French to Alain that sounded like an insult. Simcha slipped in between them and intervened with a description of the movie. "It's about an old Arab man who sweeps floors at Nouasseur for both the Americans and the French. It's the last few weeks of Ramadan. He's exhausted from the sunrise to sunset fasting. His American boss tries to get him to eat and drink in the afternoons. Offers him really good food. The old Arab resists. The American gets angry. He tells the Arab that if he refuses to eat and drink again the next day he would be fired immediately. The Arab desperately needs the income because he has a wife and six children who are all dependent on him. He tells his French boss about this dilemma. The French boss goes to the American boss and explains how important Ramadan rituals are to Muslims. The American boss does not fire the Arab."

Jilly giggled.

The next day Simcha gave me her copy on the movie. It was excellent. She had interesting interviews with Isnard and his staff and pictures of the actors. She had the ability to liven facts with entertaining comments on personalities. She knew how to begin and end sentences, paragraphs, and the article. She used language well. I gave it space in *The Minaret* and sent it to *Stars & Stripes* with a comment on who she was. I thought the combination of the piece and her bio would interest a broader audience than we had on base.

As we discussed how I would present her story, she impressed me with what she knew about producing a newspaper. She knew that layout problems involve column inches, not words. She knew that presenting pictures with captions at the right place is fearsome because it must appear natural and effortless though it is exactly the opposite. Most of all, she won me over as a journalist when I saw that her ego was not involved. Anyone who has ever had responsibility for putting out a minor publication knows how valuable that can be. Convincing writers such as chaplains, Red Cross directors, and health specialists who provide columns gratis that a few changes are in order can be an ordeal. They see themselves as experts and language as insignificant.

What most fascinated me about Simcha was her chameleon mystery. Sometimes she was playfully mischievous. Other times she presented herself as a zealous anti-colonialist, especially where French colonialism was concerned. Then there was the practical Simcha who sought a career in the United States. Jilly was Simcha's opposite—uncomplicated, easy to understand, and predictable.

Jilly playing with Moroccan children.

Chapter Six

The Medina
Casablanca

I was becoming more comfortable walking in the medina. My first time was a riot of colors, smells, and sounds, a chaotic splendor that left me utterly muddled. Mountains of spices and fresh cut herbs, saffron, anise seed, paprika, pickled lemons, and mounds of gleaming olives; small cedar boxes inset with camel bone; fragrant leather sandals and terracotta pots; roughly-woven Berber rugs, golden caftans, amulets, and talismans. Narrow alleyways disappeared into one-foot paths. Shopkeepers seemed to sense my apprehension, sometimes aggressively pulling me into their cubbyholes. I hated some of the scenes, especially skin-and-bone children sitting on dirt floors sewing and embroidering with lightning hands.

After more visits, the medina became a cacophony. Eventually I began to learn that traffic was, for the most part, coming and going between *souks*, which are organized by craft or type of food or service. The foods *souks* became a favorite of mine. Street food in a medina offers just about everything offered anyplace else. Most Casablanca natives did not have cooking facilities in their homes. The foods *souks* presented aromas of gingerbread, roasting meats mixed with cumin, and a lot of mint and basil. One of the reasons I liked the foods *souks* was that their smells overcame the odor of moist earth and dung that was otherwise almost ubiquitous in the medina. Some of the feelings that were at first a bit unnerving, like the way you can get more and more lost going from narrow to narrower alleys, eventually became enjoyable.

I was walking with Mina Halima, on our way to a party. In addition to her job with *Imprimerie Maroprint,* Mina was in Pierre Didier's *Istiqlal* cell. In her other cell there was a man named Si Fulan, who worked at *Postes et Télégraphes.* It had been decided that he would be the person who would tell me what information I would give *Istiqlal* through him. I was to be introduced to him at the party. Pierre knew I was having the meeting, but not with whom because he was not in that cell.

"Zwina will greet you with something like, 'welcome to my home and my *dyafa,*' " said Mina, "either in some kind of French or, maybe, English if someone has instructed her how to do that. *Dyafa* means party. Try to eat and drink at least a little bit of everything offered; but don't have more than one piece of dessert."

"Why?"

"Desserts often contain hashish, especially during the last week of Ramadan."

As we started up the stairs we had to be careful to avoid pieces of the run-down building that had unpeeled from the walls and stairs. Mina was stepping deliberately and said, "About Zwina, do not underestimate her. She will appear . . . maybe silly to you. But she is very gifted. She is a jailhouse girl."

"I'm sorry," I said, "I don't know the phrase . . . jailhouse girl."

"It's a tragedy," she said. "Zwina was born from the rape of a female prisoner by a guard. She lived the first twelve or so years of her life in prison with her mother. Then she was transferred to a prison section where girls like her were handpicked by guards for nightly enjoyment. When these girls get past six or so years of that, they are no longer attractive to the guards, who have new jailhouse girls to exploit. So they are given a bag with basic clothing and a little money, then left on the street outside the prison to get along as well as they can."

When we arrived at Zwina's door, I asked Mina, "I'm not clear on your relationship to *Istiqlal*. Should I be? You're a granddaughter of El Glaoui who is in bed with the French. Isn't that a problem?"

"No one has told you? My father divorced my mother. According to Muslim law, he said 'I divorce you' three times. She was given enough money to get out of town . . . as they say in the American movies . . . but no more. She was pregnant with me. She had nothing to offer an employer. She knew how to spin, roll, soak, and comb wool. Nothing more. *Do not* question my hatred for the House of Glaoua."

"Do you have any contact with the . . . family," I asked. "Do you know any of your half-sisters or half-brothers?" I was thinking, opportunistically, of contacts within the Glaoua family.

"A little," said Mina. "Not much. Now and then one of them comes to Casablanca and contacts my mother. Usually it's a female trying to escape the hopeless misery of being used for all sorts of sexual . . . things in a harem. My mother found work in the hashish trade for two or three of them . . . and she found places for some of them in the *Bousbir*."

"The Red-Light district . . . ?" I asked.

"It's better than what they had in the harem," Mina said. "A *Bousbir* provides the resources of a small city. Stores, restaurants, even hospitals. A city of women, with male and female . . . tourists? Shall we say that? Not all of the women are prostitutes. Some are dancers, singers, musicians, bakers, cooks, waitresses . . . whatever keeps that kind of city going. Of course, it's a dangerous life, but my mother says that my half-sisters who live there consider it to be a little paradise compared to their lives in a Glaoua harem."

"I see why you're not a fan of El Glaoui," I said. "How did you get caught up with *Istiqlal*?"

"My mother is from Turkey," she answered. "Her mother detested my grandfather when he sold my mother to the House of Glaoua. After my grandfather died, my grandmother sent money to the Sorbonne for my education. When I was there, my best friends were French communists. I learned from them I should fight against colonialism. One of them knew a member of *Istiqlal*. He gave me an address and a note to hand over when I came home and found that man. I did and I've been with the movement since then."

Zwina followed Mina's script, greeting us elaborately, arms out-stretched at her doorway. "Wilkim to ma huss an dyafa." She wore a muslin caftan with flowery embroidery of a thousand colors, a gold-braided belt, and a motley array of jewelry all over her body. Her smile revealed that she had not benefited much from dental care through the years. Her greeting was so warm and sincere that I liked her immediately. I thought she could be anywhere from thirty to fifty years old, each of her body parts suggesting a different age.

The room we entered was set up for a party. There was a scent of mint wafting from tea being brewed. Decorative fabrics were hung on the walls; small tables overwhelmed by vases filled with paper flowers spread out below the fabrics. One of them, in a far corner, had a lamp with no shade providing modest light from a bulb that blinked on and off. Later, Mina told me the purpose was not to have subtle lighting but to show that Zwina had electricity, albeit undependable. Next to the lamp a man wearing a bright blue turban sat lotus-positioned on the floor, playing unappealing music on a pipe instrument.

There were a dozen or so people there, sprawled on divans and standing in circles. Everyone was elbow-to-elbow, but no one seemed to mind. Zwina disappeared into the bodies and im-mediately three very young girls in light blue haiks appeared. One held a tray of small glasses filled with mint tea; the other held up a plate of biscuits. Just as I took a glass and biscuit, Zwina appeared with a thin, pinched-cheeked man wearing brown slacks and a white shirt with banded collar. Other than Mina and myself, he was the only one at the party not dressed in traditional clothing.

As Mina introduced us, Si Fulan studied me for awhile, then gave me a thin smile. Handshaking was impossible; our hands were fully occupied with food and drinks. It was probably for the better. He didn't look as though he wanted to be friendly. We nodded instead.

Mina had told me Fulan's appearance was deceptive. "He is petite for a man, almost delicate. They call him 'the butterfly on the edge of the storm' because he flutters but does not move away. He is *aussi très ruse,* a very cunning man. I believe him to be ruthless, but only in his cause."

I didn't agree with her. I thought his appearance was not at all deceptive. He had a face like a clenched fist.

The next day, in the late afternoon, I was at the place Fulan had designated in the few words he spoke to me at the party. It was a communal bakery close to the *Bab el-Jedid* gate of the medina.

On one side of the bakery there was an open dried fruits and vegetables store; on the other, a *hammam*, which, I had been told, is a Moroccan version of a Turkish Bath. In a slit of space between the bakery and the *hammam* a young man worked a wood lathe by jerking on a piece of string.

In front of the *hammam,* a letter-writer, dressed in a blue banded-collar shirt and a western suit, sat at a portable table under a threadbare umbrella, staring with droopy, sad eyes at his pens and paper. He appeared absolutely certain that there would be nothing of size moving down the narrow street because he had taken his position in the middle of it. That might have been his only viable position because tiny shops along the street overflowed into it, a sprawling of colors and goods, leaving little room even for marketers.

Also oblivious to the possibility of traffic, a wizened man in a bulky mustard djellaba stood in the middle of the street, basting long brochettes of lamb over a fiery brazier, his wrist-flicking quick strokes driven by a surprising energy.

I felt reasonably safe there, though I had been nervous throughout the morning because Fulan told me, "Do not bring any valuables except fifty dirhams or so. Leave your wallet behind."

There must have been a back door exit to the bakery because the steady stream of women, men, and children carrying dough in through the front doors never came out. The bakery and the other stores next to it were covered with orange and blue awnings.

A man in a filthy gray djellaba, holding a sloppy pile of papers mitt-fisted, arrived at the letter-writer's table. As I watched him dramatically wave his papers at the letter writer as though they contained a threat to his life, Fulan was at my back saying, "Follow me."

I did, into the *hammam*. The *mul-l-hammam* jumped from his wicker chair at the sight of me, losing his small kif pipe to the chair. He was smaller than me, but stood there stroking his large black moustache with the ball of his thumb and wearing a white crocheted skullcap, a dirty undershirt, and brown shorts, daring me to question his authority. Then he saw Fulan and he took a few steps back. Fulan said something to him and gave him some money. The minor potentate sat down, albeit with a dark disapproving glance at me.

The anteroom, where bathers take off their clothes and later, after bathing, sit around cooling, was plain. On one side was a neglected bench with clothing hooks above it, most of them occupied by djellabas, shirts, and baggy trousers. A few men were curled up in towels on the bench, dozing. One of them, tall, thickset with rounded shoulders and a sloppy beard, sat up suddenly, glared at me, waved "get out of here" and flexed his muscles. Fulan laughed at him. We went to a corner of the room.

As we undressed, Fulan said, "If it pleases you, we meet here at this time on Wednesdays." His "Wednesdays" came out as *Wed-nez-daze*. "The police do not like to come here unless they are in large numbers. One or two by themselves would not leave here alive."

I looked around and took his meaning.

"I will not meet you outside. If when you arrive the man who is the letter writer is not there, leave the medina immediately. If he is there and I am not in here, go to the letter writer and, if he is alone, ask him if he has a letter for Abdalah."

"Instructions from you will be in the letter," I said.

He nodded.

"Then I'll need a code word or a sample of your handwriting, or both," I said. "And what if he doesn't have the letter or isn't there when I come out?"

"He'll be there because you are not to spend more than five seconds looking around this room for me and . . . stay in the doorway. If he does not have a letter for Abdalah, leave the medina immediately using only the wider streets . . . stay out of the alleys. Take the military bus back to Nouasseur, and I'll have someone contact you there."

From the anteroom, we went into a room with a pile of wooden buckets. "Take two and this," he said, handing me a brown bar of olive-oil soap. Buckets and soap in hand, I followed him as he pushed open a heavy wooden door. A chain-and-pulley-counter-weight device drew the door screeching back to a closed position.

I saw nothing at first. There were banging and splashing sounds, men yelling out, buckets clanking. Then I saw a ravishing black woman in a body-hugging wrap-around standing next to Fulan.

"This," said Fulan, "is Aloutababa. She will be your *tayeba*, your scrubber. She is expensive. But don't bring any money for her. I will take care of that. She is a deaf-mute, so we can talk openly in front of her."

Aloutababa looked at me indifferently. I was unable to do the same with her.

"If the police ever wonder what brings you here every Wednesday, we want them to find that she is the reason. They will understand this." For a moment I thought I detected a smile on his hard face, but it was really more of a sneer.

As Aloutababa put gloves on her hands, I wondered if there was any possible movement she could make that would not be sexual. While she scrubbed me vigorously, Fulan explained his role in *Istiqlal* and what he would like me to do for him. "I am," he said, "on the Information Committee. We will ask you for information, but we will not involve you in operations. We are planning a boycott of French-made goods. We don't want to ask the people to boycott everything. That would seem extreme to them. Could you find out where we would do the most damage? What kind of boycott of what kind of things will hurt them the most? Another thing, can you get us some information on the disposition and attitude of the French Foreign Legion troops in the Ouarzazate area. We want to know what they can do if we cause trouble in Marrakech. We hear rumors that they are not battle-ready. . . . It is important that we know if that is the truth."

Marrakech is a city south of Casablanca. It stands in the shadows of the High Atlas peaks . . . Berber territory. The Ouarzazate area is on the south side of the High Atlas, on an apron of the Sahara Desert. I figured the Arabs might want to seize Marrakech as a fortress from which they could keep the Berbers contained in the Atlas Mountains.

Just as Aloutababa began scrubbing my legs with long firm strokes and I was on the verge of losing contact with Fulan, he said, "Perhaps the most important thing you can do for us is show us how to promote our cause in world public opinion. We get no support from the local French press. Newspapers such as *Le Petit Marocain*, where you have your Air Force paper printed, are propaganda voices for the Protectorate. We get some support from the leftist French press in Paris, but that is a mixed blessing because it supports right-wing propaganda that Arab nationalist movements are masks for Communist agitation. *TIME Magazine* and *The New York Times* are beholden to the French for their stories, so their attitude is shaped by that. Now and then a reporter will be on the spot in a situation that cannot be manipulated. He will send a story that is favorable to our side, and one of those publications will print it. But most of what gets printed in English is not only pro-French, it is anti-

Arab. Perhaps it is the skin color, perhaps the religion . . . whatever . . . the Western press dislikes Arabs intensely."

"I think I can help a little with that," I said, "but I'm sure you know I'm limited."

He nodded and said, *"D'Accord"* as Aloutababa vigorously scrubbed my toes.

"For example," said Fulan, "months ago the Sultan sent a letter to Paris proposing establishment of a representative Moroccan government composed of both natives and Frenchmen living here and capable of negotiating with France. Not long after that, *Istiqlal* offered to take part in a government that would guarantee French rights and interests in Morocco. Neither of these offers has been given attention in the Western media."

"Because," I said, "such offers contradict the French colonial propaganda claim that the nationalists want to kick the French out of the country once and for all."

"Yes," said Fulan, "so the French pretend as though they have never seen or heard of such offers. They will . . . " He was interrupted by sounds from people and animals stampeding outside. Then I heard rifles and machine-guns and screaming. Everyone in the washing room—except Aloutababa, Fulan, and I—was scurrying out of it. As though she had trained for the moment, Aloutababa removed her gown with one decisive thrust, took my naked body to the floor with hers, and rolled me over on top of her."

"They probably will not come in here," said Fulan, "but if they do, I want them to think you are having your fun on the floor. Stay there until I return."

Medina archway, Casablanca.

Medina in Casablanca.

Chapter Seven

The December 1952
Slaughter

It was hours before he came back. Aloutababa's body and mine smelled sour-sweet from perspiration mixing unpleasantly with drying soap. We had conversations with our eyes, neither of us having any real idea what the other was saying. My heart was pounding, my face burning; despite all the sweat, my mouth was dry. Thus was my ignominious witness to a defining moment in Moroccan history.

Outside the *hammam,* French police and military assaulted the medina with a mercilessness surpassing anything previously waged. Machine guns were emplaced at the intersections of main streets and fired steadily into crowds of Arabs. The crowds were unable to figure out a safe way to go because they were the target; wherever they went, the machine gun bullets followed. Foreign legionnaires stormed through the alleys, chopping with bayonets at bodies that stirred.

The French Resident General, Augustin-Leon Guillaume, explained in a letter to the United Nations that this had been done because the medina harbored nationalists and communists who, for everyone's safety, must be brought to heel. Guillaume almost always associated the communists with the nationalists and suggested that the communists ran the show.

When Fulan did return, he had my clothes. "Dress and stay close behind me," he said.

It was night. Fulan led me at a fast pace through dark streets and alleys. We jumped over piles of dead Arabs. A few times I stumbled and found myself lying on top of a dead Arab face or a bloody body. Fulan always came back, grabbed my hand. "Come, come" he said.

Our most formidable crisis was at a French militia machine gun emplacement at the entrance to the spice souk. Only one of the machine gun crew was alive, barely so because his face was covered by gunpowder; and though he had his hands in position on the trigger and bullet-belt strap, his eyes, drenching in sweat, were meandering as though they didn't know what they sought. Fulan took the man's hands off the gun, letting him fall back softly into the pile of bodies we assumed were his crew mates.

We couldn't avoid stepping on bodies to keep moving; they were piled on one another across the narrow street. As we stepped on arms and legs, some of them grabbed or kicked at us in some kind of reflex action. Or, perhaps, they were not all dead as I had assumed.

Fulan lost his footing at the end of the pile. He fell down; and when he lifted his head, a bayonet attached to a rifle was about to be thrust into his throat by a *Goumier*. I screamed *"Assassin!"* The bayonet swung in my direction, and Fulan stabbed the *Goumier* in the leg. I jumped on him, seizing the rifle as I stood up.

"Kill him," said Fulan, "My knife is stuck in his leg . . . we've got to get going." Blood gushed out of the knife hole, and the *Goumier* screamed in pain in a deep guttural voice.

"Then let's get going," I said. "I'll take the rifle, but I'm not killing this guy. It would be murder in cold blood."

"You're a fool," said Fulan, "This filth has your face in his mind, and he's vowing to himself to find you some day and kill you."

Looking in the *Gourmier's* eyes, I had no doubt Fulan was right. They were squinting as though he was working strenuously to remember my face. I was frightened, but not as frightened as I was by the thought of opening up his body with a bayonet.

"Not in the body," Fulan yelled. "They pick clothing off of dead bodies and put it on underneath the robe. This one could have six layers of clothing on him. My knife is fully into him but only an inch of skin is pierced. In the face! In the face! Get his eye if you can."

I lifted the rifle, the bayonet pointing at this chest. "To hell with you," I said, "I can't do his face. This is bad enough."

I had a lot of leverage, standing above him, and he was fatigued from battle; my first lunge went through the layers of clothing and into his body. As I struggled to pull out the bayonet, it was snarled in the various layers of material, the *Goumier* lifted his head arrogantly, reached behind his neck, and pulled out his pigtail so that it was in full view. I knew what that meant. *Goumiers* wore pigtails so that if they died on the battlefield, Allah could pull them out of the fray. It was an honorable death. I continued thrusting and pulling until Fulan pulled me off.

We came upon people who were lost, probably shoppers who had come to the medina in search of bargains and street food. I told those who spoke English that the most dangerous thing was to move around. "Just sit here on the street. Wait for the French authorities to settle things down."

"Where is the protection we expect from the American Embassy?" asked one older American man who wore a baseball cap with the New York Yankees logo.

"What were you guaranteed?" I asked him.

We left them with Fulan leading a fast-paced getaway. After maneuvering some more alleys and roof-tops, he stopped at an apartment building and said, breathlessly, "Mina and her mother live here. They do not have much space, but this is the safe place to be tonight."

Mina and her mother, Lalla, had a one-room apartment on the third floor. They were not expecting us, but acted as though it was quite normal to be visited at odd hours by unexpected persons. Fulan left immediately. Lalla tried to make me feel at ease by smiling a lot—obviously not at all embarrassed about having around a half dozen black teeth framed by two gold ones and hair that was rusty-colored from too much use of henna. She was a scrawny old woman, but her darting movements were almost girlish. She wore a colorful caftan and her toes were embellished with silver rings.

Makeshift curtains divided the room into four small spaces. One of the spaces provided a touch of privacy for undressing. Another had a commode, poorly concealed by vitreous glass baubles dangling on thin strings. A third was somewhat of a combined living/bedroom. In one corner there was a Pfaff sewing machine, its once shiny black finish was faded with time and chipped on the edges. The wheel on the right side still shone, probably from much use. The wrought-iron foot pedal was rusty except where it had obviously been used. There were mixed smells of overheated concrete walls, the commode, and henna. In the fourth space, Lalla kept a propane tank, a tin of instant coffee, cups, powdered milk, oranges in a basket, and a horde of caged chameleons. Lalla called them *"mes petits."*

Chameleons were kept in apartment rooms in the medinas to rid the air of flies, bees, bugs, and spiders. Whenever I got within a few feet of *"les petits"*, they puffed out, their fat, pink tongues zipping at me, their eyes constantly rolling three hundred and sixty degrees in opposite directions.

At first I refused to stay there. "It's not illegal for me to walk around the medina," I said. "Tell me how to get out of here."

Mina explained, "This was not a raking over to scare us. It was a killing spree. People were shot down like rabbits—everyplace, in the street, in the mosques. They fired machine guns into crowds . . . There will be police and military men everywhere in the medina tonight with orders to detain and question anyone they come upon. . . They are gathering up the thousands of bodies lying in the streets like garbage bags . . . Well, no, of course *they* are not doing *that* . . . They are forcing Arabs to do it. . . . They would stop you . . . find out you are a journalist. They do not want anyone writing about what happened today. You would become the kind of problem they cannot allow. They might send you to one of the dungeons in the Berber *kasbah*s. . . . you would just disappear."

I decided to stay with them . . . And wondered if Lalla would loose the chameleons before she went to bed.

That night Mina told me more about Si Fulan. He grew up in Ain Chok, one of the poorest neighborhoods in Casablanca. He was spotted by French talent scouts whose job was to talk with teachers at the Koran schools about their brightest students. Once selected, Si was sent to a French Protectorate Civil Service training academy. Not only were all of Si's expenses covered by the French, his parents received a monthly stipend so long as Si performed well in school. After two years at the academy, Si was assigned to *Postes et Télégraphes,* and his father was given a job at a chemicals factory. Life was suddenly good for Si and his parents. They moved into a French-built housing complex on the outskirts of Ain Chok.

About a year later Si was called into the office of his supervisor at *Postes et Télégraphes.* His supervisor introduced Si to a Frenchman named Chabrol. "An important official," said his supervisor. Chabrol said he was there to gain Si's support. In a routine search of lockers at the chemical factory, communist pamphlets had been found in the locker of Si's father. The only way to deal with this in a way that would enable the father's job and, perhaps, even Si's position, was for the father to give Chabrol a name or two of communists who were talking to him at the factory. Si convinced his father to do this. A week later Si came home to find his parents on the kitchen floor, each dead from a bullet between the eyes. Si learned that the reason his father was given the job in the factory was to become an innocent and unknowing bait to identify some of the communists working there. Fulan's loyalty to the French turned into a deep hatred.

Lalla had been standing by, with a box in her right hand, while Mina told me about Fulan. When she thought it appropriate, she opened the box and took out a little mechanical canary in a bamboo cage. She wound it up with quick twists of her bony fingers and placed it on the floor. To her delight it rocked back and forth on its perch, chirping metallic sounds that were almost overpowered by the ratchets whirring in the base.

The next morning, I was stretched out on the floor dozing when I heard a rooster crowing and a loud thudding sound like someone jumping on a trampoline. I looked out the window and saw a woman in a candy-striped djellaba with one scarf over her hair and another over her mouth, using a thick tree branch to smash some sense into an embroidered sheet. She looked at me and glared, threatening me with her pounding tool.

"Come away from the window," Mina said, tittering. "Rooftops are sacred to Arab women. They live cloistered lives, physically and psychologically. Rooftops are their breath of fresh and free air. If my mother were at the window, she'd be welcomed to watch; but never a man, and certainly not by anyone who could be French."

Lalla answered a quick, soft knock on the door. A thick, tall woman slipped into the room. Her shoulders were covered with a shawl that hung down in a broad triangle bordered by tassels like those of a flamenco dancer. She was holding a robe and slippers in her hands. She studied me carefully and somewhat sensually, as if I'd asked her to dance with me. On another day, I learned that she had been a Jewish prostitute who, during her working years, posed as a Spanish virgin.

"Here is Mahdere," said Mina. "All she knows about you is that you need a way to get out of the medina without being noticed. She is a member of my cell."

I smiled at Mahdere. She nodded, said something in Arabic to Mina, then flirted with me while dropping the bundle of clothing to the floor. Old habits die hard. Like Lalla, her hair, at least as much of it as was showing, was rusty from overuse of henna.

I had no idea what role she was to play in my escape from the medina. Actually I had no idea what the escape plan was. I think Lala, Mina, and Mahdere enjoyed that. Not that they wanted to see a person suffer from lack of knowing what was going on. Rather, I think, they saw beauty and joy in naiveté.

She gave me a robe and hood to wear over my shirt and trousers and a veil to tie around my nose and mouth as she explained the escape plan. I was to get on the bus that takes cleaning women to work in French and other European homes. "It will be arranged that you will be in the middle of a group of women walking toward the bus. Crouch down to disguise your height."

Lalla waited at the curtain that housed the continental breakfast kitchen . . . and the chameleons. She asked me something. Mina laughed. "My mother wants to know if you like *broken* coffee. It's *café au lait*."

"I do," I said. Lalla closed the sewing machine so that it folded into a coffee table and grinned with her black and gold teeth.

As planned, and carried out by the women, I sat next to a window on the bus and slouched down immediately because four French policemen were marching a group of Arabs, roped together, on my side of the bus. My legs were near buckling. The female body odors were strong and far from pleasant, but I was grateful to my protectors.

Ever since my discussion with Fulan about how events in Morocco were covered by the Western press, I tried to follow up on his belief that the Western press went beyond being pro-French; it was out-and-out anti-Arab. Coverage in *The New York Times* of the carnage I had just lived through suggested Fulan had it right. Essentially, the Associated Press reporter who wrote the story presented a picture of orderly French institutions assailed by rioting mobs. As any civilized man would expect, the French put their muscle against the rioters, using the weapons and equipment available in an orderly and judicious manner. There were cryptic observations on the blood-shed. The report said that the number of Moroccan civilians shot down by the French police and army militias was un-known, but numbered at least several hundreds.

According to the author, barbaric acts were carried out by the rioting rebellious crowds. For example, the article said, "An angry mob seized two Frenchmen in a disused stone quarry and cut off their arms. Another Frenchman was stoned to death. All three bodies were put to the torch and burned beyond recog-nition." The French forces were presented as using the proper weapons in the proper way. It was as though there could be no question about whether or not the Arabs had any rights what-soever to protest French rule. If one had asked the reporter about this, he probably would have said that the Arabs have nonviolent channels through which they can protest. Protest is acceptable; violent protest is not.

If I had gone further and said that the Arabs had used the nonviolent channels, including their rights in the United Nations, I suppose that the reporter might have said one of two things, or both: (1) Well there you have it then. They've got a microphone and they're using it. (2) So, they made their case and lost in a fair tribunal atmosphere. What more can you ask?

The reporter saw no French indecency. But many others did, including people I trusted. I don't think that Mina lied when she told me what she saw, and that was nothing if not organized French cruelty.

I came away from my thinking about the press coverage given that gory day wondering about the power that power encourages. The French were right, in the view of many, because they were the controlling power. One was right to report the event as a rebellion rightly put down, because . . . well, how else would one portray it? After all, look at how better dressed the French protectorate forces were, how they moved in a disciplined manner, handling standard weapons with skill and efficiency. Compare the rowdy Arab mobs running amok through the streets and over the rooftops, carrying anything that can kill, maim, or punish a non-Arab body, merciless to all, children and women as well as men, bestial when it suits them, and uncompromising.

Now and then Alain took me to lunch at upscale restaurants— *Le Lido* and *La Réserve*—in Casablanca or nearby Oceanside areas. In the 1930s the Resident General brought some of France's best architects and artists to build restaurants and bistros that offered Parisian cuisine and chic. Pierre said these lunches were part of my language training and also an opportunity to learn to appreciate the best of French foods and wines. Except for my incorrigible French mispronunciations, it was enjoyable to spend that time with Alain, ever the amiable and gracious host.

This time we were north of Casablanca at *Le Restaurant Homard,* a small seafood place perched on a cliff overlooking the Atlantic. It was cantilevered in order to provide the diners with a clear view of the beach and water. A light scent of salt breeze was blowing in from the sea. I was worried that the support system, saltwater-chewed wood stilts, might collapse and provide us with too close a view.

I had learned many things about Alain's life. He was born in 1918 in Marseilles, a bastard born to a French woman who tended bar and slept around. His father may have been a Lance Corporal in the British Hampshire Regiment. Alain grew up learning that he had three things going for him: good looks, street smarts, and a talent for imitating the speech patterns of high- as well as low-class Frenchmen. When he was twenty-two, he enlisted in the French Army, was captured by the Nazis, escaped from a Prisoner of War Camp, and spent the rest of the war under the protection and nourishment of various French women.

Alain met Major Courchene in Laon, France, where he was working as a waiter. She was stationed at the U.S.A.F. Laon-

Couvron Air Base, a front-line bomber and fighter installation. He was walking through a car-park area near the twelfth-century Gothic Cathedral of Laon when he saw an American female in an officer's uniform kicking a Citroën's gas tank.

"Pardon me, Major," he said to her, "Could I provide some assistance?"

"The damn gas tank gauge says I'm empty," she said. "I know it's got to be more than half full. Some sonofabitch siphoned it off."

Alain told her to wait by the car, that he would bring gas in, oh, perhaps, twenty minutes. And he did. Then he suggested a glass of wine "at a very special café."

They were married two weeks later.

As usual, at the restaurant Alain was a model of French panache. He wore light-colored, well pressed trousers with an off-white shirt and a peach sweater. He ordered for both of us then said to me, rolling his eyes toward the waiter, "*Regardez le serveur.*" The waiter, as though on cue, turned, went across the open patio where we were sitting, and made his way down a long, winding trail to the beach. We watched him take two live lobsters from a wire basket resting in the coolness of the bay. He held the snapping claws away from his body and came back up the trail.

Beyond the bay were parts of wrecked ships and debris left over from the American invasion in 1942. My brother, Tom, who was a soldier in General George Patton's Third Army, told me about it.

"I was scared shitless," he said. "We were pouring out of the landing craft while all hell was breaking loose. French planes strafed the beach, machine guns and snipers were splattering us from above, our own ships were shelling the area . . . we hugged the beach. . . . Then Patton appeared and started cussing and kicking us . . . that got us going. He stood there on the beach for hours in that shiny helmet he wore. Didn't seem to have any fear . . . just a lot of anger at us. After that, he was Superman to all the troops."

Alain filled our wine glasses. "I have something important to talk with you about." It was a good white wine, naturally. I'd given up trying to remember the names and all the other things he was trying to teach me in his attempt to give me status as an oenophile.

"This Jacques Isnard. I don't like him and Simcha together as they are." "So?" I said. I wondered if Alain was a little jealous, as was I. "He's a smooth Frenchman like you, and he's found a role for her in his movie. He has her attention."

"But you are in a position to . . . distract her?"

"I can't run Simcha's life," I replied, perhaps too abruptly or, perhaps, the look of slight pain in his eyes was a result of the fact that when we did these lunches, we spoke only French and he allowed me to go on without corrections in pronunciation or correct verb forms.

"He's a dangerous man," said Alain. "I went to a café with him and two friends of his . . . policemen. They work at *Ghoubila Prison.* . . . They described their torture techniques—incredibly brutal. Political prisoners are left in total isolation, chained to the ground or suspended head down so the guards can beat sticks on the bottom of their feet. Some of them—anyone they think knows something useful—are taken into a special torture room. They use two electric leads connected to a hand-cranked device that produces an electric charge. . . . The other two ends are connected to the penis and a nipple . . . or, with a woman. . . . "

"I've heard of it," I said, and then I tried to say the theory is that pain applied to those two parts of the body causes you to be so confused that you're incapable of resistance. I don't know if he understood me. The look of distress was back in his eyes.

"It was the way they talked about it," he said, "those two and Isnard . . . They laughed about it and compared subjects' reactions. Isnard is very—too—familiar with it."

Driving back to the base, Alain said, "There's another thing about Isnard. He wants me to get my wife to put pressure on the base radio station to make an announcement about 'Sing, Youth' a few times every day."

"Sing, Youth?"

"It's another thing Isnard is into . . . a singing competition for Arab teenagers. Each week's winner goes on to the next week's show. After two months, one winner emerges, gets recording contracts in Paris, and so on. The idea is to get the teenagers attention on things like that rather than on taking up weapons."

"I get it," I said. "The Arab teenagers listen to our radio station a lot more than they listen to the French stations."

"*Certainement,*" said Alain. "Hearing it on your station gives it instant credibility. I believe that Isnard is actually trying to recruit young Moroccans for the French colonialist cause."

I thought of Si Fulan's recruitment from the poverty of Ain Chok. The French, I thought, are inventive in use of their various powers.

We were approaching the Nouasseur main gate. Though he had to drive the standard nondescript blue Chevrolet assigned to his wife, Alain expressed his preference for European motoring flamboyance by skidding his front wheels in the gravel, veering the front tires slightly to the right as he stopped. Not a dangerous maneuver, rather a flair.

The French guard stood at the front door of the guard post with a carbine aimed at us. The American guard jogged over to us, pistol and billy club brandished as though he were prepared to valiantly defend against an attempt to illegally enter the base. He knew Alain's games and enjoyed playing them.

Alain took out his identification, showed it to the American guard and waved to the French guard who stayed in the shack. The American guard holstered his pistol, freeing a hand to take the identification from Alain. He pretended to read it, handed it back and said, "One of these days Mon-sewer, it's off to drivers' training you go." He looked at me and said, "Maybe I'll make you write an article about it. What would you say to that?"

"What state are you from?" I said.

"Oregon," he said.

"Sorry," I said, "the McCarthy Committee hasn't cleared Oregonuts. No clearance, no publicity in a military newpaper."

He waved us on. He was in a hurry now to try to share in English and French the humor of our brief encounter with his fellow gatekeeper.

As we drove away from the main gate, Alain said, "I*snard est* . . . how do you say . . . pot stirrer?"

"Meaning?" I said.

"He goes around with the big spoon stirring things that look calm," said Alain, "seeing what he stirs up."

"So," I said, "you're saying he's stirring around in my pot to see what comes up?"

"*Mais oui*, you are very interesting to him because you spend so much time with the General; and he does not understand the style and manner of American journalists, even when they are in the military."

"But he's French," I said. "Freedom of the press has been strong in France for a long time."

"*Non*," said Alain, "he is Vichy French. There are two types of Vichy Frenchmen."

Vichy France was the name given the French Government approved by the Nazis after they conquered France.

"One type plays along because there is nothing else to do," said Alain. "The other type, Isnard is one of these, commits themselves to the *new order*—that was the Nazi label for what was happening. In the new order all journalism is propaganda. So Isnard sees you as a propaganda spinner and wants to know what propaganda you have been instructed to spin. He does this because he's trying to find a way back into the loops of power and influence in Paris. Too many people know he was a champion of the *new order*. He needs salvation, and I suppose he will try to find it by exposing something the Americans are doing that they don't want the French to know. If he accomplishes this, he gains much favor with no less than Charles de Gaulle, who is, as everyone knows, furious with American lack of confidence in the French."

"Do you know," I asked, "if Isnard is . . . officially employed by any of the French secret service agencies?"

"*Non*," said Alain. "But I have no doubt he would know where to go if his pot-stirring turned something up. He is very suspicious of you. He's learned that the Commandant spends more time with you than anyone else. That is *bizarre* to him, even given the story that you are the General's press agent, and he is a man obsessed with his image in the press."

"So, what's his explanation . . . or yours?" . . . "Tell me. I'd sure like to know. I've been going around thinking I'm the General's press agent. If I'm something bigger than that, by all means tell me."

Medina.

Chapter Eight

The Officers' Club
Nouasseur Air Base

"Cracking, *mon editor*, definitely cracking," said Jilly, "I had heard, but little did I realize." She was leaning on top of the upright piano I was playing, holding a glass of champagne, looking attractive in a light-blue dress and pearl necklace.

We were in the O Club receptions room at Amelia Jackman's Final Rehearsal Party. I was glad I had a bass player and drummer accompanying me because it was the first time Jilly and Simcha heard me play, if Simcha had heard me at all above the laughter of the ring of pilots tagging along with her. Jilly had two with her. What little talent I had as a piano player was restricted to my right hand. When I was without a rhythm section, my left hand wandered slowly about the keys, trying to fake some kind of rhythmic coherence. The bass and drums left me free to concentrate on the melody lines and improvisations.

Maybe it was seeing Jilly dressed up that made me notice for the first time why I liked the way she smiled. Her smiles began in her eyes, went to her cheeks, and then to her lips. It was also the first time I smelled perfume on her, a nice rose scent.

By Amelia Jackman's standards, it was not a decent turnout. Major Courchene and Alain were there, as were a few dozen or so base officers with their spouses, perhaps as many as twenty unescorted officers, mostly pilots, a few unescorted women in addition to Jilly and Simcha, and the would-be thespians, who were there with their parents.

Jilly and Simcha didn't seem to mind being there, though the invitation had come as an order from Mrs. Jackman. She'd dropped by *The Minaret* the previous day to tell me that her preferred pianist was "off flying someplace," so I should not forget to bring my fake book. Jilly and Simcha were standing nearby.

"Married?" she said, looking them over. When she heard they were single she said, "Be a dear and bring them, Corporal. I have too few young unescorted ladies and too many young pilots."

Despite the mediocre attendance, Amelia Jackman acted as though she were having the time of her life. She always worked hard at looking young and being the life of the party. She often wore wigs, though her natural hair was not unattractive. For this occasion, she presented herself in reddish, tight curls. She wore a pink-and-white plaid silk dress with a full skirt.

At parties like this, she appeared to be filled with boundless energy. "She's perky," was usually the first thing people said when asked if they knew her. Junior officers quickly learned that if they commented on how young she looked, she remembered their names. You could hear her laugh and, sometimes, her speaking voice from across large rooms filled with people.

As I had surprised Jilly with my piano sounds—or was she just being nice?—Alain surprised me with his singing. "Casablanca" was a movie everyone had seen, so Major Courchene suggested I urge Alain to sing "As Time Goes By." His French accent and flair for the drama of the words were perfect. I supposed that every woman in the group of people who gathered around us after the first four bars or so, fell hopelessly in love with him—if they hadn't already done so.

After we played our final set, the rhythm section and I joined Jilly and a group of pilots for champagne at the bar. Simcha was at a table in the corner of the room with Alain. They didn't look like they were having a good time. Their faces were solemn and their bodies barely moved.

Just as I was tipping glasses with Jilly, I heard Mrs. Jackman's voice. "Corporal," she said, giving a formal nod to the others at the bar, "I have a marvelous idea. I want to take a group of officers' wives to see the new Governor's palace. I think you are just the man to arrange it." There was an unusual edge to her voice. I wondered if she had enjoyed too much champagne, though I'd never seen her under the influence.

She was referring to the new *Mahakma* for the Pasha of Casablanca. It housed three Moslem Courts, fifteen rooms for state functions, and luxurious living quarters for the Pasha, his wives, his concubines, and his numerous children. Mrs. Jackman's eye for the beautiful and exotic was not at all at fault. The new *Mahakma* was an opulent sight from the outside, and they said the inside made the outside look as though it had been done on a tight budget. The problem was her sense of what she was suggesting. Non-Muslims were not allowed inside it, especially female non-Muslims.

"Mrs. Jackman," I said, "it's not possible. I'll ask Simcha to explain why."

She looked frozen in a scowl until her tight lips opened and said, "I don't want to have anything to do with *her*." She wheeled around and stormed away.

"Poor you," Jilly said, "you know nothing about the Simcha flap, do you?"

"What is it I know nothing about?"

"There was a hot-in-pursuit pilot who was all over Simcha. She told him she liked girls, not boys." Mrs. Jackman's gone daft.

"So," I said, "Mrs. Jackman heard about it?"

"Luv, everyone in this room except the piano player heard about it. The General's wife is so bloody hot, I think her wig's gonna go up in flames."

"Excuse me, Jilly," I said, "I've got to talk to Alain."

"Of course," Jilly said, "Head his wife off at the pass and all that. Don't you think it's marvelously funny. Simcha shooting down that pilot."

"Sure I do. But you've been around Americans long enough to know how up-tight they are about homosexuality. It's even illegal. And for women . . . it's considered so revolting that it's not only illegal—it's unspeakable. And anything Americans in general are up-tight about, military culture is twice as up tight about it."

"Bollocks!" said Jilly. "I don't bloody believe this rubbish. You're mad at Simcha. What a . . . Mister editor, Simcha was making a joke. She was being nice. She could'a got rid of him by telling him he's repulsive. That would'a been OK with you. Lord. I expected more from you."

I walked away, over to the table where Simcha and Alain were sitting.

"I need Alain for just a moment, Simcha," I said. Then I'll walk you to your car. We can go someplace, or you can just go home. I figure you're miserable here." She nodded indifferently.

When I had him alone I asked Alain to work on Major Courchene. "I really don't want her in my office tomorrow morning demanding I kick Simcha off the paper," I said."

"You Americans," Alain said. "It must be difficult to live in your own skins. *Mais oui, certainement.* I will do it gladly."

While Simcha was getting ready to leave the party, Kate Thule, a teacher at the dependents' school, came up to me to show some pictures Jilly and she had taken at the school during a nuclear air raid drill. The pictures showed children crouched under desks, their arms wrapped around their heads.

"I'll do an article on it, if you want," she said.

I knew Kate could write from previous work she'd done for *The Minaret.* "Sure," I said," but, please keep excessively gory stuff out."

"Like what?" Kate was one of those schoolteacher types who makes questions sound like an intimating oral examination on "this week's material."

"Like pictures of what the human body looks like after being exposed to radioactive materials," I said, "And don't promote the idea that all civilians should wear dog tags for identification of bodies too ravaged for any other kind of identification. I don't care about the adult population, but scaring kids with this stuff does no one any good, and it could do some of the kids serious harm."

"Do you forget that we are in horrendous danger?" she replied sharply.

"Kids are in danger from a lot of things," I said. "Showing them gruesome pictures of bodies squashed in car wrecks, for example, doesn't help kids avoid such accidents."

"I don't accept the analogy," she said. "Public information about nuclear warfare is to help people prepare, and that is both doable and morally required."

"Prepare for what?" I said. "Civil defense films assure us that simple precautions like walled-off basement corners stocked with two weeks rations and a radio tuned to the emergency radio station should be enough for survival. The government says that such homemade precautions could broil its occupants to a crisp or squeeze them like a grapefruit."

"Is this not good," she said, now adopting a Socratic style, "having competitive voices working at getting to the goal we all desire—survival." She was beginning to breathe heavily.

"I think you have this nuclear scare stuff wrong," I said. "The possibility of a nuclear war is as horrible as it gets, but our pretense to be able to protect people in the area where one falls is sheer wishful thinking. Fear of the bomb is a new growth industry. Let me give you some examples. Many newspapers are carrying radiation readings alongside daily weather reports. *Popular Mechanics* magazine published a fallout shelter blueprint for the do-it-yourselfer. Psychologists are advertising themselves as experts on traumas related to fear of the bomb. Hollywood is preparing box office sellouts on the end of the world. The Federal Reserve designated banks for post-nuclear warfare check cashing. A farmer in Iowa, who built a fallout shelter for 299 cows, is advertising the shelter as a safe thing to do as well as an income-tax deduction . . . Kate, this is a new product and service being made available on the American market. The truth is that if they start falling there is no hope."

She stared at me as though I'd hit her on the head with a baseball bat, soft enough to leave her standing somewhat conscious, hard enough to get her confused attention. I should have known better. I suppose it was an outlet for all the other things going on that night. I was completely disgusted with the General's wife and frustrated about not being there to help Simcha when she most needed it.

Kate took the pictures back, said something about not understanding me, about things beyond my head, about maybe meeting her sometime to talk about the meaning of what I had said, about hating to have to go find her husband because he was probably enjoying himself impressing a pretty young nurse with tales of being a fighter pilot unless "he's already in her pants. Oh shit, sometimes I really hate this life."

She walked away, wobbly-legged and aimlessly just as Jilly came by with a circular tray holding two champagne glasses. I took a glass, Jilly took the other, yelled "heads up!" and then floated the tray like a Frisbee toward the center of the room. The game caught on. Trays were floating dangerously around the club. It was a typical military party. As the night progressed, the singing was louder and the dancing bolder. At this point, the General and his wife and other serious people would go home.

Simcha and I left the party and went to her car. "Why don't you spend the night in the Minaret office. You can use the sick room," I said. "I'll be working for fifteen or so minutes; and then if you want to talk, we can or you can just go to sleep."

"In the comfort of that broken-back cot with the fleas and bed bugs," she said, "marvelous." At least she smiled.

After I said good-night to Simcha and closed the door to the sick room, I went to work on the B-47 article and discovered that though my files were locked someone had opened the drawer where I kept notes and first drafts. I had rigged all my drawers. First, I bent parts of the sides. You had to forcibly jerk a drawer to open it. Then I used a system of spacing between files that would be affected by the jerking. Even if the intruder guessed that he had changed the spacing, there was no way that he could guess what the original spacing was.

I called the General. In minutes he was standing next to me looking at my files. "Who taught you this system?" he said.

"Guys I worked with when we did the undercover on Atlas."

"Hmmm," he said. I couldn't tell if he thought it was brilliant or stupid. "Anything missing from the B-47 file?"

"No. I number each sheet of paper consecutively and always know the last number I wrote down."

"Any suspects?" he asked.

"The Soviets, of course," I said. "But I have no idea who their agents are in Morocco. They'd do anything to get info on the B-47."

"Maybe," said the General. "Or, the new French agent Hedgie told you about has found his way here."

"Have you met Jacques Isnard, the movie producer?" I said.

"Yup, I told Major Courchene she could allow him to do some filming on base. Actually I had no choice. It is a French base, after all."

"Her husband, Alain, told me Isnard has buddies in the French police . . . the kind that do the heavy torture stuff."

"I'll have our criminal investigation people sniff around," he said. "If it's warranted, I might pass it on to CIA. But, Lord, I hate getting those people involved."

He walked around the office a while touching the tops of desks as though they might be concealing clues. "You don't keep anything about the bird cage . . . right?"

"Absolutely nothing," I said.

He was beginning to say something else when Simcha came out of the sick room. She was wearing only a blouse, her brown legs in full and enjoyable view. "Back in and close that door," the General said sternly to her. "I'll find out tomorrow if you're involved in anything here you shouldn't be." He gave me a hard look and left.

I followed Simcha into the improvised bedroom and sat down on the cot with her. She was crying. I maneuvered my chest under her back and put my arm over her shoulder. She positioned her head on my chest and said, "*Merde*, I won't even ask what that was all about."

"Aircraft secret stuff," I said. "No big deal. As long as there are military aircraft there'll be secret stuff. I think someone broke into my files."

"Is it trouble for you?" she said, lifting her head up.

"I don't know," I said

I tried to find my hankie to dry her face. I don't know why doing simple things like that at such crucial moments can be so frustratingly difficult. I had to jerk my hips up to get to my rear pocket, pushing up the back of her body, but I did get the hankie, and she giggled, which made my embarrassment worthwhile.

She settled back. I reached around, wiped her eyes and cheeks. Her brown skin was softer than I expected. She closed her eyes as I stroked them. When I finished, she turned her head and looked at me, her eyes wide and full of my image. "I'm going to lose it all," she said. "They'll never let me back on this base—the general's wife will make me *persona non grata*. Can you help me? This place is my only hope, the only way I can get to America as a journalist."

"I talked to Alain," I said, giving her my hankie because I thought she might do a better job with it than I was. "He will persuade the Major to not demand I let you go."

"She's crazy about Alain," said Simcha, "but I think she'll have to bow to the General's wife, who *sans doute* wants me off this base."

"I don't think so," I said. "The General's wife needs me more than I need her, and I think she knows that. So, she'll hang around nursing her shock, but she won't have the courage to demand something that could be refused."

'What do you mean," said Simcha, "she needs you more than you need her."

"Think about it, Simcha, I don't need her for anything. She needs me to open doors for her to have her photographed and to have me around to say she not only knows the base editor but can give him orders. She and I know it's not like that, but I play the game and that helps her. She knows I'm playing so she's ready to take requests from me at any time."

She put her head down on the pillow and took my left elbow into her hands, "Can I stay here tonight?" she said.

"Of course," I said.

"And you?" she said.

We went to sleep cuddling one another. In the morning we made sleepy love as the muezzin from the village *Petits USA* chanted his first call to prayer. Simcha, like Jilly, seldom called me by my first name. When she did the "J" was "zh" and the "i" was "ee" and the "m" as she ended the sound was an invitation to an open-mouthed kiss. As the muezzin chanted "Allah is Great, there is no God but Allah," I preferred Simcha's whispering my name as we touched and explored one another.

Author in front of French Foreign Legion Post, 1952.

Author at Casa Restaurant, 1953.

Crew of B-47 Strato. Author on right, 1953.

Chapter Nine

Cyprus

I was the only passenger when the C-130 Hercules plopped down on the tarmac at RAF (Royal Air Force) Akrotiri. The crew was in a bad mood. They were originally scheduled to fly to the states for a week of Christmas holidays. Being reassigned to fly me to Cyprus in a cabin designed to carry forty paratroopers, jeeps, and other equipment did not sit well with them. As usual I wore civvies and brought enough for three or so days in an overnight bag Jilly had loaned me. She and the others at the paper thought I was gathering material for a feature about opportunities for American military R&R on "Aphrodite's Island."

An Air Force sergeant opened the door and gave me a dark look. The crew didn't know what to make of me. They probably thought I had connections—a senator's brat or something like that.

I stepped out of the plane into a pleasant, richly-scented breeze and saw a jagged line of mountains not far away. One was snow-capped. Then I noticed an RAF lance corporal sitting behind the steering wheel of a jeep parked at the bottom of the ramp. He was waving me down, patting the seat next to his. Behind him were two RAF privates with a Bren machine gun and tripod between them. All three wore red berets, khaki shirts with Bermuda shorts, knee-high rugby-like socks, and well-polished brown boots. The motor was running. As soon as I sat down and put Jilly's bag on the floor, the jeep lurched forward as though we were in a race.

"I'm Drive," said the Lance Corporal out of the corner of his mouth. "The ugly old guy right behind you is Bren the elder. Next to him is his holder, Bren the younger. They're bloody bad shooters so we don give em any ammo. I keep them and the gun sitting there to scare the natives."

The elder said, "Drive's pissed cuz they took his driver's license away. He starts cleanin the loo tomorrow."

I tried to turn to say "Hi", but the jeep was making a wheel-squealing left turn off the tarmac. My body jerked back involuntarily as we looped around a Canberra photo-reconnaissance plane and two fighters. "Drive likes to let the road know who's boss," yelled the elder. Then both Brens and Drive chortled and I had the feeling I was their morning's entertainment.

We squealed onto a dirt road that ran between corrugated iron sheds, a Quonset hut, and some Bedford lorries. The base appeared to be strictly utilitarian, surrounded by ten-foot wire-mesh fences, security lights, and sand-bagged machine gun posts. It reminded me of World War II movie scenes of hurriedly built American air fields on Pacific islands. The smells of aircraft and jeep fumes mixed warlike with the distinct odors of sweaty khaki and the oil on the Bren gun.

About fifty yards ahead three armed guards stood blocking an opening in the fence. Drive screeched the jeep to a full stop, grinned, slipped into neutral and revved the engine. The guards crossed their bodies with rifles, crouching in battle-ready positions.

"Ten," said Drive. One of the Brens said "six." The other one said, "twelve, max."

The pedal slammed the floor. My back jolted. We were steaming straight at the guards who were now pointing their rifles at us. The two Brens yelled "Yeh, yeh, yeh."

We sped past the guards who had jumped out of the way laughing and cursing.

"Elder wins," shouted Drive.

Not long after we left the base, the road started to climb into the snow-capped Troodos Mountains. Drive's enthusiasm was confined by gravity but not by the twists and turns. There were no protection railings, precautionary warnings about steep and narrow passages, or protocols about what to do should a car going up see a car coming down, which, I was sure, would at best be at the last minute.

Drive appeared fearless, which was all right with me so long as the sheer precipice drop offs were on his side. "We're taking you to a hotel in Nicosia," Drive offered.

"You mean," said the elder, "you're trying to *not* get us there. Bloody hell, Drive, slow down."

"Bugger off, too dangerous," said Drive.

The elder grasped my shoulder and said, "Drive has him a little theory. He says the faster you go the less chance you'll get blown away if you hit a Greek home-brewed bomb. Bet you know about home-brewed bombs, Paddy."

"Paddy?!" I protested. I didn't know exactly where the humor started or stopped, so I was cautious.

Drive jerked his head towards me, which made me even more nervous about his driving. "Hain't your name Heefee?"

I considered telling them that I was half Irish and half Czech, and it really didn't mean anything anyway, but decided to say, "No, I don't know anything at all about them."

They laughed again. At what I wasn't sure.

A few miles later I looked down and saw a huge, fluttering pink blanket. "Probably three, four thousand today," Drive said, "yesterday there were more. Ever seen flamingos?"

I just shook my head. It was an incredible sight.

"This is their favorite stopover between the Caspian Sea and Africa," Drive volunteered. "It's a salt lake no deeper than a rifle bullet. One of our lads studies them. Says there can be as many as ten thousand on some days. But he's from London. Can't really trust them blokes."

After that we bounced on a road that was at its best rocks and ridges slightly smoothed over by splashes of blacktop. There were villages of mud-brick houses surrounding churches, with more houses strewn randomly at various distances from the village centers. Now and then, I saw a villa of some style in a flowering garden. More frequently, I saw scraggy goats nibbling between rocks.

We descended through a dense cloak of pine trees then took a sand-and-stone road through a green belt of wine country with whitewashed villages. In some the slogan ENOSIS AND ONLY ENOSIS was painted in white on houses and makeshift billboards. Smells of burning peat mixed with those of pines.

"Keep your guard up when the letters are in red," said Drive. "And don't intrude when they're in white." I knew what he meant. ENOSIS means "union" in Greek and was a symbol for the Greek-Cypriots right to kick out the British occupiers and become part of Greece. When the letters were white, it was an expression for peaceful ejection of the British. When they were red, it meant that the British were to be forced out by guerrilla warfare. Cypriot resistance fighters were organized under the banner of EOKA.

Drive was an interesting and useful tour guide. He particularly enjoyed surprising me. When we passed a gathering of thirty or so old wooden huts around a hundred yards downhill, he said, "There's one of the problems. The thinkers in London are flooding us with fresh troops to deal with the uprisings but, as is the way with the public school crowd, they don't make any arrangements for them. Those huts were built by Captain Bloody Kitchener seventy years ago. But it's all that's available. . . .

"Oh, by the by, "my orders are to take you to a meeting at Kitchener's little village. Wait. Then take you to your billet in Nicosia."

The interior of the building where the meeting was held contradicted the exterior, a reversal of Potemkin villages. If this building were an example, the old-wooden-hut appearance masked state-of-the-art facilities.

Gil Tompkins greeted me as I went into the meeting room. At first glance, he was an almost handsome man, medium-sized with a face so bony that his skin was drawn taut between the bones. He wore a safari suit over a crisp blue shirt, a straw hat positioned to make him look dashing, and Texas-style ankle boots. Appropriately he bore the odor of Old Spice. Gradually the initial impression was dampened by a realization that everything he had on was too clean and well-pressed. I wondered if he had kept the Abercrombie labels and price tags attached so that he could try to return the outfit when he returned home.

He introduced me around. It was a UKUSA gathering, so there were representatives of Britain, Canada, Australia, and New Zealand. They were all military except for Tompkins.

The British spokesperson, a Colonel Caine with a waxed handlebar moustache, a British upper-class accent, and strong pipe tobacco smells, announced himself in charge. "Now that we're all at the table, let's move on," he said. "As you know, our countries have agreed to share and organize our anti-Soviet electronic intelligence systems. I am authorized by my government to tell you about an exciting new development in our radar technology."

"Taking notes, all right?" asked the Canadian.

Colonel Caine looked pleased to have his authority recognized, but shook off the request with a scolding facial wiggle.

"Let's be sure we're together on the basics before we get into our latest. Most of the world's communications pass through high frequency radio, and all radar operates by transmitting radio frequency energy to a distance as far as the horizon, searching for those signals as well as objects. Anything that presents an obstacle to the radar transmission scatters the energy. Part of the scattered energy returns in the direction from which it came. By comparing the returned energy with that sent out, and in particular by measuring the time taken for the energy to go and return, the obstacle and its distance can be determined. When we pick up high frequency transmissions, we get the text. Of course, the good stuff is encrypted, but we've got chaps rather good at deciphering."

I had the impression that the audience was unappreciative of his elementary mini-lecture.

He nodded around the room and said, "All right, then. Now we're playing around with something new, called over-the-horizon radar. With it we can bend our radar transmission over the horizon and, well, eventually the transmissions might go on for quite a distance. We're already listening to and intercepting messages throughout the Arab countries, Israel, Greece, Turkey, and most of the Russkies' underbelly. With this new toy we'll go much further."

Colonel Caine invited each country's representative to offer a brief report on our own electronic spying. He had shown and told, now we were challenged to match him. There was an awkward silence, broken by Tompkins volunteering me to talk about USAF Security Service operations in northern Turkey. "He's a Russian-language specialist who knows what we're doing," Tompkins said, as though he had personally trained me.

I was surprised. The orders to all of us in Security Service were direct and clear. We were not to say a word about the operations to anyone except members of our team. But, he was my superior. I wondered how much he knew about the Trabzon station.

I stood up and went to the head of the class. I said "we're flying EC-135s along the Turkish-Soviet border. Now and then we violate Soviet airspace in order to trigger defense systems. We catalog the operating frequencies of the radar, the speed with which the antennas rotate, the rapidity of the pulse rate, and the length of each pulse."

"You're looking for the Russkies radar order of battle," said the Colonel, as though he knew it all along. "Where does the Russian come in?"

"We monitor voice transmissions, translating as we listen," I answered.

"This would give a nice, though brief, advantage for your bombers," said the Colonel. I was glad to let him take over, so I just nodded.

"You'd have a program of their electronic countermeasures," he went on. "So you could plot an almost undetectable route into the USSR. Jolly good stuff."

I nodded again. There was a lot more to it, but he seemed satisfied, and Tompkins was looking like a proud father, so I was glad to be able to leave it at that.

Tompkins gave me a cue to sit down as he stood up. "What Security Service gets their hands on is sent to an entirely new group called "The National Security Agency." It's essentially civilian. So autonomous that it won't officially exist. Its budget will be known only to a handful of people in Washington. It'll eventually have the greatest pool of cryptographic talent in the world."

The Australian representative said "Hear, hear." I think Tompkins missed the sarcasm in his voice. "Well and good. But my people think the Americans are holding out on us. For example, we've not seen a report from Belbasi for weeks."

He was referring to the seismographic facility we ran on the outskirts of Ankara. It felt tremors from all but the smallest Soviet nuclear tests above or below ground.

Tompkins said, "I'll check on that."

"And get back to me on it?" said the Australian.

"Naturally," Tompkins replied.

The officer from New Zealand, a tall and tanned perfect specimen in a well-creased khaki uniform, raised his hand, I could hear the sleeves crinkle.

"Yes, Major," said the British Colonel in charge.

"This is a bit off shift," he said, "we in New Zealand are worried—well, awfully worried—about the U.S. plan for nuclear warfare. Eisenhower tells us you have no plans for limited nuclear warfare, only for total nuclear warfare. We think that not only puts us in danger; it puts us, and, dammit, the whole world in jeopardy of extinction."

Tompkins coughed falsely and waved his arms. "I am not authorized to speak on that subject," he protested.

When Colonel Caine announced the meeting was over, I left the room, Tompkins at my side. "We'll pick you up at six tomorrow morning," he said flatly as people who like to show they are in charge often do.

Just as I was getting into Drive's jeep, Colonel Caine walked up and said, "Moment, please." He led the way to an outdoor toilet, I wondered if Kitchener had used it, opened the door to make sure no one was inside, then closed it and said, "I interrupted you because I didn't want that discussion about spying on the Russians to go any further. I don't know if you or this Tompkins . . . odd duck . . . know anything about the RB-45 project. If you did and blurted it out . . . well, that could mean a lot of trouble for Ten Downing Street. Do you know what I'm referring to? If you don't we'll just leave it go at that."

I did know about the RB-45 program, and I knew why Prime Minister Churchill would have to resign if it were made public.

After the euphoria of victory in Europe, there were key political figures in Britain and the United States, like President Truman and Prime Minister Churchill, who assumed that the Soviet Union would attempt to overrun Europe. Plans for war between the former allies were developed, always in deep secrecy, because, especially in Britain, there was considerable pro-Soviet sentiment. Those who believed in the peaceful intentions of the Soviets bristled when they heard of contrary suspicions. Revelation of a war plan pitting Britain and the United States against the Soviet Union was, for them, an abomination.

In as much secrecy as possible, the United States and the United Kingdom worked on a joint nuclear air strike capability and a joint aerial reconnaissance program. The operational war game was this: The Soviets overrun some areas in Europe. What do we do?

According to this war game, the US/UK response is to launch a nuclear attack on those areas. It is the only rational response because the US/UK forces do not have the manpower and conventional weapons that can match the manpower and conventional weapons available to the Soviets.

Nuclear attacks require radar scope imagery. British pilots were trained to use American RB-45 reconnaissance aircraft, at that time the most technically advanced aircraft to do this, at Barksdale Air Force Base in Louisiana, under the disguise of British-American air refueling trials. The pilots then flew RB-45s to Sculthorpe Royal Air Force Base in Norfolk, from where they flew missions to produce radar scope imagery of strategic European cities.

If the day had come when it was considered necessary to attack a European city with nuclear weapons, the RB-45 imagery would have been invaluable for success.

I found out about this when I was working out of Trabzon with the USAF Security Service. After finishing the reconnaissance radar of strategic cities in Europe, the RB-45 unit became a partner to what we were doing in the southern part of Turkey. The RB-45 did not have the technology on board that we had on the EC-135s, yet it provided excellent radar coverage of Soviet air bases in Belorussia and the Ukraine.

Yes," I said to Colonel Caine. "I know about that program."

"Would you have said anything about it?" he asked.

"Sir, I would not."

"What about this Safari bloke, Tompkins? That was a bloody stupid thing he did, putting you on the spot to talk about highly classified operations."

"I don't know," I said. "I hope he doesn't know about it."

"You're a bit of all right," he said. "You remind me of one of my sons."

"Fancy a beer, Paddy?" said Drive.

"Thought you'd never ask," I said.

"Bloody affirmative!" said both Brens.

The four of us were back in vehicle, on our way to Nicosia. Drive whistled tunelessly for twenty minutes or so, then took a sharp right onto a path barely wide enough for the jeep. We were in the back entrance to a village. Drive slowed down and stopped in back of a drab stucco building. He and I walked around to the front. Down a path a hundred feet or so, a white church sat among a patch of carob trees, the steeple rising higher than anything else in sight.

There were paths, mud-brick houses with wooden-beam sagging roofs scattered haphazardly, somewhat connected by unusually long lines of laundry sagging on cords. It was obviously the village wash day, the one day a week when women in the village can use the local stream, flowing creek, or, in extraordinarily fortunate locations, a river. In this village the water was a fast stream of crisscross muddy-green torrents. Jilly would have loved taking pictures here.

"Tip number one, Paddy," said Drive. "This is a general store in a Greek village. You can get almost everything including beer here. You can't get beer in a Turkish village. Muslims tee-total. Bloody awful . . . ain't it?"

I looked around. It was a maze of narrow alleys feeding into the one street. It was peaceful and traditional, except for the heavily sandbagged police station—a small stone building with a stalwart Commando guarding the front door. He looked angry and determined, and his finger was too close to the trigger of his Sten. I watched him watching us. "Pay no heed, man," said Drive. "He's never been a good one. Now he's worse. Christmas furlough canceled. Extra duty. All that. But even if he lets off a few, he'll miss you and hit a Greek cow. Then there'll be all of hell to pay. Whitehall'll be in dithers."

The store was a gathering place. Smells of sausage, wine, beer, and burning wood contrasted with the clear essence of pines outside. There were men bent over *tavli* boards, men smoking hookahs, men sitting around and arguing, men drinking beer or wine, and arguing. Most of the men wore frazzled turbans or knitted headwear, threadbare suit jackets, and blousy trousers tucked into boots. Many had elaborate moustaches. There was a picture of Archbishop Makarios next to an ad for Carlsboro beer.

A thickset, olive-skinned man standing behind the counter wiped his hands on an apron and acknowledged Drive's request of "*Keo, parakaló,*" with a glance at Drive's four outstretched fingers. We walked away, Drive clutching the bottles between the fingers of both hands. A small man in a lumpy brown suit with a clean threadbare shirt buttoned tightly at the collar, who was sitting in a rocking chair at the door, broke off some yellow cherries from the bunch he was eating and handed them to me. His face was thick and weather-aged. I'd never seen yellow cherries before. I foolishly said, *"Merci,"* and he graciously nodded as though to say, "It's all right, we were all young once."

As we drove away from the village, we passed a stoop-shouldered priest with a patriarchal beard talking to a young shepherd as though he were giving him advice. I wondered if they had confessions in the Greek Orthodox Church.

After another half hour the beer was warm, the cherries too soft and sweet, but I was enjoying myself. We were on the Mesaoria, a great plain that surrounds Nicosia. It is bare except for some dusty, desiccated pepper trees that haphazardly dot the landscape. I could see misty outlines of the medieval Venetian slanting curtain walls that encircled three miles of bastions, castles, churches, and gates.

Cyprus is a historical phenomenon. Everyone who was anyone in international trade and the Crusades left their footprints here. Lusignans were in control three hundred years. Venetians, eighty-two. The Turks stayed three hundred. The British had been here for seventy-eight. And along the way Richard the Lion Hearted stationed his Crusaders here and married in a castle he built for the bride.

Perhaps as a symbol of conquest or perhaps for more practical reasons, conquerors throughout the world have used the major structures of their conquests as the basis for their own. In Nicosia the Turks used the magnificent Venetian Cathedral of St. Sophia as the basis for Selimiye Mosque. Even before I saw the Venetian walls, I saw Selimiye's frail fountain-points.

I had not been at all prepared for Morocco. It was a place seldom reached in the books I had read. I had a sense of familiarity with Cyprus, particularly the Crusaders' history there. One of my nuns passed around pictures of Richard's marriage castle, and I dreamed of being a knight crusader.

"Don't forget, Drive," said Bren the younger.

"Lad, why do you think I'm pushin this thing?" Drive said.

The hotel Drive took us to in Nicosia was called Ledra Palace, named after the first name given the capitol of Cyprus by the Hellenic Greeks. It stood just outside one of the Venetian walls that looked impenetrably thick. The Ledra might have been palatial at one time. And for this time, in this part of the world, it was certainly decent. The lobby had been decorated for Christmas by someone who had no idea of what they were doing, as they tried to follow what they saw in an old British magazine. There were paper Christmas trees and stars pasted on the thick stone walls, red and green lights dangling from the reception and concierge desks, intermingled with paper gingerbread men and Santas stapled to red and green crepe paper. The overall sense was of displacement, confusion; it looked all wrong except for the earnestness with which it had been done.

Drive came into the Ledra with me. He didn't hesitate when I invited him to have beers on me. As promised, Bren the younger had driven off in the jeep. "To the beach with a local lovely," Drive confided. "It counts as duty. We don't have enough water at the station for bathing so going to the beach once a day is not only duty, it's bloody required." Just before he drove off, Bren the younger said to me, "I saw a picture of a beach in Casablanca. It was all tents, no people."

Bren the elder went off to play in a soccer game at the British Regiment of Cyprus fields. "It's a honor match between army blokes and us," he said. He put the Bren and tripod on his shoulder, grabbed his kit and winked at us.

The walls of the Ledra Palace bar smelled of heat and the Mediterranean. Drive chugged down a Keo beer, came up for air and said, "See those two Jerries at the end of the bar." I saw two men in leather flight jackets.

"They're soldiers of fortune, waiting for the right weather conditions to fly two British Lightning Jets into Yemen. Problem is that this model of the Lightning has a short range, so you have to go in perfectly. He demonstrated the flight with an outstretched hand, taking me from the airstrip at Nicosia to Egypt and the Suez Canal, to Djibouti, then to the landing strip at Sanaa.

I caught up with Drive and ordered two more Keos. "And then?" I asked. "Who gets the planes?"

"The fighters will be used by royalists against republicans," Drive said. "Or maybe it's the other way around. I don't give a bloody twitch."

The next morning, Christmas Eve day, at precisely six, a big guy who could have been American or British, but was surely a bodyguard, came into the Ledra lobby, nodded to me and indicated I should follow him. A Land Rover was parked in front with Gil Tompkins posed in the back seat in a fresh outfit from Abercrombie.

"First," he said, "a little trip into the mountains."

We were the only vehicle on the flat, straight road leaving Nicosia. "Do you know Cyprus?" Tompkins asked, in the way that someone might ask if you know a certain person.

I looked around the countryside for five seconds or so, then said, "No."

It either went right past him or he didn't care for it. "Beautiful island," he declared.

The scenery was getting interesting, so I hoped he would shut up. We passed fields of olive trees and were climbing into the Troodos Mountain range. I could see in the distance a road snaking upward, a black lace on the glossy snowcap of Mount Olympus.

My wishes weren't answered. Tompkins continued, "Beautiful and vital to the national security of the free world."

I saw a village tucked away in a mountain recess, small houses cuddled around a church.

"The British monitor radio traffic from the eastern end of the Mediterranean in these mountains. They gather intelligence and we trade them ours for it."

I nodded and pretended to be paying attention. Then he did capture my interest, telling me about a new spy plane called the U2. "The British will allow us to fly it out of Akrotiri. This is an aviation phenomenon. It flies at altitudes unreachable by any radar system and can do surveillance photography that's so clear you'd think the pictures were taken from ten yards away."

When we saw the radar dome, Tompkins said, "The man we're meeting is a Lieutenant Mason, and he's . . . well, eccentric, so be prepared. Keep in mind that he's one of the RAF's top people in cryptology, and he's also an expert in Arabic language and culture.

Lt. Ronald Mason was indeed eccentric. He was standing in the dome entrance, wearing a woman's dress, knee stockings, and mountain boots, cheerfully hollering "hullo, hullo."

We got out of the Land Rover, and he walked out to greet us . . . with a very masculine stride. "First, gentlemen," he said, "take a look around. You can see most of Cyprus from here."

It was quite a landscape. The coastal lines and deep turquoise waters of the Mediterranean were clearly defined.

"What is the only land mass you can see from here? Guess, gentlemen!"

Tompkins laughed, with a little embarrassment, and said, "I never rain on another's game, Lieutenant. Please reveal it to us."

I didn't know either, but it never occurred to me that I should.

Mason pointed behind us. "Turkey!"

I saw only cloud cover.

"On a clearer day, of course," Mason added, chuckling. "And down there. See there. Remains of a Crusaders' castle. This was their stopover."

The remains were distinct enough for me to imagine what I'd only seen in pictures when I was in school.

"Righto, now I'll show you our stuff. Ever seen a radar dome? We call them God's golf balls."

During the next few hours, I was provided with tea and shown how the observation station operated. That was mildly interesting. Lt. Mason's hobby was much more so. He was a world-class ornithologist because he had invented a new method of tracking bird migrations. He used the radar station.

"Here," he said, handing me a publication of The British Ornithology Society, "my discoveries on the movements of demoiselle cranes. Lead article!"

After that, Tompkins took me to a Turkish coffee house in Yagmuralan. The owner, who was bent over a *tavli* board when we walked in, knew Gil from trips to Washington to visit his brother, who was the owner of a D.C. restaurant and sometimes a source of information for Gil's Cyprus unit.

"We have two things to add to your agenda," Gil said as we sipped strong Turkish coffee. "First, we want you to find a radio frequency in Morocco for Sharq al-Adna, the British propaganda radio station in the Middle East. You'll meet the director tonight at a Christmas Eve dinner. Second, and this is where things get exciting, we want you to help us hold a meeting here in Cyprus of Moroccan nationalist leaders."

He looked at me with the kind of smile that I know means I, too, should find this to be exciting stuff. My reaction led him to take on a sales-pitch tone. "The Greeks and Turks joined NATO this year. This is a Greek-Turk island, a perfect place! De-Gaulle's making noises about pulling France out of NATO, but for now he's got to go along with us on this. We tell the Moroccans we want to help them unite for effectiveness. We tell the French we're trying to quiet things down in Morocco."

He did a "Father knows best" gesture with his hands and shoulders, throwing in a self-confident laugh. Perhaps because I was not reacting appropriately, he switched to a stern voice.

"Shit. We're paying more than half the costs of the French war in Vietnam. They don't dare give us lip on this. We pretend to include them in the meetings, but we keep them out of the real talks. And, we let the Moroccan guys we bring here know what we're doing. That will bond us. The French will be out of Morocco in a year or two. We'll hold on to our nuclear strike bases."

He paused to take a drink of coffee. The bodyguard was sitting facing the front door. I wondered where his automatic weapons and hand grenades were stashed.

I took a large swallow and tried to sound sincere in saying, "interesting."

"Oh, it's much more than that. It's a thoroughly well-planned moment in history. If you help pull it off, you'll become an agent of extraordinary importance."

I was thinking, but not about what he wanted.

His right hand reached into the inside of his jacket, and I discovered that the advertisements about the storage space of Abercrombie safari outfits were not exaggerated. He pulled out a very large, thick map and a collapsible pointer. It was a map of Cyprus. I obediently cleared the table. He put the map down and extended the pointer one notch.

"Here," he said, using the pointer to keep me on board. "Yagmuralan. We're here." He moved the pointer a finger nail. "Here. Mt. Olympus. Where we came from." The point swept upward to the northern coast. "Here. Kyrenia. OK?"

"Thoroughly clear," I said.

"We'll start the group off with a dinner at The Ledra Palace." He was folding up the map and speaking as one who did things like this all the time. "The next day we'll take them to the RAF Observation Station to show what kind of intelligence-gathering power NATO has. Mason, of course, will not be there. Arabs get up tight about things like that. We'll have a Madison Avenue dog and pony show ready for them up there. Then, a grand luncheon here, hosted by carefully chosen Turks who can spread the word about advantages in having Muslims cooperate with Christians. We'll give 'em a chance to nap after that, then we head for Kyrenia Castle where we'll hold two days of meetings."

He seemed very satisfied with himself, particularly with the way he had stowed the map and pointer away in its pocket. I didn't know where to begin, so I admitted that to him.

"I suggest you ask me specific questions," he said. "We want your input."

"OK," I said, "a Greek Colonel, George Grivas, is threatening to come here and lead a guerrilla war for Enosis on the island with armed troops recruited from Greek-Cypriot youth. The Turks can't accept that, even if the British would. There have already been some incidents. All indications are it'll get worse. Won't that affect the plan?" I was careful, I thought, to not refer to it either as "our plan," or "your plan."

He smiled smugly. "Covered. The Greek military runs Greece today, and the CIA runs the Greek military." It was one of those smugly confident pseudo-logical arguments for which mere mortals have no acceptable response.

"Grivas, too?" I asked him. "He's rogue. He's on a personal mission." Grivas had once been much in favor with the Americans and British because he ran the infamous fascist terrorist Organization X that massacred ELAS, the military arm of the Communist Party in Greece. He was a Cypriot native by birth and a feverishly ardent champion of Enosis.

"They know how to control him."

I didn't believe that. Grivas was known to be his own man, passionately dedicated to Enosis, unusually skillful in guerilla tactics. And, as members of ELAS could testify, he was as ruthless as they come. In addition, he had a charisma about him from which legends live for thousands of years. Cypriot youth referred to him as a Greek-Cypriot Robin Hood.

But I was in no position to put up an argument, so I asked, "What about the Berbers?"

"We want you to identify the man who can tell us which nationalist leaders to invite and how to deal with the Berbers on this. Maybe one of those mountain chiefs would want in."

"The only organized group is the *Istiqlal*," I said, "and they're outlawed. If you invite an *Istiqlal* leader, he'll be arrested by the French. If you tell the French you're holding a meeting of nationalists leaders but not inviting any *Istiqlal*, they'll be suspicious of either your grasp of the situation or your intelligence. . . . And I have no idea who the leaders are. Even my contacts don't. . . . Well, one of them might know someone who knows one of the leaders."

Tompkins drank some more coffee and looked around the restaurant as though deep in thought. He leaned back in his chair and took on a pose that I suppose was his idea of how a senior Harvard professor of physics might explain the laws of gravity to a delivery boy.

"Let's get one thing straight," he said. "This plan didn't pop out of Mamie Eisenhower's head one afternoon at the beauty parlor. An interdepartmental group, involving Air Force Intelligence, the CIA, and the State Department's top experts on Morocco and the Mediterranean, worked it out after a month of meetings. You're lucky to be involved."

I had made a mistake. I forgot that people with grand notions don't really want your views, only your applause. They are consumed by the brilliance of the plans in which they take part. So I shut up, which seemed fine with him.

"That's Audrey Sandworth, Dick's wife," said Tompkins. We had just arrived at a small mud-brick house surrounded by an orange grove in Polemidia. He was referring to a raven-haired woman wearing a Greek-style maxi dress who was waving us in from the open front door. "Hostess extraordinaire," he added.

She was indeed. The warm greeting at the door was followed by comments and manners that made me feel special, as though she'd waited a long time to have me in her home. She did that with Gil as well as with me. She probably did it with everyone. But I didn't care. It was Christmas Eve. I wanted to feel good, have some fun.

Dick Sandworth was less skilled at entertaining though dressed well for the occasion in a white dinner jacket, pale blue shirt, and white bow tie. He was walking around the table—on which there was a platter of moistureless slices of lamb and soggy Yorkshire pudding—filling our glasses with a Cypriot red wine that had a good taste even though it smelled sweet, when Tompkins asked him to "fill our Moroccan friend in on Sharq al-Adna."

"It is important to understand," Dick said, standing, holding the wine bottle against his chest as though posing for an ad, "Shark al-Adna is an Arabic-language radio station for which we provide entertainment, news, and commentaries." I thought that perhaps he wore a toupee because his hair didn't move in the right directions when he frowned, as the British sometimes do when concentrating in public. "Our purpose is to get their attention and then get the Western viewpoint across."

I said, "Was it originally operating out of Palestine? That's what I've heard."

"Yes," he answered, "before my time with it. Then it was an anti-Israel operation. We're less so now, though we do stay to a very pro-Arab position. We transmit Egyptian music, readings from the Koran, and commentaries from a 100,000-watt medium-wave transmitter that is easily heard throughout the Middle East and could be heard . . . with some static at times . . . in Morocco. All of our on-air speakers use Cairene Arabic. You perhaps know that Egyptian music is very popular in Arabic-speaking countries."

He went on to explain the significance of the Cairo accent. Arabs from one country have difficulty understanding those from another. The Cairo accent is understood by most Arabs. "The frogs use Lebanese Arabic-speakers." He chuckled the way the British do when mocking the French. "No one outside of Lebanon understands them. And, some Lebanese are Christian, so all Lebanese are suspect until actually seen in a mosque . . . on their knees."

"There's serious competition," said Audrey. "The Egyptian nationalists have started a station called *Sawt al-Arab* . . . it means 'Voice of the Arabs.' They tell Arabs to turn out their colonial masters, one way or another."

"They're reaching from Morocco to Qatar," Dick said soberly.

"And," said Audrey, as though playing a trump card, "they have Umm Kalthoum."

"The diva of Arab song," I said, "she's already a legend."

"Herself," said Dick. "She sings a while. Talks about her life growing up poor and destitute in a village along the Nile, the terrible oppression her family suffered under King Farouk and the British."

"She's good," said Audrey. "We colonialists should be intimidated by her."

"Awww-drrry," said Dick.

Tompkins announced he was "tasking" me—as though he had given me a grocery-shopping list—to set up the "wherewithal" to get the Voice of Sharq al-Adna into Morocco. "I've found the perfect man to help get it done," he said, smiling at our hosts, "Yunus Bahri."

Audrey looked shocked. "That pig!"

"My god," said Dick, "I thought he was dead."

I then learned that Yunus Bahri was a living legend, or a dead one as Dick had thought, in Arabic-speaking radio circles. Originally an Iraqi journalist who published a pro-Nazi newspaper in Baghdad, he launched and ran from 1939 to 1945 Radio Berlin's first-ever Arabic language service. He was Joseph Goebbel's pride and joy. His trademark opening line for his broadcasts—spoken in the Cairene accent he mastered at Cairo University—was *"Huna Berlin! Hayiya al-Arab!"* "This is Berlin! Long live the Arabs!"

"You know," Dick said, "he's still on the British wanted list as a war criminal. He recruited Arabs in Germany for an SS espionage operation in England and France."

"Which makes him useful to us," replied Tompkins. "We know how to find him, and we can turn him over to you anytime we choose."

"He'll be working for a British radio service," Audrey said, with no attempt to conceal her disgust.

"Tell me," Tompkins said, "that the British don't do the same thing all the time."

I asked, "Who will be able to hear it in Morocco? The French have receivers in their homes. Our Nouasseur Air Force station's music has captivated French teenagers. But your average Moroccan doesn't have a radio."

Dick said, "coffee and tea houses. That's where they gather around the radio, like Americans did in country stores long before your time. Coffeehouses are where your average bloke talks politics. And sometimes talks strongly. King Charles II closed the London coffeehouses because they were places of sedition."

"And," said Tompkins, with the casual arrogance of people who have access to vast resources, "we're giving Bahri as many radios as he needs."

Audrey downed her glass of wine in one long swallow and said, "Dinosaurs, that's what we are. Dinosaurs. The age of colonialism is dead. We just do not realize it."

"There's an information officer here on the island," Dick said, "Lawrence Durrell I think his name is." Dick was in a British absent-minded rambling mood now. His words were spoken slowly, each syllable carefully crafted. Not to any of us. He was talking to the wall. "Poet. Rather well-known in those circles back home. Lives in a Turk village like a native. He's written some thoughtful reports for the Governor."

Audrey said, "Dicky," and fluttered her hands.

"Oh . . . sorry, luv," Dicky apologized. "It's this Durrell fellow. The way he writes. Distracts me somewhat. He told the Governor the present situation should be captured and manipulated while it was still in the operatic phase, so to speak, and capable of being turned to our advantage. There is a good chance of our gaining fifteen years or so on the promise of a democratic referendum. With that in hand, we could begin overhauling the entire administrative machinery, especially the police, so that the Greek-Cypriots got a fairer shake."

"Makes sense," Audrey said.

Dick smiled softly, "Ah, yes, but no one's listened to poets for hundreds of years. They listen to Athens radio, though . . .

praising these crazy kids who join The Youth Organization of EOKA."

"Is it true," I asked as I tried to slice into Audrey's slice-resistant lamb, "that the young men who are recruited swear to give their lives for the cause, no matter what they are asked to do?"

"I swear in the name of the Holy Trinity," said Dick, "that's the oath they take. They swear to sacrifice their lives if that's necessary to achieve the liberation of Cyprus. And, Athens radio tells them they are heroes. The other day three British soldiers were killed where they slept by a time-pencil bomb. The kid who did it—a sixteen-year-old—was caught. Athens radio glorified him."

That was the way it was in the capricious world of alliances, spy craft, and colonialism. The current leaders in postwar Greece were a military group put in power by the British and Americans. By themselves the military group would probably have lost in their battle with ELAS, the left-wing Greek anti-Nazi resistance movement, for control of postwar Greece. The Americans bought the equipment for Athens Radio and had military installations on Greek territory. Athens Radio supported the overthrow of the British in Cyprus, though the two were NATO allies. Then, of course, there were the glaring inconsistencies running through the American-French alliance.

"Most of those kids who join EOKA and learn to make time-pencil bombs have nothing better to do," said Audrey. "You must see some of that in Morocco, Jim, even though the French are far more decent rulers than the British."

"Oh, knock that off, old girl," said Dick. He turned to me and said, "Audrey's a Francophile, but a legitimate one. Raised there when her daddy was French correspondent for *The Times*. She even did service with the French underground when the Nazis had the country under boot."

I looked at her, hoping she'd explain. "I was trapped there," she said. "I was a free-lance correspondent. One of those who couldn't bear the thought of leaving when a really big story was breaking. The Germans were very cozy with foreign journalists

. . . hoping, I suppose . . . that we would paint a nice picture of their occupation. That gave me opportunity to help the resistance. I did what I could."

"And she's loved the French bunch ever since," said Dick.

"You get it wrong every time, Dicky. I don't love the French bunch, as you put it. I do think the British are treating the French miserably, using them but not trusting them. But far worse is the way the British treat the Egyptians. You and I are part of that." She turned a scornful face at me. "And you Americans. You have so much navy and air force presence here that the Mediterranean is being called *An American lake*. The French are cooperating, and you give them nothing but lies."

"Makes us lucky to be their allies, luv," Dick said with a big grin.

"Allies, maybe," answered Audrey, "but I think they're already catching on to how totally deceitful we are, even with our own people."

"Audrey," Dick protested, "don't tell me you're going to go on about ol' Cat Eyes again?"

"Cat eyes?" asked Gil, toying with a piece of pudding that slid off his fork onto his safari jacket. I wondered if they'd count that against him when he tried to return it.

"During the war we resorted to a lot of things to trick the Jerries," said Dick. "One of our tricks was to tell the British people something untrue that we wanted the Jerries to believe in order to distract them from discovering the truth. We told the British public we had developed a group of RAF pilots who could see in the dark like a cat does because we had concocted a very power-ful carrot juice. The Jerries spent a lot of time trying to find their way to the formula. Of course, the truth was that we were the first in getting together a radar system that worked."

"That was bad enough," said Audrey. "Now the government's doing Black Propaganda, saying anything to discredit anyone we consider an enemy no matter who gets hurt by the lies."

"That's rather strong, my dear," said Dick.

"Don't pretend, Dicky," Audrey said icily, "you don't know about the smear campaign orchestrated by the Foreign Office's Black Propaganda team claiming that Greek Cypriot School-girls are required to prostitute themselves with fellow members of EOKA. The Foreign Office Information Research Department hands out this garbage in official daily reports to British and foreign journalists. Here in Cyprus, Greek-Cypriots are hired to hand out pamphlets about how the foreign press is reporting on this prostitution. Some of the pamphlets have pictures of Greek Cypriot Schoolgirls who, supposedly, have told their priests about it."

"Dick," said Tompkins, laughing, "I heard some juicy gossip about British officers running a female impersonator club."

Dick grinned. "Oh, now there's a pair. Ted and Lesley. They came here as RAF Soviet Air Force analysts. Did their work rather well, it's said. More interestingly, they started their own entertainment troop dressing up as female impersonators. They were shipped out to Gibraltar rather like in the middle of the night. They had important skills, so the Government offered them another posting . . . providing they stopped their entertaining business. They took dishonorable discharges and started the first night club in Spain featuring female impersonations . . . Franco says they must be communist infiltrators and insists that the British government get them out of his country."

We were laughing until Audrey interrupted, "Whatever became of that floozy German girl who was Bahri's mistress?"

Driving back to the Ledra Palace Hotel Tompkins said, "Those two run the biggest numbers station in the world. Ever hear of The Lincolnshire Poacher?"

"The Lincolnshire Poacher" was known around the world in certain circles. The listener sits and waits patiently as the short-wave buzzes and hisses. Eventually he hears the first fifteen notes of the folk song played on a glockenspiel. Then a soft British-accented female voice announces the numbers.

I had dinner Christmas evening at the Ledra after walking around inside the brooding Venetian walls. It was as though I was inside the pages I had read as a boy, miles of moat, a donjon, spires, redoubts, and drawbridges.

Though there were no more than ten diners in the restaurant, a trio—they looked Turkish—performed as if they had a real audience. The piano player used a fake book and left it in the bench when they were finished for the night. I didn't have anything else to do, so when I thought I was the only diner left I had the waiter bring me a bottle of red wine and signed for it and the meal. He was pleased when I told him I wouldn't need any more service but would like permission to play the piano. He said "Mer-ry Christ-a-mas, sir. Of cours-e you may."

It was a baby grand. Well tuned, with good bass resonance. I played an hour or so from the fake book. When I got up from the bench, I heard someone applauding lightly.

She was sitting at a table with her own bottle of wine. "Sarah Miller," she said when I walked over to her. "Thank you for making the night less lonely." She looked to be in her thirties, attractive in a simple white satin blouse. Her light brown hair waved down the sides of her face, coming to rest on her shoulders. Her eyes were hazel. "Please join me," she said. "I have a message for you from a large gentleman in Cairo."

"Who likes to eat couscous at Shepherd Hotel?"

"No," she laughed, "pigeon on the Nile."

"Got to be him," I said. Her perfume was light jasmine.

"He wants you in Cairo to do a story for release to American newspapers," she said. "You'll interview the new government public relations officer, Colonel Sadat. Hedge'll fill you in when you get there. He's cleared it with Jackman. Can you get yourself to the American Air Rescue Squadron field at Dhahran a few months from now?"

"I think so," I said.

"We'll bring you by British transport from there either to Alexandria or Abu Sueir. Hedge'll meet you wherever you land.

Come as an officer. The new government people are all Egyptian officers."

I nodded and said, "I knew it was too good to be true."

She smiled and leaned her head slightly, keeping her eyes on mine. Her hair bounced softly on her shoulders. "There's a Grundig 960 receiver and a bottle of Glenfiddich in my room. In an hour or so BBC Overseas will rebroadcast the King's College Choir Christmas Eve Carol Service. Would you like to join me . . .Oh. . . by the way. . . that's not included in my assignment."

Now and then in life, one confronts the need to make a difficult decision. That was not such a moment.

Drive picked me up at the Ledra the following day to take me to Akrotiri for the flight back to Nouasseur. He told me that Young Bren was dead. A Greek-Cypriot girl reported it. They were swimming. They got out of the water. Young Bren said I'll race you to the towels. He won, reached down for his towel and was blown to pieces.

Sahara Desert near Ouarzazate.

Chapter Ten

Port of Casablanca

As was our procedure, I went to see Eddy Boynton indirectly. Eddy believed that in the kind of work he did, the shortest distance between two places was not a straight line. I was dressed in a blue-striped seersucker suit, straw Panama hat, and all the other trappings of a tourist vigorously shopping.

I took a taxi to the Port of Casablanca bazaar area where a collection of closet-size stores, vendors with handcarts, and children holding their wares in outstretched hands sell goods from around the world, most of which are sold by seamen to the vendors at cheap prices because the seamen had not paid for them.

The arrangement was for me to spend an hour or so shopping in the bazaar, then to hire a carriage owned by Eddy. During the time I was shopping, one of Eddy's people would observe to see if anyone was following me. If a tail was spotted, the observer would signal the carriage driver, who would take me to a bus stop rather than to Eddy.

Eddy knew enough about me to know that I was not everything I appeared to be. He had worked for Atlas Construction Company when I was a member of a team of investigators who invaded their file cabinets for three nights and found evidence that the company kept two sets of books. Atlas had a cost-plus contract with the Air Force to build an air strip at Nouasseur that could be landed on by a B-36, the largest airplane in the sky. The set of books they gave the Air Force showed considerably higher costs than the set of books they showed the home office in New York. Eddy owed us because we made a deal with him that allowed him to escape prosecution as part of the Atlas fraud.

Eddy Boynton came to Oujda, Morocco, as a twenty-year-old supply sergeant with the American Fifth Army in 1943. The Fighting Fifth, under General Mark Clark, was the first American Army to initiate combat on the European mainland, at Salerno, Italy, eight months after its arrival in Morocco. During that eight months, Eddy did what any good supply sergeant did when his unit found itself in a very foreign country. He became a master at exchanging American goods for foreign goods. To do this he had to learn how to work in the legitimate, and more importantly the illegitimate, Moroccan markets. He discovered the value of American things peculiarly American, like Camels, Lucky Strikes, and Coca-Cola, and he exchanged them shrewdly for things not available to the Americans through their normal supply channels, like girls and hashish.

During those eight months, Eddy fell in love with an Arab girl. That, coupled with the profitable skills he had learned in the Oujda region, kept him in Casablanca after his Army discharge. He earned a comfortable living as a go-to guy for American businessmen who wanted to operate in Morocco, as well as for Moroccans who wanted to do business with Americans, in the legitimate, gray, and black markets. American businessmen had an unusual advantage in Morocco because of the Barbary Pirates.

Morocco was the first country to recognize the new republic of the United States. In 1787, Thomas Jefferson, John Adams, and Benjamin Franklin persuaded the Barbary pirates to lay off U.S. merchant shipping and signed the Sultan of Morocco to a treaty of friendship. This was facilitated with bribes totaling 10,000 dollars. The treaty gave American businessmen in Morocco freedom from import controls and the right to work in any currency.

In 1948 the French prompted the Sultan to set up import controls on all business activities and nationalities. It was a set-back to the American businessmen, most of whom, like Eddy, were ex-GIs who had come in on landing craft during World War II and stayed, making very comfortable livings for themselves because of the Treaty. They protested to the U.S. State Department, which sent a lawyer to the Peace Palace at The Hague to square off with a French professor of international law with a solid reputation, in front of the 15 black-robed, white-bibbed judges.

The professor argued that the treaty was an archaic document and that all other nations operating in Morocco accepted the import controls. The State Department lawyer argued that the French had violated international law during World War II when they allowed the Nazis to turn Morocco into a fortress to repel an Allied invasion. That is something you can't do with a Protectorate. Also, he said, today the French were trying to fuse Morocco into their own economy, which was a further violation of protectorate rights and responsibilities.

The court ruled in favor of the American businessmen. Eddy Boynton and the rest of that group knew that they needed the State Department.

Eddy's office was in a four-story building at the Port that was used as a warehouse with offices. The building's sea-damp smell was the only thing that was consistent with how it was used. Occupying at least two acres of space, it was constructed in the very grandest Franco-Moorish style, with arabesque arches, filigree ironwork, soft cornicing, and elaborate fretwork on the façade. The French built it in the nineteen twenties as a symbol of how majestic they could present themselves, even when putting up a warehouse.

Like his clothing, Eddy's office had a good-natured shabbiness. There were letters, bills, and invoices scattered on his simple table-desk along with an ashtray filled with pungent butts of *Gitane* cigarettes. Traditional Moroccan oil paintings dangled slipshod on blurry walls.

"I have a favor to ask," I said. "It has to do with information." He tilted his head slightly, his face tightly drawn, which was his way of saying he was perhaps listening. No commitment. Eddy was a skinny person who used a lot of body language.

"The nationalists," I said, "are planning to tell people they should stop buying French products. They would like to be more specific so that people will take them seriously. They would like to know, what would be the best choices, what would hurt or at least aggravate the French most?"

His face relaxed. He appeared relieved to find out I was seeking harmless information. "Tea," he said, "cigarettes, textiles and machinery. Wait until the shipments arrive, then boycott. Hit them when they're overstocked. Tea arrives on the tenth day of the month, cigarettes on the fifteenth. Textiles on the twentieth. Machinery on the twenty-fourth. And French movies . . . especially movies produced by *Centre Cinématographique Marocain*. Do you know that outfit?"

"As a matter of fact," I said, "I know one of their producers, Jacques Isnard. Know him?"

"Is that a serious question?" Eddy asked.

"Yes," I think he might have broken into my private files."

"Isnard is more than a movie producer. Does that help?"

"Yes, Eddy. It helps a lot," I said, "And one more thing, please. I'll be going to Ouarzazate with two young ladies, a photographer and a translator. I need a reliable place to stay."

"I think you do," Eddy said. "There's a former Legionnaire who runs a decent enough place for sleeping and eating. *Chez Dimitri*, he calls it."

As I was leaving Eddy yelled out, "you do know, don't you, that trade goes two ways."

I stopped and turned around. He threw his legs up on the table-desk and grinned. "Wool," he said. "Moroccan wool, especially the *aboudia* type, is at least the equal of France's finest wool. The French don't want anyone to know this. And they desperately need to keep the *aboudia* wool coming in."

"Eddy," I said, "I'm glad I came."

"Remember that," he said.

I went to General Jackman's office as soon as I got back to the base and told him what Eddy said about Jacques Isnard. He seemed short of time. So there was no vodka or music. He was trying on military dress jackets. Standing in front of a full-sized mirror, he stood to one side then another. Discarded one, put on the next.

"Do you think you could talk to Didier's sister-in-law," he said. "Didn't you say she was spending some time with him. Find out if he's asking her questions or anything like that?"

"I'm going with her and Jilly to Ouarzazate in two days," I said. "I'll see what I can find out."

"First to Marrakech, right. I think that's what you said."

I nodded and said, "I'll see Hedgeworth's contact there, then go on to Ouarzazate to scout out the Foreign Legion's capabilities for *Istiqlal*."

"Remember . . . careful, son . . . shit." A button had broken off the jacket he had just put on. "Oh, and there's another thing. There's a delegation from Washington coming in tomorrow. They'll explain to me our new President's policies. Truman'll be glad. Eisenhower is not buying into the idea of limited nuclear warfare. As you know, there have been rumors of this for months. Now it's official American policy, and Eisenhower wants everybody to know it—a nuclear weapon is the same as a bullet."

Jackman threw the broken-button jacket on the floor and said, "Ike's not blinking. We're on full alert to use everything we have."

View toward the Casablanca waterfront area.

Mosque in Koutoubiz, from medina.

Chapter Eleven

The Trip to Ouarzazate

The night before Jilly, Simcha, and I were to leave for our trip to Ouarzazate, we slept on cots in *The Minaret* Quonset hut. I said we were writing an article on the French Foreign Legion station at Ouarzazate, considered to be the last outpost of Western civilization in the Maghreb.

I had assembled two cots for them and put a box on each of the cots. "If you still want to do this," I said, "we sleep here tonight and leave first thing in the morning. There's clothing in the boxes . . . it's what you'll wear. I have some other boxes with water, things like that, including extra camera film. The cameras are in the jeep."

"Why like this," said Simcha.

"I'm nervous about a few things," I said. "I'll call Pierre. Let him know you'll be gone about a week."

She nodded. She trusted me. That made me feel very good.

"*Mon* editor," said Jilly, "let's look at your kits." She lifted the lid on her box, pulled out some of the items, and said, "Oh, lookee, Simcha, our bloke's been shoplifting at *Harrod's* Safari Shop.

In each box there were two pairs of desert boots, three pairs of heavy khaki socks, underwear, brown T-shirts, fatigues and fatigue hats. The fatigues were three sizes larger than what they normally wore.

"There's one more thing," I said. I held out scissors and a comb. "You must cut one another's hair. I want the result to be unattractive. Actually, ugly would be perfect."

They understood.

Jilly took the comb and scissors. As she butchered Simcha's hair, I showed them the Browning and the Walther PPK I carried. "Either of you know how to use these?" I asked. Jilly said she thought she could, "in a pinch." Simcha asked how to use them. "You point and pull the trigger," said Jilly, "that's really all there is to it. Except . . . do be braced for the jolt it'll give your upper arm. But . . . won't be as bad as this haircut, luv."

"Bloo-dy," said Jilly, "it looks like it's underwater."

We were on the Haouz Plain, close to Marrakech. Because of its plentiful oases, it was the crossroads of ancient caravan routes that had crossed the Sahara desert from Timbuktu. Originally the purpose was to take goods north to Moroccan ports. At some point in time, a few caravans began trading with one another at the Haouz oases. Eventually people from the north began to bring goods to the Haouz and traded there with the caravans of silk-veiled Touaregs from the Sahara and tribes from the Algerian border. In time cattle dealers, olive-growers, tanners, makers of agricultural tools, leather-merchants, silk-weavers, and armorers came together on a continuing basis.

Marrakech became a multi-cultured floating population of around twelve-thousand people, including wild, pale-skinned Berbers from mountain villages, black men from the edge of the desert, Arab tribes from the plains to the north and the west. A permanent marketplace emerged, then a village, then a town. Eventually Berber princes of the Alomoravid tribes who at the time were in control of Morocco declared Marrakech to be the metropolis of Morocco.

The land stretching around Marrakech was red earth fissured by streams and dotted with stray knots of palms where camels and donkeys watered.

Marrakech itself first appeared to me as a red wall in a wilderness, the entire scene dancing in vaporous curving lines. Eventually the vapors lifted, exposing sun-streaked cliffs of the Atlas with summits of pure white snow. Marrakech was now red mud walls with tops of minarets protruding above them, a last scene before the mystery of the mountains.

As we drew closer to the city walls, we passed small collections of structures made of flattened tin cans, sticks, corrugated iron, and animal hides. Each collection was surrounded by palmettos and palm trees. Some had a modest whitewashed mosque. I heard a sound, like bees buzzing at a distance. Then it was a low hum that intensified as we got closer to the city. I realized it was the sounds of human activity inside the walls.

We parked the jeep outside the bulky eleventh-century mud walls. Simcha negotiated a car-watching fee with three ragamuffin kids, then bargained with a carriage driver to transport us and our things to *Hôtel Gallia*. The French adminis-tration required coach tariffs to be posted on the back of the coachman's box but, Simcha said, it's better to negotiate the price before getting into the carriage. "If you wait until you're at the destination, the driver will haggle over price for hours."

Once inside the walls we were at *Place Jemaa el Fna*, the huge unruly square that is the physical and spiritual heart of Marrakech. What had been the buzzing sounds outside the walls were echoes of what we now heard in the square, a frenzied roar of activities.

Marrakech is a conglomeration of villages more than an urban community. *Place Jemaa el Fna* is a gargantuan market uniting the villages. It is a fairy tale place, an "Arabian Nights." Snakes slither in sinister curves from wicker baskets to the sounds of raspy flutes and ominous drumbeats, urged by epileptic gestures and hissing incantations from their wildly-braceleted keepers. Flames shot out of men's mouths. There are tall, bearded, long-robed story tellers, one with a monkey on his shoulder, surrounded by turbaned audiences. There are camels, tethered tigers, acrobats, sword swallowers, and jugglers in costumes vaguely reminiscent of Tudor heralds, acrobats, strongmen who lift donkeys up over their heads, witch doctors, dentists harshly yanking teeth with pliers, fortune tellers, cacophonies of bells, drums, fifes, flutes, cymbals and pipes, clouds of fragrant steam rising from huge saucepans full of stewed chickens and heavily scented lamb meat, flat bread piled in elephantine heaps. I was bewildered and enchanted. I wanted to run away, and I wanted to stay there the rest of my life.

The carriage took us to a corner of the square where metal-workers were pounding out dents in ploughshares brought to them by scroungy men in cloaks who sat passively waiting and observing; then on another twenty yards was *Hôtel Gallia.*

Jilly and Simcha did not mind at all when I told them I would go off on my own for a few hours. Knocking around Jemaa el Fna was fine with them, and I had arranged a meeting for them with Julio Simon, an Air Force doctor at nearby Ben Guerir Air Base, who lived in Marrakech and maintained an illegal and free clinic. I had done a piece on him that was not cleared—the Air Force did not want it known that an American officer did anything illegal, even if it was a noble humanitarian effort—so it went into my WICIW file. This was a file of articles that I believed should be printed, so I called it my "When I can, I will," collection. Jilly was pleased with the idea of the photo opportunities, and Simcha was eager to talk with the people Julio Simon treated. I wanted them in a relatively safe place. It was an agreeable arrangement.

Simcha told me I would find a queue of carriages on a street next to our hotel. I went there and showed a coal-black coachman the card Hedgeworth had given me in the Casablanca bar where we first met, to help me find Abdelqadir. The driver scratched his grisly beard as he studied the card. He excused himself and walked over to the carriage driver behind him in the queue. Coachman number two scratched his derriere as he stared at the card. Then he spoke loudly in what sounded like angry words gesturing dramatically with his hands.

Coachman one returned to me and said in a swarm of French and English that I should give some cigarettes to coach-

man two because without his help we would never find this
address. I handed over half a pack of Lucky Strike cigarettes. I
needed Simcha. But off I went.

The carriage stopped in front of a dirty stone building at the
end of an alley of cinder-block shacks with plain, silent door-
ways. The alley was lifeless except for some boys kicking a
homemade soccer ball around in swirls of dirt, a dust-caked dog
who scratched his lower body incessantly with a rear paw, and a
few unattended patches of wild sunflowers. Even though I paid
what I'm sure was an exorbitant price for the ride, the
coachman shrugged his shoulders as though to say I had taken
advantage of him. Many Moroccans did that after all trans-
actions. They mean it as a compliment, to make you feel that
you outsmarted them.

One of the boys kicking the ball around ran to my side and
told me I had chosen the best hotel in Marrakech, if not in all of
Morocco, so it was difficult to find a room. He offered his
services. He knew the owner and would put in a good word for
me. I agreed, and he led the way into a room that smelled of
stale tobacco, old wine, dust, and decay.

"Monsieur Abdelqadir," the boy yelled. Then he said something in what I guessed might be Berber. He probably said that
he found me wandering around the city and had beseeched me
to find my room here. The man standing at the hotel's makeshift registration desk—a table with keys, ashtrays, and stained
glasses spread around on it—looked up. I handed the boy a few
coins and looked at Abdelqadir. He was a tall, slim man with
cropped black hair. There was a split from his nose through his
upper lip, exposing the ends of two gray teeth. Perhaps a
harelip that had not been stitched at birth.

I approached him, said "Essad Bey," and held out a large
denomination franc note that disappeared quickly into his coat
pocket. He appeared to not even glance at it. I suspected he
knew the serial number as well as the denomination.

Without a word he led me through a labyrinth of streets,
alleys, and mud lanes roofed with rushes twisting through

housing of stones and cinder brick barely protected by rusted tin bent to look like roofs. We climbed over a camel plopped down across an alleyway, crawled under a cart pulled by a street cleaner, and dodged swill thrown from windows above us. Abdelqadir moved briskly. I struggled to keep up with him.

Eventually we came to a villa set in a garden of banana, orange, and lemon trees, with enormous cacti growing close to the walls. The trees were connected by walkways of pink sun-baked brick. Considering where we had just been, the smells of citron blossoms were a paradise. A shiny black 1937 Packard Marque, almost twenty feet long, was parked in front. It had virgin-white sidewalls (had the car ever been driven?), a curving rumble seat with three large foot plates to lead the passenger into the soft leather cushions, spare tires mounted on the sides of the long distinctive Packard engine hood, and doors twice the size of ordinary car doors.

We went inside the villa through a scalloped archway, into a vestibule with sky blue walls decorated with ancient carpets and embroidered mats. Just as the walls were tasteful, the ceiling was gaudy. We walked up gray marble stairs, past a mezzanine level decorated with potted cacti, arriving at a reception room bounded on three sides by a continuous line of window glazed in Moorish design.

At the far end of the room was the curious presence of Essad Bey sprawled on a rainbow of cushions. He wore a turban with spraying feathers in the center, enormous multi-hoop earrings, and garish rings on his pudgy fingers. A multi-colored djellaba covered his body like unruly ocean waves until it reached his bright red Turkish slippers. He waved the fingers and rings on his right hand, sending reflections to some of the windows. I wondered if it was a signal for dancing girls with veils and bouncing breasts.

It was a command to Abdelqadir, who obediently backed slowly out of the room staring blankly at the floor.

I accepted Bey's invitation, communicated by a gesture with his left hand, to sit on a chair covered in red velvet trimmed with blue and yellow fringes. Next to the chair there was a small table overflowing with sweetmeats and fruit. I selected an orange, thanked him for his hospitality, and told him I came at the suggestion of a large British gentleman who enjoys pigeons with beer on the Nile. An odor of heavy pomade came from the rainbow.

He snuggled his right hip into a purple pillow, opened both hands and moved them toward himself, suggesting he was ready to hear me.

In a swirl of English and French, we proceeded. He spoke both in a French-flavored voice. I told him I was going to the Ouarzazate Legionnaire garrison to write a feature piece on it and needed a contact there who would speak openly and was high enough in rank to authorize my photographer to take pictures.

As we spoke he smoked a kif pipe that looked like a thimble, occasionally sucking so intensely that the kif burned like a live coal and black smoke roared out of his nostrils.

He told me that I should be able to find out all I need to know from the commandant at Ouarzazate. "His name was Schillinger before he took a nom de guerre," said my host. That is an old and honorable military family name. He fled Germany a few years after Hitler came to power. A man like that cannot live with men like Hitler. He's been with the Legion ever since. Now he is the senior officer for Legionnaire garrisons and camps in the Atlas. There are many former members of the Nazi Wehrmacht in the Legion down there. You'll hear Wehrmacht marching songs in some towns. They all know about why the Commandant left Germany, but that doesn't matter. He commands their respect. Talk to him. He knows everything about the situation there. It is not good.

According to Bey, morale was all but gone in the Legion. France came out of the war with very little of what is important to a soldier, weapons, ammunition, transport, and medical supplies, and that was gone during the first year of battle with the communist rebels in French Indochina. At Ouarzazate there are two Sherman Armored Recovery vehicles, which are made to rescue fallen tank crews. But there are no tanks anywhere to be seen. "Desertion," he said, "is such a problem that the movie *Beau Geste* is banned."

I thanked him and was about to leave when he asked me if I knew about "the convoys."

I said, "No. What should I know?"

The French mine manganese up there where you are going. They convoy it out in teams of trucks. There is no room for you on a road where there is a convoy. If you're going downhill or not going around a corner you will be all right. If you are going uphill or around a corner, pray there is some place to pull off the road. Do not assume such will be available.

Abdelqadir was told to take me back to wherever I wanted to go. I did not want him to know where Jilly, Simcha, and I were staying, so I asked him to take me to *Place Jemaa el Fna*.

It was an amazing sight. What had been a magnificent scene of ordered, though to my eyes bizarre, collection of scenes from "Arabian Nights" was now as though a tornado had scattered the individual stages and stalls into bits and pieces in disarray across the vast square. Date branches sprawled on canvas awnings. Here and there, pieces of fruit. Folding chairs turned inside out. Donkeys on their sides wriggling their legs and kicking lemonade pitchers and water pipes. Empty cobra baskets lying on their sides. Everything covered with red dust.

"Dust storm," said Abdelqadir, as though it were an every-day happening.

"It was a bloody red devil hurricane," said Jilly when I found them in our hotel room. She and Simcha had poured buckets of water over one another in the room's non-operative shower stall, leaving a thick red sediment on the shower floor.

"These things start on the Sahara," said Simcha. "Think of the Sahara as an ocean. A storm at sea shows up as tidal waves that get smaller and broken into pieces by the mountains. We saw a piece today."

Hôtel Gallia rooms were positioned around a tiled courtyard two stories high, with colonnaded balconies hanging over trees of oranges nestled in burnished green leafs. Through the night I heard scurrying sounds and giggles coming from the second floor, where, Simcha said, some female slaves were kept.

Around midnight the scurrying sounds became fast-paced. Simcha yelled *"Merde!"* Jilly said, "That means shit right? How bout bloody hell."

The jeep's engine coughed erratically as we drove away from Marrakech. Jilly pulled to a stop and said, "it does this now and then."

I thought of something Edith Wharton said in her essay about traveling in Morocco, that it is one of those places where well-laid plans fall to pieces when one little cog fails, leaving one alone in untamed and mysterious circumstances.

In a moment Jilly was under the hood while the engine idled, working her mechanical magic. She returned to the driver's seat and drove on. The jeep didn't purr, but it was no longer misbehaving. Jilly said, "Praise the lord." She stopped, turned off the engine, said "Which reminds me," got out and pulled out a can that was in a box on the back seat, went to the front of the jeep and dug her fingers into a Vaseline-like grease, and applied it to the headlights. "This will keep them from getting frosted in a sandstorm," she explained to us as she spread it around on the glass bulb. "Don't you love those military training manuals?"

Jilly drove with a confidence that the jeep would do whatever she asked of it. Simcha appeared less self-assured. Perhaps because she knew more than Jilly did about where we were going. In 1953, with the exception of French Foreign Legion Posts and roads built by the Legionnaires, the High Atlas country was little different from what it had been at the end of the century before or at the end of any other century for a thousand years or more.

Many had tried. No one had conquered the High Atlas. Successive assaults by Roman legions more than two thousand years ago, Arabs beginning in the seventh century and continuing since then, by Portuguese, Spaniards, and Turks in the fifteenth and sixteenth centuries, and the French in the twentieth failed to establish political control. A village could be militarily taken but not held. Throughout all this time Berbers maintained their tribal customs. Just as the pomp and pageantry of the Moroccan Sultans was unequalled anywhere in the world, the ability of Berber tribal leaders, the nepotic caids, to remain in power in their own ways amazed the Europeans. Caids lived privileged lives in fortified *kasbahs* with slaves and harems filled with the most beautiful young local girls.

After thirty minutes or so the tarmac road gave way to dirt and rocks, the jeep going with, rather than absorbing, jolts. It was uncomfortable. It was also majestic. We were amidst streams, birds, and lushness. As we climbed we saw flat-roofed boxy wattle-and-daub houses wedged into rockfaces, watched over by buzzards at the lower levels, falcons on the next, and eagles at the summit. The mountains were reddish-brown dotted with green walnut groves until they reached their snow-capped and gray-blue summits.

Simcha told us to be aware. "We'll be going through Berber villages. God knows how we'll be received."

God didn't know, or was confused. In some villages the people waved kindly to us; in others, they threw stones. Jilly moved the jeep slowly through the friendly zones, waving her right arm, and quickly away from the stone-throwers. When we saw groups of children who weren't throwing stones, we stopped and handed out baseball caps. Most of them wore wraps made of sacks and were bare-footed. If women appeared, we gave them henna. If there were men around who looked as though they might want to assert themselves, I passed out smokes and lit them up with a Zippo lighter. As I had hoped, the clicks of its head opening and closing fascinated them. It was crude diplomacy, but it seemed to work.

The biggest challenge was how to deal with the boys swinging squirrels. When we drove away from some of the villages, we were challenged by boys twirling strings around their heads like lassos. At the end of the strings were live squirrels.

"If you give them money or anything else," said Simcha, "there will be another gang of boys doing the same thing as soon as we drive away. It's your choice. Baseball caps will not do in this case. Cigarettes would."

"A little money?" I said.

Simcha nodded. For the equivalent of around one dollar, we bought safe passage through four squirrel-swinging gangs.

In the valleys, Berbers plowed terraced fields of barley and corn with hand-made wooden plows pulled by mules and camels. The neat rectangles of crops were shaded by olive and almond trees. At higher altitudes there were clusters of huge cedar trees providing protection from the wind for shepherds tending sheep and goats. Women were rinsing clothing in streams that rushed down from snow-capped mountains. Some of them waved and laughed at us while they were beating their wash on the rocks.

Though Simcha didn't really speak Tamazight, the Berber language, she had been around Berbers enough to know how to communicate with them, using a combination of Arabic, Tamazight, French, and body language.

After ascending on a road that wove through eerie moon-scapes, we came upon a wedding ceremony in a village that was fairly large compared to the others. Simcha said it was a market center, also used for weddings and other ceremonies by people in that area. Many of the women bore indigo tribal tattoos on their foreheads—simple symmetrical arrangements of lines and dots—with elaborate henna designs on the palms of their hands. Their jewelry was large, plentiful and gaudy—silver belts, necklaces of coral, amber, and shells, richly-beaded earrings, heavy bracelets and rings. Most of them wore the *gouna'a*, an overgarment of black cotton cloth embellished with designs made of yarn.

Two whole sheep stuffed with pigeons, rice, and nuts were turning on spits to the sounds of crude pipe and percussion instruments.

A few miles outside of Tahanaoute, the village Simcha selected for our overnight stay on the way to Ouarzazate, we came to a blind turn and saw a Berber with a rifle slung over his shoulder standing alone in the middle of the road. Jilly said "Bloody hell," and slowed down. When we reached him we could see a mass of Berber tribesmen on horses, donkeys, and camels down the hillside about fifty yards from us. They were armed with swords, muzzle-loading rifles, and saddle-mounted mortars. They looked up at us. One of them yelled something. Some of the horses stirred. The man in front of us stood aside and waved us on.

Not much further up the road, we came to an assembly of djellabas scattered on a mountainside in a audience-like formation. Some of them were sitting, some standing. Perhaps there were a few hundred of them. I thought of biblical stories about Jesus preaching to impromptu audiences. We were in a semiarid mountain patch with snow-covered mountains in the backdrop.

"Probably mountain dancers," said Simcha. "You and Jilly go take a look. I've seen them. I'll guard the jeep. Jilly, take a picture from here, then leave your camera. It'll probably be all right, but if either of you sees that no one is smiling at you and anyone seems unhappy with your being there, get back here. Don't run. But do get out of there."

Jilly and I walked far enough into the assembly so that we could see the dancers. Some of the faces smiled at us. A few appeared to be nodding a welcome.

There were around a dozen dancers, all of them boys, wearing long loose white robes reaching their feet, with cords of colored silk wrapped around the sleeves and small black scarves thrown casually on their heads, half veiling their faces. They were standing stock-still, their heads back over their shoulders. Soft monotonous drum and flute sounds gradually increased in speed and loudness until the sounds were swift and piercing. Then the dancers, while maintaining a frozen state in the rest of their bodies, suddenly moved their feet vigorously. The contradiction was arresting. The assembly of djellabas murmured approval. The rest of the dance had two motifs. One was to do with other parts of the body what had been done with the feet— quick movements in contrast to stillness in the other parts of the body. The second was to glide forward while lifting the scarf to reveal a full face then retreating with swift footsteps and pulling the scarf back down.

The local inn of Tahanaoute was tended by a gap-toothed man who looked like an old Jewish prophet. There was a huge white ball on top of his head, perhaps a hastily-arranged turban. His deep-lined face was the color of old burlap, scraggily decorated with a dirty white beard that went on below his chin until it reached his waist in a lop-sided triangle. He smelled of garlic and stale sweat.

Simcha made a deal with him for a room with three beds. She gave him some money and told Jilly and me, "*c'est bon*, the room is down the alley . . . behind the animals." There were no keys, no bar of soap with a towel, or anything like that.

During the booking negotiation, two old men on wobbly chairs studied us with dark morose eyes while continuing to carry on an intense discussion with one of their busy hands in the other's lap as the second hand supported a water pipe that gave off smells like the incense used at Catholic high masses. Their heads were wrapped in turbans; their faces and scruffy beards well-weathered. They wore shabby, rough-wool caftans and relatively modern socks that had worked their way down to heavy high-top work shoes. They almost kept their quick glances at Simcha and Jilly discrete. I could feel the struggle in their eyes as we left the room. It was one of many moments when I wondered how good I was at disguising female figures.

We took food from the jeep. Some oranges, strawberry tarts and bread for me, and the same plus flattened cheese balls coated with red wax for Jilly and Simcha. We walked past a courtyard with a small herd of goats and chickens enclosed in a barbed-wire fence. Three moth-eaten camels watched us wearily.

The room had mud brick walls, a dirt floor, three cots, and a kerosene lamp. "Well," said Jilly, "it's a good thing I brought a surprise." She reached into her bag and took out a bottle of red wine, held it like a new-won trophy, and said, "*Voilà!*"

Simcha beamed. "*Jeelee, tu es vraiment une femme extraordinaire!*"

We showered using a perforated pot outside. The camels were unimpressed. For a person who does not live around camels, their stench is appalling. After I was washed and my own odor gone from my senses, I noticed the camels' stink more than I had before. And I remembered reading about an attempt by the U.S. Army to incorporate camels into cavalry units in the 1850s. The attempt failed because the camels' stench stampeded the horses.

Later, stretched out on our cots wearing only our underwear and drinking Jilly's wine, Simcha said, "In Beirut there was a game we played. Each of us would tell the others something very personal about herself, something the others didn't know."

"Let's play!" cried Jilly, looking at me as though she couldn't wait. "But first, I have a jolly to go with the wine. She reached into her bag and came out with a pack of Camel cigarettes. "I took these from one of the old C rations packages in the Nouasseur mess hall," she said while opening it and giving one to each of us. "They're really old . . . probably arrived on one of the supply ships that were with the invading forces in 1942. They're so dry that you'll only get two or three puffs from one of them after you light it. But . . . *what puffs*! Together with the wine we'll get super tipsy."

She was right. By the time I was dragging on my third cigarette Simcha's body, in a peach T-shirt, was looking very fetching. Jilly's long, curving legs were moving in soft waves, as was the floor.

"I'll go first," said Simcha. "*Mon Dieu*, I love this game." She cuddled her brown legs up around her left side and told us about her love affair with a professor at the American University of Beirut. "He was," she giggled, "a Quaker, and married, with three grown children going to schools in America . . . Quaker schools, *natueralliment.*" She rolled her body over, turned from us, with her knee against the soft brick wall, and said, "We made love in a room with a cot in the bookstore. He was not very good at it."

"How jolly in-te-lec-chew-all," said Jilly. She inched her shoulder up against the wall, got herself into a sitting position. "I shoulda listened ta me ol' mum. She said he was a twisted stick. I met him while he was one of those Americans waiting to invade France. We got married." She frowned. "Love's a crazy thing. Ain't it. He made it through Normandy, got shot in the arm outside of Paris, came back to England. I was with him all the time they allowed in the hospital. Months after that he and I went to America . . . Bloomington, in Indiana. His folks seemed to like me. The old man worked in a factory. The old lady was a schoolteacher. There was a sister who did jobs as they came along. Nice girl. And there was a high school sweetheart. My hubby and she had kept up their love letters from the day he left Bloomington . . . Yeh, even when he and I were a number. We were divorced before I had been in America a year."

Simcha said, "I'm sorry." Jilly shrugged her shoulders and inched back down to her cot. "It's your go, *mon* editor," she said mischievously.

I told them about my failure as an aspiring jazz musician. It was not a minor misstep. It was a realization that years of practice and commitment can lead . . . nowhere. A coming upon falseness in the idea that if you work at it you can be anything you wish. "Maybe the worst," I said, "was having to pretend that I was not destroyed by this."

Jilly uncurled and announced "Cheering up time, guv." She stood on her cot, wiggled her shoulders and broke out with an imitation of Peggy Lee's "Lover." Simcha ran over and jumped on to Jilly's cot. It was a Peggy Lee duet of British and French/Arabic accents. Mostly I noticed the curves of the bodies as they moved.

The next morning's air was cool and misty. We watched the innkeeper's wife make flat bread in a beehive oven while we ate breakfast. She cooked the dough over coals on top of a perforated metal shelf. On the table there was bread next to a bowl of yellowish jam, a basketful of oranges, yogurt, mint tea and something that looked like chickpeas. "Go easy with the jam," Simcha said, "it might be *majoun* . . . if it is, there'll be hashish in it . . . maybe a lot."

As we ate I worked on my tiny Hermes portable typewriter. I did a first draft for the opening to my article on the Legionnaire garrison at Ouarzazate. I wanted to use it as an introduction to the commandant, to show him that my intention was to be supportive, even admiring, of the Legion.

A sagging bus, overflowing with berbers in djellabas, caftans, burnooses and haiks, stopped nearby. The roof of the bus was covered with men holding goats against their chests, enclosed in a makeshift safety net of ropes held up by sticks. People were getting out of the bus and walking over to donkeys that were lined up like taxis at a taxi stand, their ears flicking flies. "This is the end of the bus line," Simcha said. "After this we get into the real countryside." Jilly dashed off, camera in hand.

The donkeys were so small and bowed that the riders' feet touched the ground. Some of the passengers urged the animals forward by pushing off the ground, looking as though they were riding a bicycle. A man had positioned himself between the bus and the donkey queue with a smoking pot. I asked Simcha what he was yelling. "Locusts fried and hot," she said. "There must have been a locust attack yesterday."

Some of the other bus passengers came over towards us to purchase doughnuts prepared by the innkeeper in a way that made his wife's bread oven look high tech. His doughnut-maker was a hearth of tamped earth into which brush and fire logs were put in one side and a smoke-hole allows smoke out the other end. A pan of hot oil sat on the smoke-hole. He put the doughnuts in and took them out with a small tree branch. When he did so, the smoky and oil odors provided relief from the stench of diesel exhaust. Before the bus arrived, there had been a pleasant scent of citrus and jasmine.

Jilly was preoccupied with her camera. She didn't see a young Berber man in a skullcap and shepherd's robe coming after her with a rock in his hand. I ran out to tackle him but wasn't needed because the shrill scolding voice of the innkeeper's wife halted him in his tracks. She looked at me, threw up her hands in disgust and apology, then yelled something to Simcha. "She says he's from another tribe, not hers," Simcha said. "The bus stop and her husband's doughnuts sometimes attract undesirables."

The angry young Berber man had been deterred but not completely driven off by the innkeeper's wife. We came upon him again as we were driving away from Tahanaoute. At the first bend in the road, no more than a mile from the bus stop, we had to slow down because there was a camel in front of us. And behind the camel was the young Berber, this time armed with an ax, swinging it back and forth as though practicing a golf swing. His eyes were wild and full of malicious intent. I took out the Browning, got out of the jeep, and approached him, pointing the Browning at his chest. Suddenly I realized that I had made a mistake. What if he had friends about? He lifted the ax above his head, came around the camel and charged at me. I fired, putting a bullet in his right shoulder.

He fell. Simcha came running. I yelled at Jilly to stay in the jeep and keep the engine going.

"Look at him," said Simcha, "he's suffering. We must take him back to the village." He was bleeding and screaming.

"No, no, no," I said. "Simcha. You and I and Jilly are out here all alone. We can't take that kind of a chance. We don't know how those people will react. We get out of here now. If it helps, I'll tell you that I feel like shit about this. But. We go. Now."

Then I felt a sharp pain just above my left ankle. He had managed to slice me with his ax. I sat down, pulled off my shirt, found a part of the sleeve that was not soaked in sweat, ripped it from the rest of the shirt and tied it as tight as I could around the bleeding cut, keeping my eye on him. He glared back at me contorting his face to keep from screaming any more. Alarms were going off in my head. Jilly drove the jeep to where I sat. She and Simcha helped me into the back seat. Jilly threw a first aid pack to Simcha and jumped back into the driver's seat. The jeep's tires screeched. Simcha untied my shirt knot, packed sulfa power into the wound and bound it with a clean white bandage.

"Good shot, guv," Jilly yelled. "That shoulder wound will heal nicely. I didn't know that *mon* piano man was an expert marksman."

The jeep protested Jilly's speed. It rocked violently from ruptures in the road's surface. There was a riot of pain coming from my leg. I saw reflections of the bright sun sparkling minutely between stones, probably from the invisible vegetation jawed at by goats. "I was aiming for his heart," I said.

After an hour or so Jilly pulled off on a rugged dirt road, then followed a rutted track into a cork forest, "to get some help for the wound and some petrol for the jeep," she said. Her destination was an Aircraft Control and Warning squadron. It consisted of a radar van and tents.

The soldiers were all members of the Georgia National Guard, except for the officer in charge of equipment maintenance, Bert Wolf, who was called "Kraut" because his father had fought in the Kaiser's army in World War I. "A recent commission?" I asked him. He smiled. He knew what I meant. He dated Jilly now and then, always dressed in civvies because it was against regulations for officers to date anyone in the enlisted ranks.

"No," he answered, "ROTC Rutgers."

By the time we left, Jilly had filled her gas cans and tucked two bottles of cognac in her bag. She and Simcha were wearing pith helmets with Guardsmen's nicknames scribbled all over them.

Between there and Ouarzazate, we went through a zigzagging series of blind twists and corners. Aleppo pines clung to crumbling rockfaces. Streams that had worn their way into long crevices glinted in the sunshine. Pastoral nomads walking across a stretch of wild grass with dusty, raw-hide tents on their shoulders glanced at us indifferently. Mountains become more rounded, houses built higher. The roadway mutated as frequently as the landscape. Sand and stone gave way to clay with jutting rocks and then the jeep would hum along on a smooth stretch of tar and hard dirt.

We stopped briefly at Anefgou. Mina Halima had asked us to take a few pictures there because it was her mother's village. Like other Berber villages we had seen, it appeared from a distance to be an adobe castle or a giant sand castle. The buildings were tall and continuously joined together, with a few crenellated towers. We came upon a funeral for a woman who had died of old age. There were women standing around on the side of a decrepit mud brick building with a roof of stones on wood. They were all staring at us with gloomy eyes. Except for a few male infants, they were all females of various ages. It was a timeless picture that could have been seen hundreds of years ago. Everyone was wrapped from head to toe in clothing patterns that suggested Mother Country cloth that was deemed undesirable by French merchants. Berber women didn't wear veils. They appeared more independent than Arab women. The Berber women and men are lighter skinned and taller than Arabs.

"No wonder Mina's mom stayed in Casablanca," said Jilly. "Simcha, would you ask them if I could take pictures?"

While Jilly was taking pictures, Simcha and I sat on the ground by an arroyo. "I have some questions about Jacques Isnard," I said.

She looked at me, tilted her head and said, "Questions . . . ?"

"I don't have a more subtle way to go about this," I said, "I have too much respect for you to play games here. I suspect that he might be more than a movie producer."

"You think he is . . . spying on the American Air Force?"

"That, or maybe something else," I said. "I don't care about the something else. I do care about the spying on the Air Force part."

"*Très intérressant*," she said. "And so . . . what do you want from me?"

"Does he ask you about things at the base? About airplanes, weapons . . . that sort of thing."

"But he knows I know nothing about any of that."

"So your answer is . . . ?"

"*Non.*"

I decided to let it go. I didn't really have the skills to do this kind of interrogation.

"*Mais*," she said, "he asks me questions about who I see at the base, coming and going, so to speak. He wants to know if there are visits by generals . . . or civilians who look important."

The creek bed was almost dry; the last of the season's waterfall from the mountains splashed casually on its stones and snaked complex routes around them. "Is that all there is," I asked.

"How do I know?" said Simcha. "I don't even know what we are talking about. Are we going back to the night at the *Minaret?* Are you jealous of Isnard? You haven't given me a nod of any sorts since that night. What is your purpose here? Do you want to compete for me? I would adore that. But remember that Isnard is serious competition. And there are others."

"Our relationship," I said, and as I spoke I could feel the unnaturalness in my voice, "is one thing and what I'm asking you about now is another thing."

"Perhaps, then," she said, "we should speak first about you and me, and then about Isnard and me. Do not jump to the Frenchman's conclusion that I have no doubts about an affair with you, that I'm just waiting in girlish anticipation of hearing you declare for me. I have serious reluctance about going further with you."

"Bloody, you two. So serious. Planning a wedding and then a divorce?" It was Jilly yelling at us as she approached the creek bed.

After Anefgou we came to a wide stony pink and beige desert plain with palm trees that led to Ourarzazate. The jeep bumped downward through ever warmer layers of air. There was a dissonance of odors. Orange blossoms and sun-baked excrement.

"Inside that hunk of mud," said Jilly theatrically, "T'hami El Glaoui, Lord of the Atlas, keeps his dancing girls and secret cellars of French wine and German beer." She was sitting with her hands on the steering wheel.

We were parked in front of *kasbah* Taourirt, an imposing fortified castle built with mortared mud and, according to legend, bodies of slaves who died on the job. It is three stories high and could fill two Big Ten football stadiums. At the four corners crenellated towers rise above the copper-colored walls. Between the towers are spikes and stepped merlons. The façade is pitted and decorated with geometric patterns in negative relief.

We were facing the iron-bossed double doors to the forecourt. They were easily twice my height and opened only from the inside, at that time, by a giant Negro slave using a foot-long key and his colossal shoulder. We watched him open it twice, once for a small caravan of camels, the other time for a Berber war-rior, wearing a blue indigo turban and dark brown burnoose, who danced his horse in small circles to show his displeasure for the wait. When the doors creaked and rasped open, an angry crow flew out of his nest on top of the tower to our left, expres-sing his fury with raucous caws.

In front of the walls there were acacia trees, bright green fans of date palms and scrub grass jutting out of the semi-desert dirt. That day three Berbers slept on their kneeling camels in shade provided by the walls. Inside the walls there was a courtyard of uneven rubble surrounded by a flurry of staircases cut into the walls and huge hand-hewn ladders.

You'd like to take some pics, wouldn't you," I said.

Jilly nodded. "It's a bloody wicked itch. Make me an over-night Margaret Bourke White it would. God . . . it's hot as an oven here."

There was a reason the House of Glaoua built the formid-able Taourirt *kasbah*. It stood in the confluence of three major oasis valley systems, the Ourzazate, the Dadès, and the Drâa. To have military clout at this juncture was to have control over vital trade routes.

Simcha was at *Chez* Dimitri, an *auberge* owned by a former Legionnaire. Dimitri was his nom de guerre; he was actually a larger-than-life White Russian who couldn't go home again. Ouarzazate was dominated by some of Glaoui's most fearsome fighters and the garrison's Legionnaires. Glaoui's men usually stayed inside the *kasbah*. The Legionnaires roamed the streets at night, drunk and unrestrained. There was no other source of power and authority except for the small and ineffective Legion-naire military police units. Simcha was livid when I told her that was the reason I left her with Dimitri. She believed she had earned the right to be with Jilly and me.

I couldn't tell her the real reason why I didn't want her with us. Years after all of this was over, people like Jilly and I would be far gone from Morocco. But Simcha might still be here. And there was also her family to consider. Hopefully my decep-tion would never be known, but there was a possibility it would. If it were, Simcha would surely be brought in for questioning, perhaps even a rough-handed interrogation. Members of her family might also be questioned.

We were too early for our appointment with the Ouarzazate Garrison's commandant, and Bey had warned me, "don't be early because he will be making sure all the shoes are shined for the photographer."

The garrison was a mile or so down the road from the *kasbah*—a square of white barracks surrounding a parade ground, en-closed in protective walls painted a deep burnt sinna. As Bey had said, two Sherman ARVs stood in a corner, along with two open-top, tracked Bren Gun Carriers, an old American Bantam shooting break wagon, two Panhard armored cars, four Fiat "Go Anywhere" trucks, motorcycles, bicycles, camels, and awesome white Arabian horses.

Two Legionnaires kneeled at attention behind a belt-fed machine gun in front of a flagpole with the *Tricolore* hanging on top. Their shoes were shined to brilliance, as were their cartridge belts and the machine gun. Though their faces were shaded by the visors of their kepi caps, I could see they were not smiling. A fluttering caught my attention. It was a falcon clawed to a gloved hand of a Berber in a pale blue caftan. I was comforted by its position . . . far away across the parade grounds.

The commandant's office was Spartan to a fault. There was a metal table with European-type folder files stacked neatly on one side, a straight back metal chair where he sat as we talked, and two chairs for Jilly and me. He was a square, Prussian-type, German, appearing to be the kind of man qualified for the Legion's officers' corps, who, according to the stereotype is a bachelor with the temperament of a condottiere, dreaming of action, whose only possessions are his African footlocker and who is only happy on bivouac. There was a *Gitane* cigarette box on the table showing a black gypsy girl dancing against a blue desert sky. Next to it were three wooden matchboxes. One was decorated with a painted camel, another with a vintage car, and the third with a palm tree.

I suggested we begin the interview with his reading what I wrote as a first draft for the beginning of the article; that is, Simcha's French translation:

> There is an indelible image of the French Foreign Legion. Lines of hard, disciplined men in their white képis, blue greatcoats, white trousers and blue waistbands marching out of fortresses of dried mud to do battle against enemies who always outnumbered but never outfought them.

The Legion is an army surrounded by romance, myth and intrigue. It has a history spanning a hundred and twenty-five years and a reputation for brave deeds that is difficult to beat. From fighting Russians Cossacks in 1853 to their ongoing battle with Vietnamese in Indo China, they have always been in the thick of the action. Started by King Louis-Philippe in 1831 as a means of funneling foreign layabouts and criminals into high-risk African garrisons, the Legion exists today as an implicit contract with the world's dreamers, drifters, adventurers and those in a hurry to change identities.

The contract says this: Fight anonymously for France's overseas interests, and we will provide you with a new identity and a new family. Despite its long-standing reputation as the last holdout for cutthroats and desperados, it is one of the most disciplined and elite forces in the world.

In this article we look at the Legion garrison in Ouarzazate, French Morocco, which sits in harm's way on the apron of the northern Sahara desert.

As the Commandant read, a tall Berber man with a pock-marked face came in to serve mint tea into small tulip-shaped glasses. He wore the traditional *Goumier* uniform, a brown and white striped robe, turban, goatskin sandals, and a very long knife. *Goumiers* were known for their capability to walk incredibly long distances without provisions, eating raw plants and, if necessary, their slain enemies. They raped and plundered when they could stop to do so. At least, that was their reputation.

The *Goumier* poured from a tea pot with a long, curved pouring spout and held the pot high enough above the glass so that the effect was a thin green waterfall that stopped miraculously at the glass's brim with a flick of his wrist, not a drop spilled. The commandant looked up from his reading, "Sorry, no sugar or milk today." He spoke English with an Alsatian accent. The Berber left silently, as he had entered. Jilly rolled her eyes in awe.

When the commandant appeared finished with my draft, he nodded casually and asked me what I wanted.

"The next line," I said, "will tell the reader that the commandant of the Ouarzazate garrison told me that the primary mission of his battalion . . . whatever you tell me it is, sir. Then I'll describe your office. We'll have a picture of you sitting at your desk or wherever you wish. Then, if it's all right with you, you'll take us out the door and I'll describe what I see. I'd like to interview a few people and take some pictures, as you decide. I know you are limited by security considerations, but I would like to give our readers your sense of preparedness for your mission. Everyone understands that supplies are short for the French military throughout Morocco, so I don't think we'll offend your superiors if we get into that. However, it's up to you. And if you say anything, then regret having said it, please tell me and I'll keep it off the record. I'm here to write an interesting and inspiring story for American military forces, not to write an *exposé*."

I told him I understood a little German. Though I was far from fluent in German my pronunciations were better than my French. It was like that with Russian also; that is, I was more comfortable with it and listeners didn't look as bewildered as they did when I tried French. Perhaps my tongue was built to twist itself around guttural sounds not smooth ones. Or perhaps it was the fact that the first foreign language I spoke was Czech, which I spoke with my bedridden grandmother.

He nodded casually again, the way a military man does when he's not sure whether to show deference or command. He gave us a short history of the battalion and its battles, including what some of its companies did in Indochina. Then he recited the duties of his command. "The Legion," he said, "is the face of French authority in this area." We have no serious trouble with the Berbers in this area because it's controlled by T'hami El Glaoui, who is far more the enemy of the nationalist movement and the Sultan than he is of the French. The House of Glaoua has never recognized the Sultans' authority.

He walked over to a wall map of North Africa and moved his hand across it as he told us that before the Arabs came in the eighth century, the Berbers occupied all the territory from the Siwa Oasis in Egypt to the Atlantic Ocean in the west and from the Mediterranean in the North to the Niger River on the southern borders of the Sahara. The Arabs took most of that away from them, including vast amounts of fertile plains. The Berbers were left with inhospitable mountain ranges and the Sahara Desert. The House of Glaoua has been the most powerful symbol of Berber revenge for hundreds of years, and this Sultan and this El Glaoui have brought the feud to a higher . . . more personal, level of hatred. The last time El Glaoui was in the Sultan's court, the Sultan's second-in-command called El Glaoui a nigger in front of the Sultan. The Sultan nodded instead of punishing his subordinate. El Glaoui stormed out.

"Nigger?" I said.

"El Glaoui's mother, Zora, was an Ethiopian black concubine," said the Commandant. "We call him The Black Panther. He's menacing in appearance and in what he's willing to do to get his way, but he's also flamboyant. He's built a golf course just outside of Marrakech where he entertains royally. Winston Churchill has been there a number of times."

"What's his source of income?" I asked.

"Hashish . . . prostitution," the commandant answered. "They say he has 27,000 public women in Marrakech who pay him a percentage. And he has some mines, a lot of land, water rights. Then there are tributes paid him by the Berber caids he supports."

He talked about what the Legion was currently doing in the Atlas—maintaining roads, patrolling towns, directing traffic at mountain passes after avalanches, escorting French officials and their wives. I asked him what the Legionnaires think of that kind of duty.

"I'll tell you because you might find a way to work this into your article," he said, "but I request you do not have it coming directly from my mouth."

Legionnaires, he said, go through a training that is severe and demanding. Unmatched by any other military group in any country of the world. That training is for fighting. For nothing else. A legionnaire's morale is based on his ability and willingness, without any hesitation, to be the most fierce fighter anyone has ever seen. Any duty not connected directly with that . . . lowers his morale. A month of doing things like that destroys his morale.

"However," I said, "legionnaires built all the roads in these mountains. I thought it was something you took pride in."

"That was the 1920s," he said, "when building a road was dangerous. There were landslides and Berber snipers shooting at them with rifles stolen from a live legionnaire or taken from a dead one. And there was the mission of bringing civilization to the savages. The word Berber means barbarian in Greek."

What I heard him telling me was that he had a serious morale problem in his battalion. I said, "Thank you for sharing that with me. I won't repeat it, but I'll let the reader draw his own conclusions from the contradictions between what being a Legionnaire means to a man and the kinds of jobs he is doing here. Civilian readers might miss it, might even think it's good that the Legionnaires are so flexible. I don't think a member of the American military, especially one who actually fights, will miss it.

"How's the food, the medical services, equipment, and so on," I asked.

The commandant looked away as though he wanted to change the subject. His profile was like a dark reddish-brown rock, and I noticed the multicolored tattoo drilled into his muscular right arm, a standard Legionnaire decoration.

"I think," he said, "the American military has the right to know some things. They are here and they are allies. Our provisions are . . . not good. Our only decent arms and equipment were given to us by the Americans and the British. Paris would leave us with only bolt-action rifles if it were left to them. The Legion is not prepared to do much against an Arab uprising. Like morale, everything is in short supply. Most of what we have now, even the socks . . . are provided by the Americans. But we don't have much. We count the bullets. . . . There's a Berber saying, *An empty sack cannot stand upright.*"

"Can I say in my article that you told me you are short on supplies, if I leave out the comments on Paris?"

"*Ja*, I say it in my reports every week. If someone in Paris doesn't like to read it in a newspaper, maybe they'll start reading reports from the field." He looked away from me and cursed using a German phrase I didn't understand. "Once," he said, "we were like crusaders, Jesuit Priests, if you will. Bringing Christianity to lost souls. Our swords drawn, our commitment passionate. Today we are like priests without a god. One can do that, but not for long. The old songs, the rituals, lose meaning when the purpose has fled. And the purpose flees when you no longer have the weapons to pursue it."

I felt guilty for getting what Si Fulan wanted, because the Commandant was grateful for something in which I had no part. It was, I thought, underhanded, and that bothered me because he was, it appeared, a man of honor. I supposed that Hedgeworth would laugh at those feelings. I heard him saying something like, you bloody amateur kid, you think you can outsmart an old hand like this guy? Ask yourself what he's getting out of this because he knows exactly what he's doing.

"What about El Glaoui?" I asked the commandant. "Would he help? He has a lot to lose if the French were forced out and the Sultan was completely in control."

There are hundreds of local Berber areas ruled by caids, he said. They are sometimes willing to follow El Glaoui's leadership but not always. Last year there was an incident so embarrassing to El Glaoui that the caids refused to march with him for six or more months.

It had to do with the moral support the Sultan gave to *Istiqlal*. This infuriated General Alphonse Juin, who was Resident General then. Juin kept after the Sultan to sign a declaration denouncing *Istiqlal*. The Sultan's Viziers drew up their own version, which the Sultan did sign. It was so nebulous that Mohammed V said, "I have no idea what I am saying. So be it."

Juin was livid. He wrote later, "Understanding that I was being trifled with, I severed all relations with the Palace." He turned to T'hami El Glaoui, who had for years demanded more from the French than a declaration by the Sultan that he censures *Istiqlal*. T'hami told Juin to depose Mohammed V.

General Juin proposed to El Glaoui that he gather an army and surround the Sultan's palace with an ultimatum: abdicate or go under my sword, and promised no opposition from the French. El Glaoui agreed, and probably was immediately relishing the prospect of the Sultan's refusal to vacate his throne.

"What followed," says historian Gavin Maxwell, "was a piece of trickery so gigantic that it must be difficult to find its parallel in the history of any nation."

T'hami pulled his caids together into a massive army of mounted warriors and charged northward to Fez without telling the caids what Juin and he had in mind. Some caids thought the Sultan would host them at a great feast, some thought they would march in parades glorifying their tribes. They arrived at Fez and surrounded the city with their tents. French armored troops surrounded the Sultan's palace.

Juin told the Sultan that he was surrounded by Berbers who wanted his head. The only escape from this, Juin advised him, was to sign a declaration against *Istiqlal* with far more teeth in it than his previous one. Mohammed V consulted with his viziers. They produced a signed declaration condemning "a certain party" and praising France's generosity. Nothing had changed. Everyone would know that if the Sultan intended to denounce *Istiqlal,* he would not have said "a certain party."

But Juin was satisfied. The truth was that Juin could never have allowed French guns to be silenced while the Berbers overthrew the Sultan. Mohammed V had powerful friends and supporters in the United States, Egypt, and in French intellectual circles.

A humiliated El Glaoui and confused Berber caids turned around and went home.

We saw one of the living quarters. A Legionnaire snapped to attention as we entered. Each bed had been stripped and draped with a red cover. The sheets had been tightly rolled into sticks and placed as saltire crosses on the red covers. A brown blanket was folded into squares at the foot of the bed. Next to the bed was a broom made from palm leaves leaning against the wall at a forty-five degree angle. I attended a Catholic High School staffed by Marianist Brothers in Cleveland. The brothers routinely made attempts to recruit students. Not with a big push or even a shove; it was more like a jobs fair where the student is shown what's involved in a certain line of work. Included was a look at how the Brothers of Mary lived. The Legion barracks reminded me of the Brothers' dormitory.

When we were outside, the Commandant said to Jilly, "Here's a picture for you, if you like." He was looking at two dark-skinned legionnaires brushing one of the Arabian horses. They were dressed in short red jackets embroidered in black, wide red sashes, with baggy blue trousers.

"Do you know Spahis?" he said. "They are Algerian, sometimes Tunisian, cavalrymen. There are four of them here."

"Are Spahis the ones who ride in parade on Bastille Day in Paris?" Jilly asked.

"Yes," said the Commandant. "They are the elite of the Legion. They are like the British Queen's Guard. Our four have gone to Paris the past six years for the parade. Two of them are good enough to ride flank."

That night Dimitri served couscous, wine and beer. We sat with him on hassocks around a mound of semolina interlaced with vegetables. Under the mound were bony parts of a chicken. We ate the chicken by tearing it into pieces, pouring oil over the torn piece, with our hands. As we ate, there was entertainment. First, three women dressed in colorful robes with elaborate tattoos on their faces and hands performed story-telling dances, accompanied by a man playing a one-string fiddle, a boy playing a type of mandolin made from a turtle shell, and a tiny man, dressed in an oversized djellaba and unexplainable tattered top hat, playing on a large drum with curved sticks.

The next act began with three drummers who walked around in a circle to their own loping beat. They were joined by a fiddler and a tall, thin man in a white gown along with a heavy-set attractive woman wearing an identical gown. The man bellowed angry sounds while the woman seemed to be responding in a high-pitched wail.

Throughout the dinner, Simcha avoided interaction with me, looking and talking only to Jilly and Dimitri. Jilly skillfully described our meeting at the garrison as rather routine, "really nothing you missed ol' girl, unless you like tea that tastes like diesel fuel."

When we were finished with our dinner, Dimitri asked if we would like to see "some *Gnawa*." I didn't know what he meant. "*Mais oui*," Simcha said, "*mais oui!*" Dimitri disappeared for a few minutes, then returned with a black woman in a white robe and two black men in black robes. One of the men had a lute; the other had iron clappers. The three sat on the floor.

Simcha said, "*Gnawa* is a performance by descendants of black slaves. Berbers and Arabs bring in groups like this one to purify houses after death and to cast evil spirits from the mentally ill. We must be very silent now until they leave."

After a few moments the lute sounded low monotonous tones. The woman's body began swaying very slowly. In five minutes or so she was in a trance. Then the iron clappers loudly called her to attention and the lute sounded eerie high-pitched phrases. The woman shuddered and moaned for a few minutes, then collapsed. The men carried her out of the room.

Later that night the three of us and Dimitri sat drinking wine, smoking black tobacco *Casa Sports,* and listening to scratchy recordings of Edith Piaf's *"Mon Légionnaire"* and *"Le Fanion de la Légion,"* while Dimitri regaled us with tales of life in the Legionnaires. Simcha had some trouble with his heavily-accented French and wine-soaked tongue but provided a translation.

He joined the Legion in 1920, a few months after his White Russian Cossacks' regiment had been defeated by the Reds. Some of his regiment's officers fled to Germany and England with their families and valuables. Dimitri and some of the other rank and file riders who had neither families nor valuables joined the Legion. Along with some former Polish Cossacks and Prussian light cavalry, they were the first Legion cavalry unit in Morocco.

The 1920s were the days of Abd el-Krim, who defeated the Spanish troops in Spanish Morocco because they were harassing him in his Rif Mountain enclave, and then, under a banner declaring a New Rif Republic, el-Krim went south with an army of over a hundred thousand troops. In a few months his army steamrolled over thirty of the sixty-five French border outposts. The Riffians were unstoppable, until Dimitri's cavalry unit galloped into the battle.

Neither side showed any mercy. Abd el-Krim's troops tortured their captives in ways that surprised even the more experienced and hardened Legionnaires. At some outposts Legionnaires immolated themselves rather than be taken. Dimitri said he saw a Riffian infantryman holding the head of a Legionnaire by the ear. "He looked at me," said Simcha valiantly translating, "laughed and spit in the dead face."

When el-Krim was almost at the gates of Fez, Dimitri's regiment attacked. They completely surprised el-Krim's troops because their riding and killing skills had never been seen in Morocco. In twelve hours of unrelenting slaying, el-Krim gave it up and managed to escape. Later he signed a surrender document. I saw him come into the camp to sign the peace agreement, Dimitri said. I remember great wood fires. The sun had risen, but in those mountains it is always bone-chilling cold in the mornings. He wore a heavy brown burnoose and rode a white horse. Two Spahis accompanied him, along with a French officer and the local caid who had been the middleman in negotiations between the French and el-Krim.

Here was the man whose name created terror. There was no emotion in his face. He was surrendering to the will of Allah. All of us stood at attention. He dismounted with the same stoical indifference, as though he were paying a morning call. He then walked over to the general who was there to accept the surrender. He bowed to the general, courteously, not hurried, and not at all deferential.

Dimitri raised his glass and toasted the bravery of his enemy, saying something like "to courage in battle."

I asked Dimitri if this was the same Krim who was exiled to Reunion Island in the Indian Ocean. He said, *"C'est lui!"*

I knew of Krim. He escaped from Reunion Island shortly after the end of WWII, was given asylum in Egypt, and became one of the leaders of the North African Independence Movement. His guerilla tactics didn't win in the end, but they left a legacy of warfare that inspired Ho Chi Minh, Mao Zedong, and Che Guevara. When told by an American general how Ho Chi Minh operated, Generalisimo Franco said, "He reminds me of Abd el-Krim."

We had three army cots with mosquito nettings in our room. I sat next to Simcha on hers, wanting to make peace with her. "On two conditions," she said. "Tomorrow morning before we leave, we spend a few hours on the desert. And you promise to never leave me alone until we are back in Casablanca." I said, *"D'accord."*

"I have a third condition," said Simcha.

I looked at her. "That you tell Alain," she said, "to work on your pronunciation."

We went out on the Sahara early the next morning. The air blowing from it was like hot air from a blazing furnace. Simcha and I climbed the highest nearby dune and looked out on the desert land sea. To the west it was a stormy surge of waves. To the east, flat and bronze-colored. Jilly sat at the bottom so she could click pictures of us with the absolutely clear blue sky over our heads. The molten sun was spread behind her shoulders. Then she untied her desert boots, wiggled out of them using her toes and took off her socks to ease walking on the sand. "Scorpions," I yelled to her. "Remember that other military manual?" She laughed and walked off. She had spotted an opportunity. On another dune a man in a black djellaba was on his knees, facing Mecca, his body flowing with his prayer. In the background there were a dozen or more hardscrabble trees in a swirl of dunes.

Nouasseur Air Base

"It'll be a great story for you," said Major Albright, Amelia Jackman's preferred pianist. We were at the O Club bar. He was telling me about an Air Rescue Mission he was launching. A C-47, on a flight from Rome to Nouasseur, ran out of gas at night over the Atlas Mountains. The aircrew and passengers, a total of ten, bailed out and the aircraft crashed.

"We're taking a twin-engine amphibious, two helicopters and one transport," said Albright. "There's room for you. We're leaving crack of dawn tomorrow.

"I can't make it," I said, "I'm leaving for Egypt in a few days, but I have a good person to send, Sergeant Jilly Hopper. She's an excellent photographer and getting to be a decent journalist."

"This is rugged, tough stuff," said Albright. "We never know what we'll run into. I don't know . . . a woman?"

"She can do it," I said.

The next day I told Jilly about it. As I expected, she was eager to do it, "If," she said, "you promise to help me write the article." I knew she was saying that to make me feel good. That was all right with me.

Chapter Twelve

General Jackman's Office

"I envy you," said General Jackman. We were in his office for my *Off to Egypt, My Boy* meeting. He handed me a copy of Baedecker's little red handbook on travel in Egypt. "It's the 1885 edition. A treasure. It's too valuable for me to chance having it lost. I'll be out of the office all day tomorrow. Spend the day with it here. Help yourself to the booze and records while you're at it. This is a travel guide . . . probably still the best there is on Egypt. Not a political analysis. But pay attention to the pages on what the Egyptian army officers did in 1882. It's the template for what's going on today."

"What I know," I said, "is that up to last year the British controlled Egypt. That the king was a puppet . . . a self-serving puppet who stashed away a lot of gold in Switzerland while dancing on the Brits' strings. The Egyptian army overthrew him, set up their officers as rulers, and they're giving the British fits about the future of the Suez Canal."

"That's it," he said. "Trouble is that the Brits don't understand that those army officers have the people behind them all the way because their goal is to restore dignity for the Egyptians first and then for the entire Arab world still under colonial control. That numbers the days for the British in Egypt. Now, about the 1882 business . . . the Egyptian army championed the same cause, to save the country from being totally raped by a corrupt King . . . the Brits sent warships to shell areas where the uprisings were strongest and put a few thousand troops on ground. That was the quick end of that. But this is different. If the Brits try to use military muscle, we'll have to get between them and the Egyptians."

"Because," I said, "the U.S. stands for nationalism and is not a supporter of colonialism . . . ?"

"Yep. Crazy world isn't it," said the General. "The Cold War makes for strange bedfellows. We need the Middle East quiet enough for us to maintain our military bases there in relative calm. If the British put those Egyptian officers down, we'll have to surround our Middle East bases with thick layers of troops, and that won't be enough to keep them safe from some very angry Arabs. We'd probably have to pull out. So, of course the Russkies are courting those Egyptian army officers."

"Supposing the British did a repeat of 1882, what would we do?"

He looked at me and shook his head. "Try to talk them out of doing it. Pray. . . . Something else comes to me. Other than Hedgie, don't expect any British Foreign Service people to be like those you met in Cyprus. The Cyprus bunch is new school, technically oriented, concerned with intelligence gathering. The Egypt bunch . . . they're old school in the worst of ways. Victorian throwbacks. Won their spurs in India, playing cricket at their exclusive clubs. For them the greatest period in history was when the sun never set on the British Empire. I still remember the first one of them I met . . . thin to the bone, very tall. Wore expensive clothing deliberatively disheveled."

Sometimes the General would express his disgust by posing a description as a dumbfounded question as he did when he said "deliberately disheveled?" sounding as though he wanted to say *"Why, in God's name, deliberately disheveled?"*

"His skin," the General went on, "had been so overexposed to Indian sun that it was bloated and looked as though it was covered with iodine. Now and then he looked at me incredulously and said *'Oh, do you really think so.'"*

Dhahran Air Field

Saudi Arabia

"Sir, no military food, anyplace on the globe, can match what you're about to have," said Tech Sergeant Charlie Morris.

We were sitting in the dining hall of the USAF 7th Air Rescue Squadron at Dhahran Air Field in Saudi Arabia just inland of the Persian Gulf. Sergeant Morris was flight mechanic for the twin-engine amphibian that took me from Akrotiri RAF Base in Cyprus to Dhahran. The plan was that the British would take me to Egypt the next day. Dhahran Air Field was typical military for air rescue missions in remote areas. There were a few transport aircraft that carried large lifeboats. Helicopters. Six by six trucks. An ambulance. Quonset huts, and tents.

The "sir" address had to do with my being uniformed as a captain, as Hedgeworth had requested. Sergeant Morris had been assigned to take care of me between flights. He was a career airman "from everywhere and nowhere," as he put it, "because I grew up as a military brat and enlisted right out of high school." I was uncomfortable posing as an officer, getting deference from a real soldier like Morris.

"The cooks are Italian chefs, the waiters are also Italian," he said, "left over from the Eritrean and Somaliland colonies. The U.S. Government gives them one of two contracts. If they provide satisfactory service for three years, we provide return passage to Italy. For five years exemplary service, we provide passage to the U.S. and American citizenship. A C-47 flies in fresh vegetables, fruits, and meat from Eritrea every day. I tell you, we've got food and service to write home about!"

"And the bad news?" I said.

"The only time we can leave this base," he said, "is when we're practicing or executing rescues or working on desert survival menus or going to Cyprus or Egypt or . . . of course, home. The King doesn't want his people to know we're in the country. Just wants his monthly rent check—bet it's a big one."

"Desert survival menus?" I said.

He grinned. "We collect anything that crawls, slithers, walks, runs or in any way moves in the *Rub al Khali* Desert sands—spiders, snakes, lizards, foxes, gazelles, and things I don't recognize. We send them to the states for evaluation of their benefits or hazards to survival in the desert. So, if a flyboy has to ditch in the desert here, he knows which he should eat and which he should kill. The pilots call it the guide to Saudi Fast Foods."

The next morning I was jerked from sleep by Morris shaking my shoulder. "We've got to get, sir, right now!"

He tossed my trousers at me as he gathered up the loose ends I had scattered around the tent before collapsing on the cot, exhausted from the trip and the squadron's generous servings of beer, wine, and bourbon.

"It's still dark out," I said, "so what happened to leaving in the morning?"

"Big sandstorm on the way," he said, throwing my possessions on the bed. "Pack 'em up, quick. There's a Brit transport out there ready to take off. It can't wait much longer. Once the storm gets here, nothing takes off for hours or days. . . . Never know. Move it, sir."

It was pitch dark on the airstrip, except for lights on two helicopters and what I guessed was the British transport aircraft. The helicopters were making first-stage chopping noises like mating calls to the soft roar of the transport's two engines. The motorbike on which I sat behind Sergeant Morris provided a soggy chatter.

When we arrived at the ladder to the British transport, there was no time for anything except having instructions screamed at me by a British airman who helped me strap into a parachute and bucket seat as the aircraft taxied.

We arrived mid-morning at RAF Abu Sueir, a British Garrison and air field close to the Suez Canal. My Brit attendant who had strapped me in swiftly and too tightly got friendly once we were clear of the sandstorm. He shared some coffee from a thermos and told me about himself and what he was doing in that part of the world.

"Fact is," he said, "I'm a light anti-aircraft bloke. They sent us down here just last year to protect the Canal from this new Gyppo military bunch. If you're hangin over with us a bit, let me warn you. There are no Gyppos you can trust . . . They're takin pot shots at us, booby-trappin vegetable and fruit carts we use, ambushin our vehicles. The other day we caught four Gyppos trying to blow a ship with a mine . . . wanted to block the Canal entrance. We eat food from tins and the tins' probably taste better'n the food. We sleep in tents. At night the bloody worst crawling things in this world attack us in our cots. This place is royally cocked up."

Fortunately I didn't stay at Abu Sueir. Hedgeworth was there with a Bentley Mark V and a burly driver named Omar el-Bashir who had the perilous look of a mastiff. His face was thick and black with puffy charcoal lips.

Hedgeworth was holding a bottle of red wine. "You look older. Maybe wiser," said Hedgeworth as he poured wine into tin cups. "Must be the uniform. How's Jackie?"

"I suppose," I said, "he misses having me around to take care of him."

Hedgeworth roared in laughter. I felt victorious. I had made it. I was in the club. Not at his or the General's level surely. But my foot was in the door. Omar started the motor and turned the steering wheel with a huge left hand, perhaps even larger than Hedgeworth's. He kept his right hand on a Sten machine carbine, the type British airborne troops made famous during World War II. The windows were bullet-proof thick. I wondered if this was to make me feel more, or less, safe.

We were driving from Ismailia to Cairo, closely paralleling a waterway unaccountably called Sweetwater Canal, a large ditch dug out of the semi-desert between the Nile and the excavations for the Suez Canal to bring equipment, materials, and water to the workers building the Canal in the late nineteenth century. What I saw was a river of pea soup emitting stench that filled the car though the windows were tightly closed. People were washing clothes in it. Relieving themselves in it. Drinking from it.

Now and then I saw feluccas, small wooden boats with one or two triangular sails extended by long spars slung to a low mast , gliding toward the Suez, weary donkeys bearing loads of wood and rushes, herds of goats scattering and reassembling as though they were tethered to invisible ropes that allowed them only a little freedom, and *gamoosa,* small water buffalo. The Bedouins appeared to be struggling just to keep at what they were doing. Most of them wore dark and mucky djellaba-type clothing. Some of the children suffered from bilharzia, which comes from water such as that found in Sweetwater Canal and reveals itself in huge scabs on the face, especially around the eyes.

The road was an asphalt of sorts, put together by pouring oil on sand. This combination hardens during the cold nights. The landscape was harsh and rocky. Housing was constructed by using discarded oil drums as walls with roofs made from reeds and bulrushes. Now and then there were blindfolded mules making circles around waterwheels, inspired by Bedouin children whacking them with sticks.

It was the most wretched poverty I had ever seen. I was glad that Hedgeworth was providing wine and camaraderie, despite the schizophrenic result I felt.

He picked up a folder that was on the floor between his legs. "I have a nice little surprise. Do you remember . . . in Casablanca I told you we were on to a top-level French agent."

"The one getting numbers station messages from a Brit?"

"Yup. Turns out there are two of them. I've got pictures and bios right here."

"And the Brit?"

"Audrey, the wife of Dick Sandworth, the Sharq al-Adna guy. Remember Sarah? She gave you a message from me in Cyprus. She told me you met Audrey and Dick. Bloody bitch Audrey was using the same equipment she and Dick use for The Lincolnshire Poacher."

"What was she telling them?" I said.

"We don't have all that yet," he said. "But we do know she told them about meeting you. Were you under cover that night?"

The look on my face was certainly enough to tell him I was not. My dislike for Gil Tompkins was seething. And I recalled Audrey's Francophile comments, how she favored French colonial administration over British.

The first picture he showed me was not a surprise. It was a shot of the agent from the waistline up. The upper quarter of his left chest was covered by medals and ribbons. The markings on his shoulders indicated he was a colonel.

"Meet Adolphe Chevetteraux," said Hedgeworth.

"I know him as Jacques Isnard," I said.

"What's his cover there?"

"He's a movie producer . . . I think he invaded my files."

Hedgeworth leaned back and looked out the window at the canal. A decrepit two-story wooden houseboat was being pulled by a dozen or so bedouins connected to the boat by ropes tied around their chests.

"As soon as we get to Cairo, I'll advise Jackie to pick up Isnard," said Hedgeworth. "We've got to find out how much he knows about you. Do you have any interrogators at Nouasseur? No, I don't think so. Too bad we can't use the French. They'd get it out of him. I'll tell Jackie to ship Isnard to Cyprus. We've got boys there who can do this."

"Whose the other one," I said.

"André Coronet, another colonel in the secret service," said Hedgeworth, opening the folder. He and Chevetteraux are De-Gaulle's favorite team. They pulled off some remarkable tricks in French IndoChina. Coronet's had a relationship with Audrey for years."

He reached into the folder and showed me a picture of Alain.

It was a few hours drive from where Hedgeworth showed me Alain's picture to az-Zaqaziq, a city on the Nile River delta northeast of Cairo, where Sweetwater Canal begins. I was dejected. Hedgeworth had been right when he told me, at that first meeting in Casablanca, I would never be able to spot the new French agent who had been sent to Morocco.

If it had been up to me, I would have sat silently through the saddest two hours of my life. But Hedgeworth would have none of that. After I told him about my relationship to Alain, he said, "This is more complicated than Chevetteraux because Coronet's married to an Air Force officer. Between here and Cairo, you and I are going to figure out how to handle it. Let's show one another that we can do it. Right now I suspect I've a lot more confidence in you than you have in yourself. Keep in mind two things. I can't figure this out by myself. You're the one who knows the situation there. Help me for Christ's sake. Don't sit there moping. I need you."

He suggested we begin by telling one another what we knew of "Alain". After I went through everything I could think of from that first day when Major Courchene introduced him to me, Hedgeworth told me about the bond between "Alain" and Audrey.

In the late 1940s Audrey was producing a British government-sponsored daily *English Hour* on the radio in Lebanon, using recordings sent to her from London. One day she put on a play that was billed as a drama about disputes between generations in a farming family. The précis on the recording did not mention that the family was Jewish. The farmer was advising his son to carve out a home in Palestine on land he did not own and to protect the home and the homes of fellow Israeli squatters-neighbors with whatever weapons were available. Pamphlets on how to militarily defend such areas were distributed to the squatters along with biblical references supporting the Israelis' moral rights to the land. An Arab newspaper in Beirut published a scathing review of the program and accused the British government of encouraging Jewish illegal land seizures as well as provoking armed conflict with peaceful Palestinians.

The radio show was canceled. Audrey was out of a job and out of favor with the crowd that does those kinds of things. It was, of course, not fair, but it is a golden rule of large organizations to diminish the embarrassing consequences of big mistakes by castigating the innocent field person with one hand while promoting the guilty headquarters person with the other.

Audrey knew "Alain" from parties at the French Embassy in Beirut. At the time he was posing as cultural attaché. She was a minor celebrity at the Embassy because of her work with the French resistance during the war. At one of the parties she received *Le Chevalier*, a silver medal with scarlet ribbon. Though it was the French Ambassador who pinned it on, rumors had it that "Alain" did the real honors much later that night.

The morning after Audrey was cashiered out of the British radio service, "Alain" visited her at her apartment and offered her a position as director of public relations with the French Embassy in Cyprus. His plan, which he did not reveal to her, was to dangle her talents in front of Dick Sandworth. Sandworth had been put in charge of Sharq al-Adna and The Lincolnshire Poacher when they were moved from Palestine to Cyprus. He was desperate for talent, which "Alain" knew. "Alain" wanted someone he could control who had access to The Linconshire Poacher.

The plan worked. Dick not only hired Audrey, "I stole her from the Frogs," he boasted, he married her. Which was not a problem for "Alain" because Audrey was his, for whatever he wished.

"Where is she now?" I asked Hedgeworth. The stink of Sweetwater Canal was now lodged in my nostrils, but it was no longer bothering me. We were smoking cigars and into our second bottle of red.

"We left her in place, as though we suspected nothing. We'll monitor everything she does. Dick doesn't seem to have a clue about what's happening feet from where he stands."

We talked more about "Alain" and made a non-decision decision. We would tell the General everything we knew and leave the next step to him.

"Now to my agenda for you here," said Hedgeworth. He poured more wine. "Tomorrow we'll meet with an *Al Ahram* reporter. *Al Ahram* is the most prestigious Arabic language newspaper in . . . sorry, you know that, of course. I want you to give him all the gory details about the December massacre in Casablanca. He'll write it as an interview, but he won't name you as the source. I'm doing this as a favor. He and I do that . . . favors . . . for one another. He's a valuable resource for me, so give him something that will arouse anti-colonial resentment."

I was tempted to ask him why the British would want to fan anti-colonial flames in Egypt, but I'd learned enough to know that this is how things are, though I'd not learned enough to know why this is how things are.

"The next day," said Hedgeworth, "*you'll* do the interviewing of Anwar al Sadat. He's the minister for public relations, an army colonel and very much within the inner circle of this new government. The subject is what they're calling Arab Socialism. They like to talk about it and welcome any chance to publicize it. Arab Socialism involves nationalizing anything that's big and works. What I want you to find out, without making it obvious that you're doing so, is if they've got notions about seizing the Suez Canal and nationalizing it. This is very big time for us. We might have to go to war with them if they do it, and . . . bloody hell, let's try to keep them from doing it. If we have to go to war over this, I doubt you Americans would support us. So, the best alliance either of us has is at stake."

I thought he was right about the American reaction should the British go to war with Egypt and also about the problem it would cause for the Anglo-American alliance that worked so well for both countries.

Hedgeworth reached back into the briefcase from which he had taken the photographs, came out with a thick brown envelope and handed it to me. "I want you to get this manuscript published. If necessary we'll subsidize." Written by a man named Mohi El Din who is very much out of favor here. He's under our protection. We'll get him out of the country soon."

I put my tin cup between my legs and accepted the manuscript, wondering where to put it.

"Put it on the floor," said Hedgeworth the mind-reader, "but guard it with your life." He was having his fun.

As we got close to the Nile, I saw farmhouses of mud and thatch, each with a pigeon tower clumsily made of Nile mud. Thanks to the General's Baedecker, I knew that almost every Egyptian farm has a pigeon tower which provides dung for fertilizer and food for supper. At one of the farmhouses, there were two pigeon towers; one was made from mud, the other was a modern concrete tower.

"An example of Arab Socialism," said Hedgeworth. "Nasser's hell-bent to modernize Egypt, so he orders these concrete towers to replace the ugly mud ones. Look at where the pigeons are." There was a cloud of them fluttering on top of the mud column; nothing around the concrete one.

Cairo

When we got out of the Bentley in front of the Edwardian-inspired Shepherd's Hotel, I looked at the crowded street. Had all of Cairo's fifteen million people descended on this place at this time?

The hotel lobby was dominated by a wall-to-wall Persian rug, a geometrical paradise of peach coral, indigo, camel, slate blue and pale sky blue colors. The British furniture, practical hardwood tables, each with two or more ashtrays, attended by extravagantly inappropriate leather chairs, were an embarrassing contrast. I was impressed to be there. So many important treaties had been signed in this hotel. I wondered where the odors came from, and from how long ago. Bitter tobacco mixed with unsuccessful attempts to hide body odor in perfume. Egyptians, starting with Queen Hatshupset in 3,000 B.C., were so fond of perfume smells that perfumes ranked second only to gold as treasures to be buried with wealthy rulers. In the early 1950s Egyptian factories produced thousands of perfumes with an equal number of odors. Some pleasant, some tolerable, many unpleasant.

Hedgeworth led me upstairs to the rooftop garden, which, according to Gertrude Stein, was "the meeting place of all Frankish Cairo for gossip in the afternoon."

The scent of magnolia blossom was a pleasant relief from the lobby. It appeared that everyone there had come to make a statement with the way he or she dressed. Some suits and dresses were as one might see at salons in Paris, Rome, or London. Others were curious, such as some women wearing two-piece suits and heavy doses of kohl on the edges of their eyelids. Some men wore ties with band-collar shirts. Others suited up in traditional checked headdresses and long tunics that almost reached the floor. There was a buzz of multilingual babble.

We sat at a table overlooking *Gumuhira Avenue* with a view of Ramses Railway Station to the left and Hajjin Palace on the right. The avenue was a raging stream of cars, trucks, bicycles, motorbikes, carriages, rickshaws, horses, donkeys, and camels moving chaotically between grand Victorian and Edwardian buildings, houses set in gardens, and perfume boutiques. Traffic never stopped, especially not, it appeared, at red lights. Buses slowed down for passengers getting off and on. Accidents were just gone around, with sidewalks becoming part of the traffic way. Sounds of car horns dueled with chugs from motorbikes and enraged brays from donkeys and camels.

Crossing the avenue required skill and luck. Bodies were darting around in quick dashes and sudden stops. Hedgeworth said that one of the bartenders kept book on how many people would be hit as they tried to cross the avenue. Bets could be placed between noon and one in the afternoon. The winner was announced three hours later by a boy dressed in ancient Egyptian style, a short linen kilt with a band of cloth over his shoulder. He walked around the hotel ringing a small bell, calling out the winner's name as best he could. It was customary to tip him and the bartender in an amount commensurate to the winnings.

"Omar," said Hedgeworth, "will be in the room next to yours."

"A babysitter. How thoughtful of you. Does he keep the Sten under his pillow?"

Hedgeworth laughed. "Sort of," he said, grinning. "I've got to tell you this. He left home because his wife has been keeping a cobra in the house the past few weeks."

"A . . . pet?" I said.

"Not exactly," said Hedgeworth. He was coming closer to giggling than I thought possible for him. "Muslims believe that God created mankind out of clay and at the same time created another species of creature from fire. These other creatures are called Jinns, Jnun, Genies, depending on the country you're in. They mate, have children, die. Usually we can't see them. They're either invisible or have taken the form of a dog, a scorpion, or a human being. Most Jinns are wicked and enjoy injuring humans. Egyptians believe that if a snake comes into your home you must stay on his good side because he is probably a good Jinn who will protect you from bad Jinns. The wife puts milk out for the cobra in a saucer, like you would for a cat. The cobra drinks the milk and is apparently content. Omar is Sudanese. He hates snakes."

"How did he end up here, working for the British?"

"He's been with us forever," said Hedgeworth. "When he and I were kids like you, he was a camel tender for the Sudanese unit that was part of the Indian Camel Corps that patrolled the Suez Canal. My ol' man was Administrator for Canal Operations. Omar taught me the right way to deal with a camel and a lot more about survival in the desert. During the First World War, I did an undercover op in Beersheba, mapping Turkish trench positions. Omar volunteered to go with me. I'd not have come back from that job, let alone get the map done, if Omar hadn't been there with me. Eventually he became a rider in the Camel Corps. When they disbanded the Corps, I asked them to assign him to me. He's a blessing, from God or Allah . . . I don't care which."

The next morning a muezzin's call to early morning prayer wound its way into my sleepy conscious. I'd heard it many times in Morocco but this was different. This call was louder with a coil of sounds between musical registers rather than the sing-song sounds of Moroccan muezzins. It was ominous. Like being called to Judgment Day. Cairo had a profound affect on me already. The General had warned me about that. "I've seen men lose their souls there," he said. "It's as though you realize there are questions about life and the history of life you never knew existed and that this is the place to ask them."

Moguid's Pigeon Place

"Zoooo, are you pre-par-ed to tell me what tru-e-ly happen-ed at the De-cem-ber massacre in Morocco?" My interrogator was a small, skeletal *Al Ahram* reporter sitting across from Hedge-worth and myself at a picnic table twenty yards or so from the Nile. We were eating barbequed pigeons with our fingers and drinking sweet-tasting beer from a ceramic pitcher at *Moguid's Pigeon Place*. It was a good day for sailing. Triangular sails of feluccas, bent like bows from the gusty winds, glided on the cocoa-colored water, as they had for centuries. Across the Nile was the old native quarters, and beyond that the Pyramids of Giza. Here I was in *Umm al-Dunya,* Mother of the World, being interviewed by an obnoxious reporter while the dawn of history casually presented itself.

The reporter had difficulty taking notes as I described what I knew about the massacre. Fingers covered with greasy, spiced pigeon don't grip pencils firmly. So I had to go over some of the details two or three times.

That night in my hotel room, almost comfortable in an over-stuffed armchair reeking of bug spray, I read the manuscript Hedgeworth had given me: "Memories of a Revolution" by Mohi El Din. It was hand-written in bold pen strokes.

Mohi El Din was born and raised in a dervish monastery. His father was master of the order and trustee for the endow-ment, as had been his grandfather and his great-grandfather. Mohi was being groomed to replace his father in the monastery, but the British unintentionally changed all that by forcing the King to accept the Anglo-Egyptian Treaty of 1936, which gave the British exclusive rights to equip and train the Egyptian military, and permission to build as many military bases in Egypt as they wished. According to the British, the treaty was necessary to protect commerce on the Suez Canal. Mussolini's invasion of Ethiopia in 1935, as the British saw it, was the first step in his strategy to seize the Canal. Rather than deny the Egyptian view that the King signed the treaty with a British revolver at his head, London claimed the treaty protected Western civilization from the Fascist jackboots of Mussolini and Hitler.

At the time, Mohi El Din was fourteen. "I very quickly became active in the political environment," he wrote. "My fellow students and I were outraged, and I was on my way to becoming an ardent believer in nationalism and patriotism."

It was those emotions that led him to the Egyptian Military College, which, though formally under British tutelage, "echoed with intense nationalistic feelings." Eventually he rose to the rank of major and served on the Army's Revolutionary Command Council that engineered the *coup d'état*. He was completely committed to the Command Council leadership until he came to believe that Colonel Gamal al-Nasser, who had been the inspirational leader of the army's revolt and became President of Egypt, had no intention to promote democracy because he did not trust "the people." As Mohi El Din saw it, Nasser wanted to be the King's replacement, without British supervision. He voiced his feelings and became persona non grata overnight. Within a week he was accused of being a communist and was labeled "the Red Major."

Gezira Island
Cairo

General Jackman's Baedecker's 1895 edition of the little red handbook on Egypt describes Gezira Island as "Paris on the

Nile." Mansions of salmon pink and blindingly white stone stood majestically on clean streets lined with tall palms and laurels. This is where the wealth of Egypt had isolated itself from the abject poverty of Egypt during the past hundred years or so. The island is not geographically isolated. It is one short Nile bridge away from central Cairo. Most of the mansions had been originally constructed for European businessmen and embassies. They were currently being taken over by the new government and the streets were being renamed. The street we were on had been called "Rue Willcocks" from 1908 until a few days before I arrived, when it was officially renamed "26th of July Street," commemorating the date of the Free Officers coup d'etat.

Hedgeworth was taking me to the interview with Anwar Sadat. "Remember," Hedgeworth said, unnecessarily, "I need to know what they're thinking about the Suez Canal. After I introduce you I'll leave the house and wait in the car."

We stopped in front of a Mediterranean-style villa of huge white stones with a red-tiled roof supported by heavy beams. Beneath the beams were ornately carved ornamentations as green in color as the palms nestling the building. In contrast, pots of red flowers led up to the entryway steps.

I had not told Hedgeworth I'd done my homework on Sadat. He was born into a peasant family of thirteen children in a delta village north of Cairo. After graduation from the British military school in the late 1930s, he was posted as a second lieutenant in the signal corps in the Sudan where he met Gamal al-Nasser who brought him into the small revolutionary group of officers who were destined to overthrow British rule.

The British arrested him for treason a few years after the end of World War II. He spent four lonely years in prison yet managed to teach himself English and French. When he got out he acted for a while and was involved in several small businesses. Nasser contacted him a few months before the 1952 revolution, and on the day the King abdicated, Sadat became the new government's public relations minister and Nasser's most trusted ally.

Sadat was frequently mentioned in Mohi El Din's manuscript. According to El Din it was Sadat who labeled him "the Red Major" in newspaper articles. Because of that and because El Din thought Sadat was a bootlicking opportunist, the manuscript was not a rave review for Egypt's Minister of Public relations.

Hedgeworth and I were taken to Sadat's office by a young officer who said he was "the Minister's adjutant." When we entered the room Sadat was standing in front of his desk wearing a black suit, white shirt with black tie, and black loafers. There was an old ten-by-twelve-foot tapestry on one wall, a biblical scene in a medieval setting. A soldier was carrying an old bearded man with a crowd around. Underneath the tapestry was a Queen Anne sofa that had ornately carved wooden legs and back with seats covered by green and gold striped silk. On one end table, there was a black and white picture of Sadat standing in uniform. On the other, a head-and-shoulders color photograph of Nasser in civilian clothes, his smiling face surrounded by a clear blue sky. On the opposite wall there were illuminated recesses containing figurines and ceramic pieces.

Hedgeworth introduced us. The Minister carried an odor of bitter pipe tobacco and had oriental eyes that stared boldly into mine.

When Hedgeworth left, Sadat invited me to sit on the sofa next to Nasser. He sat next to Nasser himself and said, "What questions would you have me answer?"

"I want to write about Arab Socialism," I said. "Can you help me? I'd like to begin with your feelings about the British in Egypt." I wanted to draw out what I thought would be contemptuous rage. He denied me the chance.

"The *Ingleez*," he said, speaking in a carefully-measured pace, separating syllables as though they were individual words, "did some good here. Now it is the time for them to leave. We will miss them. However, we will do well when they are gone. They and the King gave us a civil service that lived from bribe to bribe."

"Why is Arab Socialism an improvement on what the King and the British were doing?" I asked him.

He took one of the pipes—there were ten or more—from the rack next to his picture. I looked out the window in the rear of the room and saw a banyan tree with those grotesque yet fascinating roots that stretch from branches to ground.

Sadat put the pipe stem between his teeth then drew it away. "Arab Socialism," he said, "organizes Egypt so that each person can play an important role in the modernization and economic development of his country. First we must rid the country of the greed that comes from private ownership. We are nationalizing businesses and breaking down large landholdings so that any one individual can own only enough land to feed him and his family. Otherwise we would have Egyptians replacing the *Ingleez*. The people would be left as miserable as they were before the revolution."

"Other revolutions have tried that," I said, "and found that the new landowners have to borrow money for seed, fertilizer, and so on. Then the money lenders take over where the large landowners left off."

He smiled confidently and said, "We have establishd cooperatives which provide the new landowners with all they need, including a government agency that buys their products, sells them at affordable prices to our non-farming people, and has enough money left over to invest in industrial growth. President Nasser says that everything from pins to rockets will be manufacturd in the new Egypt."

I knew that Nasser was a friend of Tito's, so I asked Sadat, "Is Arab Socialism a form of communism?"

"A form of . . . perhaps. More than a form of capitalism, of course. But communism denies God. In Egypt, *Allah Akbhar*."

"Will you nationalize everything?" I asked.

"Yes," he said. "But gradually."

He explained, as one might to a child, that drastically rapid nationalization would destabilize the economy. "The economy is a complicated set of interrelationships," he said in professorial tones, "that must be slowly, patiently, adjusted to achieve the mission. We nationalized the banks first. That was absolutely essential. Without that none of the rest could happen. First we carried out the agrarian reform. Then we nationalized the insurance companies, large shipping companies, and, of course, all heavy and basic industries."

A woman in a yoked granny dress and head scarf entered the room with a tray and placed it on a turtleback marble coffee table in front of us. She carried an odor of acrid perfume that was stronger than the coffee and tea on the tray. I was glad she left quickly.

"Wheech do you like?" Sadat asked, pointing to a china expresso of thick black coffee, a tea cup of reddish tea, along with a dish of sugar and two square almond-smelling cookies.

"Coffee, please."

"Would you want water with it?"

I declined, took the cup and saucer in hand and said, "How do you know," I said, "how far to go and when?"

Sadat took the tea in hand and cradled the cup, looking into it as a gypsy consults a crystal ball.

"We have a National Planning Commission assisted by professors from the Harvard Business School and anthropologists and social welfare experts and agriculturalists," he said, as though that settled everything. "We are going very slowly with our transformation of the countryside. Our intention is to free the peasant people from the tyranny of their traditions. Feudalism, nomadism and tribalism will all be extinguished in time."

"It's ambitious," I said.

"Yes. It is. We are grateful to Allah that we have President Nasser to guide us. In the middle of one discussion with the experts on how we would build industries, the President interrupted. He asked how the workers in these new industries would live. Will they bring their own housing? He asked. We all laughed, and we saw his wisdom. Someone suggested that we should build housing for them at the same time that we are

building the factories. The President complimented that suggestion, but of course that was what he had thinking all along."

"Will you nationalize the Suez Canal?" As soon as I asked, I
knew it was bad timing.

"We are in a war to win something for the Egyptian people
and eventually all Arabs. It is like General Lee against General
Meade at Gettysburg." He put his cup down, took a bag of
tobacco from a pouch he kept in a side pocket, stuffed it then
damped it into the bowl, lit it, puffed vigorously to get it going,
and said, "At the officers' school each of us had to pick a major
battle in history to analyze. I analyzed the battle at Gettysburg.
We are like the rebels at Gettysburg. But . . . we will not lose
because we will do anything that is necessary to win. What is
Egyptian is Egyptian. *Ingleez* frustrations cannot change that.
God is with us." He waved the flame out just as it was about to
burn his flesh and tossed the match to the floor. "Are you not
asking about Operation Susannah?"

"I don't know what you're talking about," I said.

"Oh . . . so they are keeping that from you. I am not
surprised."

"What is it?" I asked.

It happened the day before my arrival in Egypt. Israeli
agents had persuaded four Egyptian Jews to plant bombs in
several buildings, including the American Consulate. The plan
was to leave evidence behind implicating the Mulsim Brotherhood, Egypt's most prominent political party, and currently at
odds with President Nasser. The ruse would have worked, had
not one of the bombers told his lover, who, in turn, reported
what he said to the police. Eventually the police rounded up the
Israeli spy ring.

"Will you write about this?" he said dryly.

"No," I said, "unless it fits into the overall theme of your
vision for Egypt."

"Just as you will not write about the Israelis attempt to get
nuclear weapons. From you, of course."

I said I knew nothing about that.

"You sit there in calm arrogance," he said. "You Americans have the power to wipe the rest of us off the face of Allah's planet and you pretend that power is not there. Have you no idea how that makes us feel?"

"I think we're way beyond the boundaries of this interview," I said.

"I see," he said. "Here is something that fits . . . I believe. Do you know what an Islamist is? Why the Muslim Brotherhood is a deadly threat to everything you believe."

"The Brotherhood's goal," I said, "is to keep Egypt and other Islamic countries from becoming Western-style nation states."

"Yes, you are quite correct. Their credo is that God is their objective, the Koran is their Constitution, the Prophet is their leader, struggle is their way, and death for the sake of God is the highest of their aspirations. That's dangerous thinking for Egypt, for all Muslim countries, and for America and the rest of the non-Muslim world." As he spoke he interrupted himself several times to puff on his pipe in a way that indicated he was annoyed by the Islamists.

"I've heard," I said, "that the Brotherhood is very angry with President Nasser because he broke what they thought was a solemn promise to turn Egypt into an Islamic state."

"That's the stuff that comes out of camels' asses," he said, getting more angry. "The President tells us he will not be distracted from achieving justice for Egyptians. If that means he must mislead the enemies of this search for justice, he will do so. Do you know of that example of the firemen and the building on fire?"

He was calming down from his irritation, so I told him I did not, which was true, and that I would like him to tell me about it, which was not.

"There is this building on fire. It is in the middle of many buildings in a large city where many people live." He set his pipe to rest in a large marbled ashtray. "A fire crew is sent to put out the fire. A large part of the city and thousands of people are in danger. On the way to put out this fire, the chief of this fire crew notices that the streets are dirty. He orders the crew to clean up the litter and bathe the streets. The fire from this building spreads to other buildings. The city and its people become ashes."

"So," I said, "the leader who loses sight of what is the most important problem to solve . . . who wastes his resources on an immediate but minor problem . . . is not a good leader."

He smiled. I was an apt pupil.

"The President," he said, "has great courage in fighting these distractions. He even put Sayyid Qutb in jail."

I had heard a little about Qutb, who was considered to be the father of modern Islamist Fundamentalism and the most famous personality of the contemporary Muslim world. His ideology had spread throughout the Muslim world, particularly to Saudi Arabia and Afghanistan. When I studied Russian at Syracuse University, as a new recruit in the U.S.A.F. Security Service, one of my instructors, going at that time by the name of Grishko Baguta, told us that the West would prevail over the Soviet Union, but would not see what was coming next, a conflict with Islamists that would defy our mindset and confuse our military strategies and tactics. I didn't remember his warning because it made sense to me at the time. I remembered it because of the way he phrased it. "You will be an Alice in Wonderland. You will try to understand in the way you have learned to understand. And that will not work."

I learned a number of things at that interview, one of which was: Always request a glass of water to go along with Egyptian coffee. It is almost too thick to swallow.

Chapter Thirteen

Giza

"Our parents named us after Coptic calendar months so that we would remember our heritage." Amshir Makram 'Ebreid was speaking.

"Whenever we were asked about our names," added her sister, Nasi, "we could steer the conversation to Coptic history."

Hedgeworth laughed, circled the wine bottle across our glasses and poured himself some more.

The four of us were having dinner under the sprawl of a massive 100-pole tent next to the Great Pyramid in Giza. This came after we attended the *Son et Lumière* show in front of The Sphinx, which was diminished by the narrator's propaganda inserts about how only since the 1952 revolution has slavery been done away with in Egypt.

Amshir and Nasi were lovely raven-haired women in Egyptian-silk caftans that draped suggestively over one shoulder. Amshir's was coral with faint floral patterns. Nasi's was pure white. Each of them had the right kind of shoulder for the effect. Their bodies were lithe; their skin was smooth and brown. They were, what was called in Egypt at that time, "bluestocking," referring to eighteenth-century clubs for women who had intellectual and literary interests. Amshir, a medical doctor, lived with Hedgeworth. Nasi had won honors in French at the University of Poitiers and now taught French literature at Cairo University. I was hoping she was not living with anyone.

Chapter Thirteen

The dinner was less enjoyable than the calendar girls. It was *mulukhiyah*, Egypt's true national dish. As Amshir explained it to me, spinach leaves are chopped vigorously until they become a green paste. A mixture of rabbit broth, butter, garlic, and green coriander is poured over the paste. A few minutes of boiling turns the sauce a blackish green. It is then ladled over plates of rice, dried bread, and lamb. The spicy smells went into my nostrils and lingered there, a bit too long. What I put into my mouth was slimy and stringy. Texture is a bench mark for whether I like or dislike a dish. I didn't like *mulukhiyah*.

It was a different Hedgeworth that night. Amshir brought out a softness, an attractive vulnerability I'd not seen in him. He would cover her shoulder with his meaty hand when telling us all a story or joke, a loving and gentle hand, enjoying being where it was.

"So," I said, "how do the calendar girls get into Coptic culture when they are asked where their names come from."

"I cannot speak for Nasi," said Amshir, "because I am a scientist and she is under the spell of French impressionism and all that." She laughed to show that she was just kidding. "I answer by saying that I am named after the sixth month in the Coptic calendar, which is different than the Western Christian calendars and the Muslim calendar. Our year begins about in the middle of your September. It has twelve months of thirty days each and one month of five or six days."

"That is the one I'm named after," said Nasi, "the little one."

"If the questioner gets interested in why our calendar is different," said Amshir, "I have him or her on my Coptic hook." She pronounced it "whook."

I looked at Hedgeworth. He nodded. "It is interesting. The Copts are Christian. They're the ones who were here when the Arabs brought Islam and took over."

Nasi, who had a nice twinkle in her dark almost-Asian eyes and a tender smile, said to me, "Ask away, Mee-ster journalist."

"I interviewed Minister Sadat today," I said. "I'd like to know what Arab Socialism means to the Copts."

"Bad news," said Amshir. "Copts are professionals or own businesses or have large landholdings. Nationalization takes away the businesses and landholdings."

"Bad news for the farmers, also," said Amshir. "They are worse off than they were when they worked for big landowners. The new arrangements force them to work longer hours. They don't sell their crops like the government says they do. They turn them over to government cooperatives. The money they receive in return and what they can do with it makes them poorer than they were before the revolution."

Fortunately for me the *mulukhiyah* was taken from the table and replaced with a large platter of fruits—grapes, guavas, melons, oranges and mandarins—piled up in the shape of a pyramid. Unwilling to risk the embarrassment of causing the pile to collapse, I took a bunch of grapes from the top.

Hedgeworth laughed, reached boldly into the middle of the pile and extracted a mandarin. The pyramid jiggled but remained intact. "Nasi," he said, looking at me with a cocky grin, "I've not had a chance to tell *Monsieur journaliste* what we want him to do for you."

Nasi stirred uncomfortably and said, "Not here, please. It's embarrassing."

"We don't have enough time to do it right," said Hedgeworth. "Don't underestimate this kid. He's a lot older than he looks. And Americans have an awesome lack of concern for politeness."

Amshir pushed her chair closer to Nasi, put her arm around her, and said, "It's all right. It's good. Let us do it."

"Nasi has to get out of town," said Hedgeworth. "There are two reasons. Nasser is wooing the college students by promising them jobs the day after they graduate. He puts them not to work but to sit around in grimy government offices. Most of them do nothing. Clever. Disguised unemployment. The students liked Nasser from the beginning and now they worship him."

Amshir comforted Nasi with a hand on the back of her head; it was coming to me that Nasi was shamed by this entreaty to a stranger. "The students have become Nasserites," said Amshir. "They interrupt classes with demands that a professor such as Nasi should stop talking about old French literature and talk about Arab Socialism . . . praising it, naturally."

"They also demand that I give lectures on the reasons for Black Saturday," said Nasi. "I think my refusal to do that is what angers them the most."

"What do you know about Black Saturday," Hedgeworth asked me.

I told him I understood it to be a mass rioting against everything British. Mobs burned buildings, slaughtered people, and looted. "I forget," I said, "what it was exactly that set this off."

"Some of our Ismailia army boys bloody lost their minds," said Hedgeworth. "They said they'd just gotten fed up with the constant Egyptian guerrilla attacks on the canal and on them. It was a running sore. They were convinced the Egyptian police were helping the guerrillas . . . and in that they were right. So they decide to render a lesson. They surround the local police barracks with armored cars, bren gun carriers, and a Centurion tank. They give the policemen in the barracks an ultimatum to come out and surrender or be attacked. The police radio man contacts the Ministry of the Interior and that damn fool tells the Ismailia radio man the policemen must refuse to surrender. The only fire power the Egyptian police have are Lee Enfield rifles. At the end of the slaughter, there are seventy dead Egyptian policemen, bodies torn to pieces, barely recognizable. The barracks is rubble."

"All Egyptians who knew about it were outraged," said Amshir."

"The news spread so fast," said Nasi, "almost everyone knew about it the following day. Street protests became gangs searching out British targets. There was smoke coming from the Opera Cinema. Rumor said that it had been set afire. Burning buildings became the way to express the Egyptians' fury. At first it was just British places, but then all European places were targeted. Downtown Cairo was a sea of crazy mobs torching cinemas, restaurants, hotels, clubs, department stores . . . around seven or eight hundred in all."

"The Egyptians," said Hedgeworth, "are still furious because the Western press made a headline story on what the Egyptians did. The Ismailia slaughter of Egyptian policemen was a footnote, at best."

"My students believe I should give lectures in which the Ismailia incident is presented in full," said Nasi.

Nasi took her eyes away from the fruit, tried to smile, and said apologetically to me, "I am so sorry. Please do not accept this as an obligation."

"If that's all there was," said Hedgeworth, "I wouldn't be asking you to help us out here. There was an attempt on Nasser's life the other day. Sadat and some others are blaming the Copts. Actually it was the Muslim Brotherhood. I know that some of those students are cooking up rumors about Nasi's involvement."

As I was thinking about that a hush fell over the tent. "Umm Kalthoum," Nasi whispered reverently in my ear.

A spotlight caught the Egyptian diva on a small stage along with some strings and percussion. She was covered sleekly and sinuously by a peach silk wrap, the seductive type that requires the wearer to be continually occupied with its slippery and voluminous folds. Such robes are considered to be modesty wraps. However, when wrapped around a well-shaped body and in the hands of a woman who is instinctively passionate, the robe can reveal the body in very seductive ways. She sang *Ala Balad El Mahboub, "Bring Me Home To My Lover,"* in the manner opera singers perform arias. Her voice was captivating but perhaps more impressive was the spellbound audience. Her standing as a national treasure might have exceeded the beauty of her voice and the subtlety of her moves with the wrap.

After the song and applause that seemed to go on forever, Umm Kalthoum talked about growing up poor and destitute in a village along the Nile, the terrible oppression her family suffered under King Farouk and the British, and how happy she is to live now under Arab Socialism." It was just as Dick and

Audrey Sandworth had described her radio appearances to me at their home on Christmas Eve.

"Well," said Hedgeworth. "Look. Whirling dervishes."

After Umm Kalthoum left, a dozen or so men were on the stage. They wore white cone-shaped hats, white costumes covering each of them from neck to ankle, and white sandals.

"It's a rare treat these days," Amshir said. "Nasser wants to get rid of traditional Egypt because he believes it hinders modernization."

"I think he doesn't like any competition to his authority," said Nasi. "He can't explain away religious authority like he does British rule. Often we get the dervishes if Umm Kalthoum is singing because she adores them . . . "

"And," Amshir said, "Nasser adores her."

I heard sounds from a reed pipe and watched the dancers march in a circle for a few minutes. The sounds from the pipe increased in volume and intensity, joined by what seemed to be a large number of unseen drums. The dancers began to whirl in place. As they did, their skirts opened out like umbrellas. They whirled faster in dazzling pirouettes and returned to moving as a group in a circle and the circle itself appeared to be pirouetting. Then suddenly the music stopped an the dancers fell to the ground, leaving a man in a black robe with white hair down to his waist standing alone. A drum sounded a slow monotonous rhythm. It was joined by other drums. The man in the black robe began to whirl faster and faster. The reed pipe blared an intimidating crescendo. The man whirled so fast that I couldn't see it as a whirl. It was a blur. His hair flared over and beyond his shoulders; it was now a bizarre quaking hat of sorts. The music went on in an unbroken stream of syncopated sounds ranging from somber to rhapsodical as the incredible whirling figure went on—before he dropped limply to the ground.

I was so absorbed that I didn't know until minutes after he dropped to the floor that Nasi was holding my hand. Later I found out more about that and was disappointed. Hedgeworth had a plan that required an appearance of a budding romance between Nasi and me.

The next morning I met Hedgeworth in the hotel breakfast room. We had the Egyptian national breakfast, *foul madamis*, a dish of dried beans dressed with olive oil and lemon. They offered French coffee, so I had that. Hedgeworth had Egyptian coffee, without a glass of water. Omar sat at another table staring out a window, dressed in an oversized djellaba to conceal his sten gun.

"You said the other day you know something about Abd el-Krim," said Hedgeworth.

"I even know a former French Legionnaire who fought against him," I said. "He was in the first Legionnaire cavalry unit."

Hedgeworth looked mildly impressed. "Fez," he said. I nodded. "Mention that to el-Krim," he said. "Warriors like him have a lot of respect for anyone who can beat them on the battlefield."

"I heard he had come here after he escaped from the French prison on Reunion Island. Am I interviewing him? Or what?" I said.

"There'll be another man at the meeting," said Hedgeworth. "He's with Israeli intelligence. He and el-Krim want you to take an offer back to your *Istiqlal* contact."

"Let me get this straight," I said, "el-Krim is working for Moroccan independence here in Cairo and there's a Mossad agent working with el-Krim . . . here . . . in Cairo."

"Yeh," said Hedgeworth, as though it were the most natural thing in the world. He was amusing himself with my naiveté again.

The Café of Mirrors

The meeting with el-Krim and the Mossad agent was to be in a tea house of Cairo's most famous bazaar, *Khan el-Khali*. Omar dropped us at *al-Azhar Avenue* on the southern side of the bazaar. Hedgeworth led me through narrow streets and alleyways bordered by small shops and carts offering spices, perfumes, leather-work, gold and silver jewelry, carpets, glass, ceramics, wood carvings, silk on spools, and silk clothing. Merchants stood in front of their cubbyhole shops beseeching us to come in for some mint tea and "just a look."

When we arrived at the Brass and Coppersmith market, Hedgeworth led me inside one of the rooms where ten-foot high shelving displayed a bewildering variety of colorful brassware that reflected so brightly one would think the room was lit by powerful neon lights. "This place has been like this since the fourteenth century," Hedgeworth said. "All the bounty of the East finds its way here.

"You are perhaps surprised to meet with an Arab nationalist and a representative of the Israeli government in the same room . . . at the same time." Abd el-Krim chuckled at his own humor before taking his first sip of a steaming tea that had a strong mint aroma.

People don't always live up to the titles and nicknames they pick up during their lifetimes. Looking at Abd el-Krim I didn't see "The Wolf of the Rif," nor did I see the man Dimitri had described when he recalled the Riffian wars. He was short and flabby in a Moroccan mountaineer robe. His eyes, with brown pupils irregularly rimmed with pale blue gray, rolled dolefully. He talked in a high-pitched voice that was irritating when he laughed at his own jokes. It was difficult imagining him terrorizing northern Morocco with his Riffian armies.

He was sitting at a café table made from a large bronze tray etched with intricate arabesque patterns. Next to him was the Mossad man. He looked as I expected. He wore dark trousers and a short-sleeved white shirt that displayed his intensely-tanned sinewy arms. It was the uniform for Israeli men, at least that's how they always appeared in pictures, whether they were at a government cabinet meeting or on a kibbutz. Behind the Mossad man there was a stuffed crocodile.

Hedgeworth and I were sitting across from them in a back room of the venerable tea house called *Café of Mirrors* because mirrors of various sizes and designs cover almost every inch of wall space. It has been managed by the same family and has remained open twenty-four hours a day since 1773. Cracks in the mirrors, deeply smoke-stained ceilings, and ancient wooden furniture gave one the impression that the *Café* had been well-used for a long time. No one remembers why each room was decorated with a stuffed crocodile in the late nineteenth century. It is a place that everyone knows about, where everyone who knows anyone goes, where famous people sit table-to-table with the unknown.

Yet, it is also a place where one can hold a private meeting, as we were. The *Café's* public and back rooms were off bounds for the Egyptian police. The back rooms were walled off from the public rooms and one entered them by getting to the *Café's* basement and then going up a stairway. Each back room had its own stairway. You did not see any stairway other than the one you used. Hedgeworth had gotten us to the basement by using a door in the rear of the brass and coppersmith's shop.

The Mossad man explained that Israel wanted to establish working relations with nationalists in Tunisia, Algeria, and Morocco. "We need some friends in the Muslim world to prevent an all-out jihad against us," he said. "The Muslim countries in our neighborhood are probably going to be out to destroy us for the foreseeable future. We don't want to see that attitude spread to Muslim countries in West Africa. That's a long-term strategy. In the short term we want Moroccan Jews to be able to emigrate to Israel without hassle from the Moroccan or French authorities."

"We offer armaments from bullets to Uzis," he said. "We want you to pass the message on to your contacts in *Istiqlal*."

"How will you get them in?" Hedgeworth asked.

"By sea, caravans, and helicopter," said the Israeli. "Depends on where delivery is made inside Morocco. We'll need cooperation from the British for sea shipments. We'll bribe some Berber caids and foreign legionnaires to look the other way when we take the stuff by caravans through the Atlas. But sea and desert shipments take a long time. For the next few months, we'll have to bring it in by helicopter. . . . We have two Hiller 360s. Someone must talk with General Jackman. We don't want the American aircraft A&W units to make records of our flights."

Hedgeworth stirred uneasily, turned to me and said, "this is new to me. We can't ask General Jackman to falsify records from the aircraft warning people. That puts him in a box."

"What is the alternative?" said the Mossad man.

"Hey," yelled Hedgeworth getting right into the Israeli's face, "cut out that crap. We're not here to take orders from you or to figure out how to do things for you." He turned back to me and said, "These Mossad guys are always so bloody cheeky."

I didn't know what to say. I thought the General could handle the request. He was perfectly capable of saying no to something he thought was a bad idea. But I didn't know what game, if any, Hedgeworth was playing. So I kept quiet.

"All right," said the Mossad man. "What do you think we should offer the General in exchange?"

Hedgeworth looked at his tea, as though deliberating, and said, "the General and I go way back. I believe he'd consider you doing me a favor as a decent quid pro quo."

"Of course," said the Mossad man, dryly. "I should have thought of that."

Abd el-Krim looked grim.

Hedgeworth picked up his tea and blew steam away from it. "I want your intelligence on the Nasser crowd's intentions about nationalizing the Suez Canal. If they're thinking about it, when they intend to do it, and what specific steps they'll take."

"Agreed," said the Mossad man.

Abd el-Krim sat back, now obviously unhappy. Nasser had been very good to him, providing him with a safe haven from French imprisonment and supporting him in his efforts to win freedom for the Moroccans. Now he was in the position of having arranged a meeting at which the British would gain significant information about something that Nasser had an intense interest in keeping secret.

"Israel has a primitive economy," said the Mossad man, "we will need some money to cross hands."

"Naturally," said Hedgeworth, smiling sarcastically. "But it can't come from the Brits."

"I'll ask my *Istiqlal* contact," I said. "See if he can come up with it."

Walking away from the Café alone with Hedgeworth I said, "I suppose I missed some of the subtleties in that meeting. But from what I saw, I was impressed by what you did and how you did it."

Out of the side of his mouth he said, "Kid, you didn't miss some of them . . . you missed a lot of them." So we were back to that. With the general's help I had decided to see Hedgeworth's put-downs as friendly. He wanted to keep me off guard, alert to my shortcomings. It was his way of helping me stay alive. "The el-Krim I just met doesn't seem like the legend. Is the legend a myth?" I asked him.

"No, not at all," said Hedgeworth. "The French had him long enough in the dungeons and torture chambers on Reunion to bring him down. His escape is one of the most bloody grizzly stories I've ever heard."

Shark fishing was a modest source of income for the people of Reunion. Even a modest source was significant for them because Reunion was France's poorest overseas administrative district. When fishermen could get their hands on a dog, they often used the dog as bait, skewering it on hooks and dragging it behind a boat. The French authorities provided prisoners to help the fishermen use dogs as live shark bait. The fishermen appreciated this because skewering a dog at sea and throwing it overboard while holding on to a rope between the dog and the boat was dangerous work. If a prisoner was lost in the process, it was of no concern to the French.

Abd el-Krim worked a number of boats, often volunteering just to get away for a half day or so from the sadistic prison guards. And, there was another reason. He worked out an escape plan. He waited for a calm day on the ocean and a physically inferior fisherman. When he grabbed the dog to skewer it, he threw it overboard and buried the two skewer hooks in the fisherman's chest. After throwing the dead body overboard, he steered the boat to the Portuguese colony of Mozambique where he passed himself off, in Spanish, as a poor Berber fisherman from Reunion whose wife had been killed by a French official because she refused his sexual advances.

Two aspects of el-Krim's life enabled him to pull this off. He was an educated son of an Islamic judge in Spanish Morocco who had excelled in Spanish schools and spent three years in Spain studying mining and military engineering. Eventually, using Arabic as well as Spanish, he made his way to Cairo, presented himself as Abd el-Krim, and was welcomed.

"He survived," said Hedgeworth, "but he will never again be the wolf of the Rif."

I saw el-Krim one more time. He had asked to see Hedgeworth and me at his house. As we got out of the Bentley, Omar's right hand firmly gripping the Sten, Hedgeworth pointed to a tomb a few doors away from el-Krim's house and said, "There lies the father of the Egyptian independence movement, Zaghloul Pasha." He pointed across the street to a large concrete building. "And that's the headquarters of the exiled Moroccan, Algerian, and Tunisian nationalists.

An Egyptian policeman dozed in his chair at the gates to el-Krim's front garden. El-Krim was sitting with three other men in wicker chairs on the latticed front porch. They left after el-Krim introduced them as Moroccan pilgrims on their way to Mecca. He invited us to sit down and asked if we preferred our coffee light, medium, or strong. He wore a long tan robe with kimono sleeves, yellow leather Moroccan slippers, and a sheer white linen cloth wrapped around his head as a turban. Now, with what Hedgeworth told me about his escape, I had more respect for him.

After coffee and polite conversation about the weather, el-Krim said, "I need your help. I must get out of Egypt. Eventually the Nasser people are going to hear about the meeting at *Café of Mirrors*. Even if they don't, the Mossad man will hold that over my head and get me to do things I do not want to do. I must leave."

"Where do you want to go?" said Hedgeworth.

"London," el-Krim said.

"Starting tomorrow," said Hedgeworth, "be prepared to leave at a moment's notice."

On The Nile

"That's the Citadel," said Nasi, pointing to the western shore of the Nile at a massive medieval fortress. We were on a felucca going south from Cairo. There were four cushioned seats. Nasi had brought a picnic basket filled with wine, flatbread, slices of lamb, roasted peanuts, and oranges. Our helmsman was a heavy bronze-faced man with rotten teeth whose tourist-trade smiles just didn't work. But there was a strong wind in the sail, and Nasi looked charming in gray slacks and a tight-fitting yellow T-shirt. It was a good day, or at least was starting off as one.

"It was built by a great Mamluk named Salah ad-Din nine hundred years ago," said Nasi. She was now looking at the orange she was unpeeling as though it were a challenge. "He picked that spot after experimentation. He hung up raw pieces of meat at different heights around Cairo. Everywhere except at that place the meat rotted after only one day and night. There, on that limestone spur, it remained fresh for two days."

The domes and minarets of Cairo were dropping out of sight as the distance between the flat banks of crumbling alluvial mud widened. Our destination was Hulwan, a few hours away. It was there that Hedgeworth was going to do one of his tricks. Nasi and Amshir would disappear into thin air. Or at least that was the plan.

Nasi conquered the orange and passed half of it to me. "Do you think it will work?" she said, in a trembling voice.

"If I were you," I said, "I'd have all the confidence in the world. I think Hedgeworth really knows what he's doing."

"Strange thing for a journalist to get involved in," she said. I had been getting the feeling that she had a hunch I was not completely as advertised.

"Actually," I said, "journalists get involved in a lot of irregular or not exactly normal things . . . part of the job, I guess."

Hedgeworth's plan was that Nasi and I would appear to be two young people attracted to one another, taking a romantic felucca ride on the Nile, nothing more. Her surveillance would most probably not follow but wait at the dock where we departed. I was amused by the thought of seeing the surveillance team hop on their own felucca and say, "follow that felucca!"

"Where do you live in America?" Nasi asked.

"Cleveland, Ohio," I said.

"Nice place?"

"Exactly the opposite of Cairo. Boring but safe."

She looked at me, bit into her half of the orange, squirted juice into her nose, giggled, and said, "I like Americans." Her hair was being blown back by the wind revealing a small tattoo, like a cross. I must have been staring at it because she said, "Our parents have it put there as a tattoo in case we might try to deny being Christians. Is there religious prejudice in America?"

I told her I was a first-generation Irishman who knew poverty and the ungenerous consequences of class, *and* the benefits of growing up in a cocoon, an Irish-Catholic parish. "At that time, in Cleveland," I said, "Catholics were regarded as, I suppose, Copts are in Egypt. But those who were prejudiced were held back by laws and the legal system. Not entirely, but substantially."

The helmsman interrupted us with a guttural moan. He was steering laboriously around one of the tiny islands that grew out of the river. We looked at him. He appeared to be making a superhuman effort to save us from colliding with the island. His act was about as convincing as his smile. But who expects Barrymore on a felucca in the Nile?

"You asked us," she said, "what Arab Socialism means to us, Amshir and me. What does it mean to you?"

"Arab Socialism is a pipe dream. You know that phrase?"

She shrugged, moving the T-shirt attractively over her breasts.

"I mean it assumes that all Arabs want to live peacefully together." I was having a problem concentrating on analytical criticism of an ideology while my libido surged. "And all you need to fuel that desire is to provide the people with an ideology of economic development."

"I'm confused," she said.

"It's an offshoot of communism," I said, "Arab Socialism tells the people to find places in an organization—it could be agricultural or manufacturing, or service, educational, whatever—and then play that role with full commitment. You're not taking orders from anyone. You're playing your role. You're free even though you're taking orders from someone. By doing this, you benefit in two ways. First, you benefit materially because you've found your most productive niche . . . by giving yourself to the organization the organization places you where you can do the best for yourself and the organization. Second, you benefit spiritually because whatever the organization is doing, it will do it better by your commitment to playing your role. All of society, all of humankind, is better off because you know your place and dedicate yourself to it."

"What's wrong with that," she said, handing me two slices of lamb, flat bread, and a slice of lemon on a sheet of newspaper.

"Well," I said, "let's suppose that you're told by your dean that the best role you can play for the good of your university is to give lectures on the Ismailia slaughter."

"And I say, I can't do that."

"Then he says that if you care for the good of your university and your country you *will* do it."

"I suppose," she said, "it would look as though I care more about the integrity of the subject I teach than I do about the university, the country, Arab Socialism, and all that." She put some lamb and flat bread, with a twist of lemon, on a sheet of newspaper and placed it at the helmsman's feet.

"That's Turra," she said, pointing to the shore. I saw a large village with whitewashed houses. A space of gray stony plain separated the houses from quarried mountains, the flanks of which were hewn away. Where the axes and machines had not yet been at work, the mountains were tawny. There were piles of rough-hewn blocks—looking more like salt than stone—along the bank, ready for transport. A fleet of boats was moored at the river's edge, some laden, others lading. A tram was being pushed by thick-bodied workers on rails that extended from the river to the quarries. Alongside it were lines of mule-carts coming and going.

"All the new buildings in Cairo come from there," said Nasi, "just as did the Pyramids six-thousand years ago."

Hedgeworth was waiting for us where the helmsman tied up the felucca. He was standing next to a man who had a remarkable deep scar running from his left ear to the cleft in his chin. A fencing wound from a personal duel? One of my mother's Czech friends had one. It's called "a smite." Though it leaves the face disfigured, it is a badge of honor.

"This is Otto Skorzeny," said Hedgeworth as he helped Nasi off the boat. "Plans have changed. For now just do what I tell you. I'll explain later."

He led us to a Kubelwagen that appeared to be hidden in a small forest of date palms. During World War II, the Kubelwagen was Germany's answer to the Jeep. It had been designed by Ferdinand Porsche and built on a Volkswagen frame at Hitler's personal request. Kubelwagens were the Jeeps' ugly cousins, boxy with angled hoods that carried a spare tire on top; underneath was the trunk. They looked like tin containers with long menacing snouts. Extra large wheels enabled maneuvering on rough terrain, and they were cabriolet so they had cover in rain or snow. Patton's troops had a long list of jokes ridiculing them; but when they tested a few they had captured in North Africa, the jokes stopped. Kubelwagens were found to be simpler, easier to maintain, faster, and more comfortable for four passengers than American Jeeps.

Skorzeny drove. Hedgeworth sat next to him. Nasi and I were in the rear bucket seats. He drove cautiously around the date palms. I was impressed by the Kubelwagen's maneuverability. We came to a dirt road and Skorzeny pushed for full speed, about fifty miles an hour.

"The Egyptian secret service found out about my plan," said Hedgeworth. "They're all over the Hulwan airport. We'll go to Abu Sueir."

"Amshir . . . ?" said Nasi.

"I sent her to Abu Sueir hours ago," Hedgeworth answered.

Later I found out that Skorzeny, a security adviser to Nasser, moonlighted by doing favors for the British and Israelis. He had caught on to Hedgeworth's plan, told Nasser about it, then informed Hedgeworth that the Egyptian secret service were waiting at the Hulwan airport. It was a living. Right now he was going to make some money by getting Hedgeworth, Nasi, and myself to a relatively safe airport.

We were driving north by northeast, toward the Moqattam Hills, in the direction of Sweetwater Canal roadway. Skorzeny said nothing. I had no idea what his voice sounded like. I imagined it would be strident.

Nasi turned her head to me and said, "Do you know about the cities of the dead? Over there to the left is one of them." It looked like a small city, with elaborate marble and granite buildings.

"That's Qarafah," said Hedgeworth. "Sultans, emirs, saints, and descendants of Muhammad are buried there. . . . But not as you might think. They're buried in permanent structures with two or three rooms, walled courts, and sometimes second and third floors. The body is interred in a shroud facing Mecca either under the courtyard or a floor of one of the rooms. A commemorative plaque marks the spot."

"How large is it?" I asked.

Hedgeworth looked at Nasi. "About three square miles," she said.

"You'll get a close look. We have to pick up some petrol and water," said Hedgeworth. "And oh will you be surprised young man."

It was indeed a surprise. The cemetery was filled with people. "It's an alternative to the streets for Egypt's poorest people," said Nasi. "All those empty rooms."

"Are not empty anymore," said Hedgeworth. "Be prepared. You haven't smelled anything like this before. There is no garbage collection or sewage services."

We were on a makeshift road that scribbled around burial sites. Now and then we stopped to avoid hitting people in the streets who appeared to have no awareness of our presence. "They can't look at us," said Nasi, "because they are not supposed to be here."

"Why?" I said.

"Since medieval times," said Nasi, "the poor have moved into the empty tomb rooms. It was acceptable behavior until . . . the West came."

"What?" I said.

"Napoleon," she said. "He came here, occupied the country, and brought Western mores, which included the moral principle that graveyards are for the dead . . . only the dead. It became shameful to live in a graveyard."

I saw wet clothing hanging on lines between cemetery buildings. The stench of garbage and sewage was overwhelming.

Skorzeny stopped on the side of a two-story sand-stoned mausoleum, got out, walked to the front of the Kubelwagen, lifted the trunk cover, and took out two large containers. Four large men in black djellabas came out of a small door of the mausoleum and moved swiftly toward him. Hedgeworth already had his right hand inside his jacket. Skorzeny was still facing the front of the Kubelwagen. His eyes told Hegeworth to calm down, as though he had eyes in the back of his head. My reaction time was much slower than Hedgeworth's, so I was still reaching for the Walther PPK in my ankle holster as he withdrew his hand from the shoulder holster. Nasi looked scared. I was, I hoped I didn't look it.

Skorzeny turned and faced the four men. They backed away touching their hands to their lips, then touching their foreheads and chests. It was as though they had seen a saint or a ghost. He said something to them in Arabic, the first words I'd heard from him. It was short, maybe three words. And it was forceful.

One of the men raised his hands above his head pointing his fingers to the left and then at his chest. Skorzeny nodded slowly. The man ran off.

"Guess they recognized him," said Hedgeworth. "He probably showed his Knight's Cross. Hitler personally did the honors. Skorzeny was Adolph's favorite *Waffen*-SS man. He sent him to rescue Mussolini after the Italians put Il Duce in prison. Skorzeny pulled off a daring glider assault on the Campo Imperatore Hotel at Gran Sasso and took Mussolini to Germany without firing a shot. This is the big time, son."

Nasi and I looked at one another. Hedgeworth chuckled. "He's known around as the gash-faced devil with a cross from hell. Nasser brought a lot of Nazis to Egypt after the war. For him they're natural and useful allies. They hate Jews and they have skills he needs. Otto's very close with Nasser. He designed a training program for the Egyptian secret service. And rumors say he's Nasser's favorite assassin."

"Lucky for him they recognized him," I said. Hedgeworth turned his bulk sideways in the seat and replied, "Lucky for them, you mean."

The man who ran off returned with a group of men carrying containers. "That's our petrol and water," said Hedgeworth to me. "We're going to Abu Sueir. From there you'll go to Dhahran. Nasi and Amshir go to Akrotiri."

Native scene near Foreign Legion Post at Ouarzazate.

Chapter Fourteen

Nouasseur Air Base

"It was easy to know what to do with him . . . but she was a problem." Subtle harmonies of Duke Ellington's "Moon Indigo" were in the background. I was on my second round of Stolichnaya pepper vodka as the General was telling me what he did when he received Hedgeworth's message about Alain's true identity.

"I turned him over to our special investigation people," said the General. "I talked to the major. I'm convinced she was completely taken in. We agreed to an honorable discharge with a signed agreement that she never speak of this. I told her I'd send the dogs of war after her if she violated our agreement, but I suspect our power to revoke her pension is enough to keep her quiet. She's from a poor family, and she certainly can't count on spousal support. She doesn't have an ideology or a cause or anything like that. She's just a person trying to survive. She was promoted way beyond her accomplishments—the gender thing. She knows she's been in over her head since she made first lieutenant. So the threat of canceling her pension is probably enough."

"What," I asked, "if the French go after her?"

"We sent a few of our heaviest-booted CIA boys to visit the right people at Quai d'Orsay," he said. "Our message was that they'd get Alain back in due time if they just sat on all of this for now. If they so much as flutter in the direction of this incident, the Americans will lodge a formal complaint with the French Government, the United Nations, and NATO Central Control. There's a hornets' nest of curious minds in those organizations, all looking for something to investigate. I doubt the French want all that dirty laundry strung up on lines in Paris, Washington, and London, and God knows where else."

"And . . . Isnard?" I said.

"Gave his ass to special investigation along with his colleague."

I drank some vodka. The general was not finished with that thought, I could tell.

"They're both in Cyprus," he said. "we may need to have you talk with your former French tutor. What we really want to find out is how much they know about what. You might be able to get things out of him that no one else can." I almost jumped at this very pleasant surprise. Maybe I was still in the game.

"Because," I said, "I have a relationship with Alain, or whatever his name is, that could be used." I was guessing.

"You *are* catching on," said the General. "But catching on and being able to do it are two different things. We might ask you to use your friendship with this guy to trick and deceive him. You might not yet be up to doing that. Oh, by the way, you'll be disappointed to hear that our friend, Gil Tompkins, has no more operational duties. You don't work for him anymore."

"Pity," I said. "What happened?"

"Oh, the day you told me he was going to run Yunus Bahri here in Morocco, I told someone in Washington that this loose cannon intended to make us work with a man the British had on their shit list. That did it."

"Guess that means there is a God in Heaven," I said—"and that I won't set up a meeting in Cyprus on Moroccan nationalism."

"I also told them about that idea," said the General, "Just to make sure that dummy got stuffed in a closet. Another thing, Sergeant Hopper and the rescue unit are not back from that search for the C-47 crew in the Atlas. I've got everything available out there looking for them. No luck yet." He finished his vodka and said, "So, what happened in Egypt?"

General Jackman didn't see any problem in letting the Israelis deliver weapons to *Istiqlal*. But he wanted me to turn the arrangements over to Si Fulan. "I don't want any American military people involved beyond that. Fulan should have a way of contacting Abd el-Krim."

"And our AC&W guys?" I said.

"We do that non-record keeping regularly," he said. "That's what records are for. Only fools try to get rid of records. Wise men don't record anything that could be a problem down the line. The AC&W mission is to alert us to incoming Russkies. Nothing more. I've made that clear to all the AC&W people."

He filled our vodka glasses and smiled. "Isn't ol' Hedge something? He knows how these things work, that I'm not the least bit interested in Israelis flying in here. But he got that Mossad guy to give him something for my being willing to not record their being here. I could learn from him forever."

"I didn't pick up on the AC&W thing," I said, "but I did notice how he's got Abd el-Krim under his thumb. One word from him to the Nasser gang about how Abd el-Krim set up a meeting that resulted in the British gaining information from Mossad on what Nasser's planning to do about the Suez Canal and . . . bye, bye Abd."

"You're learning," he said. I didn't know exactly how to take that. And he still had not commented on whether or not I was being held responsible for Alain's ruse. But Woody Herman's "Apple Honey" provided some compensation.

Simcha was angry. "Jilly and Alain are just . . . gone. And all you can say to me is that you cannot tell me why Alain is gone, and that you might be able to tell me about Jilly in a day or two. *Merde*."

We were in *The Minaret* Quonset. She was laying out the front page of the next edition.

"It's the best I can do . . . all that I know," I said.

She kept on working, turning pieces around haphazardly, muttering "merde." Suddenly she looked up at me as though it was the first time she saw me and said, "I almost forgot, Mina Halima is at the gate. She wants to see you."

"I'll go meet her," I said. "But before that . . . I want to ask you something. I'm going to Fez tomorrow to observe and make notes on the installation of the new Sultan. I could use an interpreter."

"*D'accord,*" she said glumly. "I wish we had our photographer. What a big show it will be."

I had no choice but to use Jilly's jeep. I'd never driven a right-hand side drive vehicle, so I was all over the road between my office and the gate. Both the French and the American MPs were standing in the road, probably preparing to arrest me for drunken driving, as well as for stealing Jilly's Jeep. When the American MP recognized me and the right-hand side drive vehicle, he yelled, "Now you know why we leave that one to Jilly. By the way, where's she been? Haven't seen her in a while. Usually I see her just 'bout every day."

"On assignment off base," I yelled back. Mina got into the jeep. As I was turning around the MP said to her, "Ma'm I should warn you that this man is not a real driver. Actually he ain't got a driver's license, nothin' like that. He cleans floors and waste paper baskets at our newspaper office. I could give you official and very secure passage." He thought it was such a good one that he was trying to tell his French colleague what he said as we drove off.

Mina said, "You remember Zwina? Her party . . . where you met Si?"

I nodded. "She joined *Istiqlal* the day after Mohammed V was deposed," Mina said. "They assigned her to a terror cell. Trained her to set fires. Women are better than men for this. The police hesitate to stop and search a woman. The French believe that all insurgents are men, so women, like Zwina, can walk the streets freely carrying straw baskets with benzene and matches hidden inside."

Zwina was on an assignment with Leila, a sister freedom fighter. They went to Farka's tobacco and kif shop. He sold French cigarettes, though he had been warned that to do so was treason. As soon as they were inside, they poured bottles of benzene over everything they could reach and threw lit matches into the benzene. They ran out on to the street, chased by Farka and some of his friends. One of the pursuers caught and ripped off Zwina's djellaba hood. Leila threw a basket of lettuce at him. That slowed him down. Zwina and Leila found a door slightly ajar. They pushed it open, then locked it behind them. They found themselves in a courtyard where women were peeling vegetables.

Zwina yelled at the women, "We are freedom fighters." The women gathered around Zwina and Leila and rushed them upstairs. Minutes later French policemen were in the courtyard holding Zwina's djellaba hood to the nose of a police dog. Not long after that they were leading Zwina and Leila stumbling down the stairs of the upstairs room bound together with a rope. To make sure these women who had tried to help Zwina and Leila understood they had committed crimes, three large French policemen walked around the upstairs room beating them indiscriminately with wooden clubs, shouting "we punish terrorists."

"Where is she now?" I asked.

"Ghoubila Prison," said Mina.

I remembered what Alain had said about methods of torture at Ghoubila, sending electric charges to highly sensitive parts of the body.

"I took some bread and sugarloaf in a basket to her yesterday," Mina said. "At the prison gate, they handed me a sheet of paper and told me to write the prisoner's name on it. As I did so, they sliced into the food and chopped it into rough pieces which they then threw back into the basket."

Mina was told to join a group of visitors standing in front of a blackboard. A guard dressed in a robe of white cotton wrote her name on the blackboard. She had heard of the routine.

When there were ten names on the blackboard, that group of ten visitors were led into a hall divided by two partitions with guards holding clubs standing in between. Eventually the prisoners whom the visitors had come to see were brought into the hall and lined up on the sides of the partitions where the guards were. When Mina saw Zwina, she walked to the other side of the partition so that they were face-to-face seeing one another through wire screen.

"She looked . . . an inch away from death," said Mina. "Do you remember how she dressed in the most ornate clothing and jewelry imaginable. Now she is dressed in sackcloth with no jewelry. The only things colorful are the bloodstains, black-and-blue welts all over her face, and the roots of her hair were such a strange color. I suppose they yanked her face in and out of pails of water. Her eyes have almost disappeared into her head. What I could see of them was dark gray. She looked as though she had been crying quite a lot but was now beyond tears. Neither of us said a word. We just stood there gazing at one another. The silence was sharp as a knife's edge."

Midway through Mina's telling me what had happened, I pulled over to the side of the road and turned off the engine. Absorbing what Mina was saying was impossible so long as I struggled with Jilly's Jeep. She had been staring straight ahead. Now she turned her head and looked at me, saying, "I think she has already told them all she knows. Probably they know you and I were at her party. We'll be questioned. We must tell the same story. What should it be?"

"Do you know if she knows about Si?" I said.

"I don't think she does . . but."

"Let's just tell them you brought me to a Moroccan party. And that's it."

Zwina was an example of what happened in French Morocco after the deposition of Sultan Mohammed V. The deposition was an inevitability because Mohammed V had not only refused French requests to denounce *Istiqlal* and to do other things to bolster the French presence, he had made an alliance with Sidi

Mohammed el Amin Pasha, Bey of Tunis and leader of the natives in the French protectorate of Tunisia.

Like Morocco, Tunisia was plagued by increasing waves of murder and riot as the natives fought for independence. As *Istiqlal* supported Mohammed V, *Neo-Destour*, the principal nationalist party in Tunisia, backed The Bey of Tunis. Both leaders had rejected French demands that French residents in their countries be given weighted voting rights in municipal elections permitting them to equal the influence of the native populations many times their number.

Together the two leaders presented their case to the United Nations and particularly to the United States. When pressed by the American State Department about the French claim that the nationalist movements were driven by communists, they responded that there was indeed some communist influence, but this influence resulted from French rules on labor unions. In both countries, workers' organizations asked to be given the right to form their own unions. They were refused, told to join French unions, which were led by French communists.

Meanwhile spokespersons for the American State Department said that the disturbances in Morocco were minor expressions of dissatisfactions, currently under "positive and progressive discussion."

Though *Istiqlal* and *Neo-Destour* were ideologically hostile to communism for religious reasons, they were opportunistically willing to profit from communist organization techniques. *Istiqlal* went to school on how to organize at meetings of the General Confederation of Workers, planned and run by communists. When the French caught on to how these nationalist parties were organized, they saw the communist design and concluded that the parties were led by communists.

Every Arab in Morocco knew the insulting details of how the French sped Mohammed V out of the country. After securing the support of El Glaoui and Abd El Hay Kittani, the French made their move.

It happened in mid-afternoon, at the end of the siesta hour. A column of French shock troops in camouflage paratrooper uniforms entered the Palace courtyard and easily overcame the ceremonial Black Guard, who carried parade weapons without ammunition. The Sultan was about to put a djellaba over his pajamas when the French Resident General, Augustin-Leon Guillaume, along with the chief of security police, came into his bedroom with four of the shock troops demanding the Sultan's immediate abdication. The Sultan refused. Guillaume pointed at the Sultan and shouted "You are deposed!"

Still clothed only in his pajamas, the Sultan was taken to a Residency car at gunpoint, driven to the military airport of *Souissi*, and deposited in an unheated Douglas C-47 Dakota. Guillaume, in his open light-blue Bugatti, followed the Sultan's car from the Palace to the airstrip, looking very confident in his white jacket, his black hair oiled and combed straight back.

The Sultan's two sons had been put on the plane earlier. The aircraft had no seats, nothing to eat or drink, and was not pressurized. The royal party was flown to Ajaccio, Corsica, without any luggage whatsoever. Numerous photos were taken of the Sultan and his sons, sitting awkwardly on straw in their pajamas. The pictures, printed in all Moroccan papers, were picked up by wire services around the world.

The next day, the French, being the French, sent the Sultan's three legal wives, six legal children, seven black slaves, and twenty-three concubines of various colors and nationalities, along with their wardrobes and those of the ex-Sultan to join him in Ajaccio.

The Ajaccio governor had not been told what was going on, so he made the best of it. He treated the whole thing as a visit by a reigning monarch and party, with all the customary courtesy and protocol. Mohammed V was presentd with a Napoleonic Medal, and his sons were given honorary status as members of the legendary Corsican Guard.

The deposition of Mohammed V was a colossal diplomatic blunder. A deep collective grief consumed the nation. Mina told me the people believed the country was now in the hands of demons. Moroccans gathered on rooftops at night because a revered Imam reported seeing the features of Mohammed V on the moon. Many said they saw the features. They reached out crying for the Sultan's return.

The French Protectorate declared that seeing the Sultan's face on the moon was a violation of national security punishable by imprisonment. They kept their word. Thousands of Moroccans were thrown into dungeons for declaring that they saw the ex-Sultan's face on the moon. French police and army militias tried to block access to rooftops. They failed to halt the crawling, climbing bodies. "They are like the locusts," a French journalist said to me, "they swarm over you in unstoppable numbers."

In desperation the Protectorate declared Medina rooftops off-limits. Violators would be shot or gassed from helicopters.

After three nights of blood-soaked rooftops, the Western press finally joined the Arab press in condemning what was going on. Newspapers in the Arab and Western worlds said that Morocco now looked like an occupied country under Nazi Germany.

The Afro-Asian Group in Paris asked the United Nations to condemn the Sultan's deposition. The French argued that the U.N. Charter precluded it from intervening in domestic affairs. The reference was to Article 2 Paragraph 7, which says: "Nothing contained in the present Charter shall authorize the United Nations to intervene in matters which are essentially within the domestic jurisdiction of any state."

It was a sticky argument. Legally, Morocco was a Protectorate, not a Colony. International law did not answer the question of whether a country under Protectorate status qualified for the domestic jurisdiction clause. France was not alone in trying to protect colonies from U.N. intervention by invoking Article 2. The Dutch referred to it with regard to its presence in West New Guinea; the British did the same with Cyprus. South

Africa's officials vigorously claimed that treatment of the colored people was an internal affair.

The U.N. Security Council refused to condemn Mohammed V's deposition. The Soviet Union, China, Chile, Lebanon, and Pakistan voted for the condemnation. The U.S., U.K., France, Columbia, and Denmark voted against it. One of the reasons the U.S. did not support the condemnation was that one week prior to the Sultan's deposition, the Soviets had conducted their first successful test of a hydrogen bomb. Though not as powerful as one we had tested nine months earlier, it had a scary advantage—it was an immediately usable weapon, small enough to be dropped from an airplane.

Hydrogen bombs are a thousand times more deadly than the atomic bombs that devastated Hiroshima and Nagasaki.

American war strategists were taken by surprise, because our intelligence estimated that the Soviets were at least a year away from even successfully testing a hydrogen bomb, let alone one that could be used immediately. In addition, the death of Stalin, a few months earlier, put an unknown factor, Georgi Malenkov, in charge at the Kremlin. Therefore we played a very cautious hand. One of the many flaws in how American intelligence interpreted Soviet intentions was the idea that everything had to do with Stalin. So, when he died we were clueless.

The UN refusal to condemn Mohammed V's deposition brought a tirade from *Istiqlal*. "The Great Western Powers have exerted their influence to oppose the freedom and self-determination of peoples," said *Istiqlal* spokesmen. "This is a repudiation of the principles to which their own histories pay honor and their current statesmen pay lip services. This vote is likely to result in more desperate actions by the Moroccan people. It is certain to weaken the trust of all Asian and African peoples in the good faith of the Western Powers."

Istiqlal voices were echoed loudly and ferociously throughout the Mediterranean. Millions of Muslims spread across north Africa cried out for justice. The issue was becoming Christianity versus Islam. Before, colonialism was explained as economic exploitation. Now it was being presented also as a Christian enslavement of muslims.

In Casablanca there was terrorism and counter-terrorism. French soldiers were on constant patrol in the medina, carrying submachine guns pointed menacingly at the natives. Non-Europeans were pulled out of their automobiles, commanded to show identity papers while the vehicles were searched so thoroughly that the drivers had to spend hours getting things back into place.

Whereas previously the French would not assault an Arab on the French streets—they took them into large vans, closed the back doors, and battered them—they now attacked them viciously anywhere in the city, throwing them across tables and through store windows, if the stores were owned by Arabs. They were empowered to do almost anything they wanted. If any business or establishment were considered antagonistic to the state, it could, without much more said, be destroyed.

The French tried to block labor strikes and other disruptions. Sometimes the countermoves worked, sometimes they did not. When Moroccan shops shut down in protest, police forced open the metal wickets covering shop windows. In most cases the shop owners returned to protect their merchandise. But the French were less successful with attempts to order striking workers back to work. When the workers were marched back to work at rifle points, they often sabotaged operations when back at work.

Foreign legionnaires watched the natives from the roofs of buildings. Sandbag fortifications blocked every medina gate. Non-Arab taxi drivers refused to take passengers into the medinas. Bicycle riding was forbidden in most medina streets because the authorities believed that terrorist attacks were signaled—and coordinated—by cyclists. The Moroccans pushed their bicycles through the streets toward the European quarters where they were permitted to ride. From eight in the evening to five in the morning, Moroccans were kept behind closed doors in their medinas.

Chapter Fourteen

A Moroccan writer called this period "The Year of the Elephant," referring to a legendary battle in early Islam. Abraha, the Christian King of Yemen, constructed a magnificent church at Sanaa and expected the Arabs to regard it as the center for their religious worship. The Arabs already had a center for religious worship, the Kaaba at Mecca. They declined the invitation.

Abraha was incensed. His response was decisive. He sent an elephant brigade, hundreds of elephants and 40,000 men, to march on Mecca and destroy the Kaaba. Such a force could easily carry out the order. However, Allah interfered in two ways. The Prophet Muhammad was born that same year and Allah sent an army of birds with pebbles in their beaks to form a dark cloud above the invading forces. The birds rained pebbles on Abraha's elephants and troops. The invaders retreated in despair.

French Resident General Guillaume was alarmed when he heard that the Arabs were making jewelry shaped like elephants and that almost every Arab wore one. He began to rely more and more on T'hami El Glaoui.

T'hami was delighted that Muhammad V, the man who allowed his second-in-command to call T'hami a "nigger," was exiled and humiliated. The Berber chief sent thousands of his mountain tribal warriors into Marrakech to maintain order Berber-style. The French Police Inspector in Marrakech sent an urgent message to his superiors in Rabat, saying the streets had been taken over by wild men over whom he had no control. Lives of Europeans living in or visiting the city were in grave danger, though other Europeans were enjoying the lavish hospitality of El Glaoui in the mountains. It was perhaps the high point of El Glaoui's life, if victory over a rival counts. And it did—really—count for him. His honor and the honor of the House of Glaoua had been reclaimed, because the house that had taken it away was now in disgrace.

It was one thing to whisk the Sultan out of the country, another to find a new Sultan who could meet both the political and religious benchmarks as well as being acceptable to El Glaoui. Ties between Guillaume and El Glaoui had begun back in 1919 when Guillaume, then a young and ambitious officer who had just been repatriated from a German Prisoner of War camp, came to Morocco as an intelligence officer in the native affairs bureau. A mountain man himself, born and raised in the *Haute Alpes* region of Provence, Guillaume was drawn to the Berbers, the mountain men of Morocco. He became commandant of the Moroccan troops fighting in Italy of which Pierre Didier and his Fourth Mountain Division were a part.

Guillaume personally led the Berber *Goumiers*. General Patton had heard about the fierce *Goumier* warriors, met with Guillaume and declared that a *Goum*, the name for a unit of *Goumiers*, under the command of Guillaume, would be worth three divisions of American and British troops in the Italian mountains. He requested that Guillaume, in addition to being commandant of the Moroccan troops in Italy, be personally in charge of the *Goum*.

The *Goum* distinguished itself in two ways. It was, as Patton predicted, much more effective in mountain fighting than any American or British unit, and it acquired a reputation for sheer ferocity in combat.

After considerable bargaining between Guillame, El Glaoui, and Kittani, an uncle of Mohammed V, Moulay Arafa, was selected to be the new Sultan. Arafa was pro-French and anti-*Istiqlal*, though he had not been active in matters of state prior to this moment. The next step was to get approval from the *Oulema*, or religious council, of Fez, without whose proclamation no one could be a legitimate Sultan.

In the early hours of the morning on the day after Mohammed V was dispatched to Corsica, French police banged on the sculpted cedar doors of *Riad Saada*, the *Oulema* residence house. They ordered all members to appear that afternoon at the Sultan's Palace to sign the proclamation of the new Sultan

Arafa. Two refused. One did so because, quoting the Koran—when there are two *Imams*, the second must be killed—if Arafa were named Sultan, he would have to be killed. That protestor disappeared the same day. The other objector, a Koranic professor at the Ben Youssef University of Marrakech was beaten to within an inch of his life. The proclamation was signed. Moulay Arafa was to be installed as the new Sultan of Morocco.

A week later Arafa led prayer for the first time as the Sultan-designate in a mosque of little Islamic significance. The small number of fellow prayers were carefully selected by Guillaume. That small group outnumbered prayers at other Moroccan mosques which were empty because the French promised punishment to whoever offered prayer in the name of anyone other than Arafa. To offer a prayer for Mohammed V was punishable by death. In Marrakech an *Imam* stood in front of his mosque shouting he could not offer prayer for Arafa. Within a minute he was stabbed to death.

The French tried to keep the people from speaking publicly about Mohammed V. The people responded in crowds of fifty thousand or more, shouting for the return of Mohammed V.

Fez

French Morocco

Elaborate precautions were taken to ensure the safety of Moulay Arafa at his investiture ceremony. The Sultan-designate had barely escaped two assassination attempts the week before.

The first was a daring attempt by a boy whose father managed to have him tied to the ceiling above Arafa's bed and camouflaged with painting on his body to blend into the scene. The boy had a knife that enabled him to cut himself loose and was to be used as the instrument of assassination when he fell on top of the sleeping Sultan-designate. Unfortunately for the boy, he had not practiced. He lost balance while descending and plunged the knife into his own gut.

The other attempt was classic Moroccan. The assassin rushed the vehicle in which the Sultan-designate was being transported. As often happened, this assassin was blistered by bullets and deep-cut by swords and knives long before he saw his target's face.

Such failures were not discouraging to those determined to see Mohammed V returned as Sultan. Actually they were celebrated as victories because they demonstrated the rejection of this Sultan-designate.

Arafa was unacceptable as Sultan not only because he was not deemed a worthy successor to Mohammed V; but also because prior to this investiture ceremony, he had signed over all his legislative powers to a council consisting of Frenchmen and Moroccans handpicked for their allegiance to maintenance of the French Protectorate.

In the only speech he gave touching on politics after the *Oulema* proclaimed him Sultan-designate, he condemned the *Istiqlal* Party and declared that the nationalist movement was an offense to Islam, and, he added, now that it is in collusion with the communists, it is a dangerous threat to the Arab world. The speech was written by Guillaume and delivered in a small, barely-known mosque. All Moroccan newspaper editors were there, including Pierre Didier, and they all gave major coverage to the speech because Guillaume made them aware he would have it no other way.

Simcha and I, with two Foreign Legionnaire snipers armed with Brown Precision rifles, were on the third floor of a building overlooking the ceremonial procession. Pierre Didier had arranged it.

The installation was to take place in Kairaouine Mosque, built in the ninth century to accept 20,000 worshippers. The procession started about three hundred yards from the mosque and went along a wide boulevard. Moulay Arafa traveled in the

Imperial coach, an old-fashioned London four-wheeler pulled by white horses and decorated in green, gold, and white. Inside, Moulay Arafa was dressed in pure white.

The sides of the coach were lined by the Sultan's Black Guard Officers, magnificent men in red tunics with bulging green and white turbans, riding gray horses, their faces black as coal. Each horseman carried a tall lance flying the green pennant of Islam. Black Guard non-commissioned officers with submachine guns stood at five-yard intervals facing the crowds lining the boulevard, alert for the smallest suspicious movement. French Legionnaire snipers were on every rooftop as well as in some of the windows. The rifle barrels glistened in the sun.

Immediately behind the Imperial coach rode T'hami El Glaoui mounted on a bay horse. A repeating carbine rested on his left arm. At this point in his life, El Glaoui traveled this way or in a black Bentley Mark VI.

He was ensuring, it appeared, that he was perfectly suited to be the new Sultan's bodyguard, despite rumors that he was suffering from two or three incurable diseases. His tall thin body was statuesquely erect in the saddle, though his body was tortured by pain. He bore the scars of sixteen wounds, all of which had been treated with red ants. Berber medicine men knew how to sew up wounds but did not know how to disinfect them. The stitches festered quickly and burst open. The medicine men gave up stitching and began putting live red ants on wounds after holding the two edges of the skin together, leaving part of both edges protruding. The ant instantly closed its very powerful mandibles on the skin and was then cut off with scissors; the mandibles remained closed on the skin, acting as clips holding the edges together. Over time various problems including infection resulted from these treatments.

With pipes, drums, and rifles eight thousand Berber warriors stood on a nearby hillside next to their horses. In front of the mosque there was a band in pink djellabas holding long brass trumpets.

When the coach was close to the mosque, eight thousand Berber rifles saluted Moulay Arafa from the hilltop. The sound shook the building we were on. El Glaoui attempted to fire his carbine when that sound subsided. His carbine malfunctioned. He tried again with a frustrating effect. I did not see it, but was told that he brought down a stork that happened to be passing by. T'hami El Glaoui, a genius at creating legends about himself, said that the stork was an evil jinn sent by Mohammed V to bite Moulay Arafa in his neck with a deadly poison.

Usually the designated Sultan dismounts from the Imperial coach and enters the mosque on foot. This time the coach was driven into the mosque with Arafa sitting trembling within it.

Simcha said something in French I didn't understand. The sharpshooters snickered but kept their eyes on the scene below.

All of these happenings, from the humbling deposition of Mohammed V to the cowardly behavior of Moulay Arafa at his installation ceremony, were well known and bewailed in Arab streets.

The morning after the ceremonies in Fez, I went to General Jackman's office to discuss this new Moroccan situation. It seemed to me that our strategy to be on the right side of a victorious nationalist movement was coming apart at the seams. Moulay Arafa had denounced Istiqlal and El Glaoui had always opposed it. The French had removed the one man who, in their view, stood in the way of their maintaining power in Morocco, and replaced him with a marionette.

"We have to hope that the French have overplayed their hand," said the General. "And we have to do whatever we can to make this backfire on them. There are signs that the alliance between the Resident General, El Glaoui, and Kittani shows wear and tear. The Resident General told me he was finding Kittani repulsive these days because the *Chereef* wants guarantees of considerable autonomy for his *Zaouia* tribes. He said that El Glaoui is pledging full support for the Protectorate so long as Mohammend V is exiled. He also said he doesn't trust El Glaoui as far as he can throw a camel."

"And," I said, "El Glaoui probably feels the same way about the Resident General. Though I suppose T'hami would say 'two camels.'"

"I have clearance from Washington," the General said, "to ask Hedgeworth to urge the Israelis to get more weapons into the hands of the nationalists as fast as they can. This is the time to push things forward. Talk to your *Istiqlal* contact. Find out what weapons they need most."

I went to my office. Jilly was sitting at her desk. She looked limp and exhausted. I wanted to hug her but instead sat on her desk facing her, as close as I could get without touching her, and said, "Welcome back. We worried about you. . . . And we missed you. How . . . ?"

"We never found the survivors of that plane," she said. Her words came slowly and deliberately, as though she needed to take a breath after each one. "We were taken prisoners by some mountain Arabs who kept us in a cave for days. The chief came to see us and set us free. Strange looking bloke. He had a white beard and blue eyes. Looked more like a Scandinavian than an Arab. Said his name is Abd El Hay Kittani, that he couldn't release us sooner because there was too much danger for us being loose in that area."

Kittani held a banquet for Jilly and the others before providing them with camels for transportation back to Nouasseur. His last words to them were, "Please tell your General Jackman that Abd El Hay Kittani and the *Zaouia*, my people, are friends to the Americans."

"I met Kittani at the Didiers," I said. "Maybe he realizes that he is the most dispensable of the three conspirators. I hear the French and Berbers brought him into the plot at the last minute. If he gets us on his side, it's a trump card."

"Why did he go along?" Jilly asked.

"When the Sultan was a teenager," I said, "Kittani's brother refused to bow as the Sultan passed him on horseback. Kittani's brother was flogged to death on the spot."

"Guv," said Jilly, "can I try my hand at writing a piece on this?"

I thought about it. "OK, with some limitations. You can't say anything about the reason you went there. We don't want to reveal that there might be some live American flight crew alive and lost in those mountains. Say that you went to observe a training mission. I'll work with you on it if you'd like."

She smiled. "I'd like. But now I need sack time. I'm bloody knackered."

It was so good to see her and so hard to just let her go from me so quickly. I didn't know how to express how I really felt. I said, "Of course." I wanted to say, "Please stay with me. I have really missed you."

By the twentieth day of Moulay Arafa's reign, nearly thirteen thousand people had been arrested on charges of treason. Morocco's dungeons were fuller than they had ever been in the country's history. The new Sultan hid in his palace most of the time, insisting on an impenetrable guard when he went out of it. Press correspondents from the United States and Europe descended upon bloodstained Morocco like petrels who arrive after a storm to eat dead fish off the shores. Stringers hoping to land pieces in prestige publications such as *The New York Times* and *TIME Magazine* hung around *The Minaret* office looking for leads. The local press was now fully censored to prevent reportage of daily riots and bloody encounters.

For centuries Morocco had been a scene of blood and destruction, but this was an unparalleled moment in its history. Each new day saw an increase in riots and explosions. The French had unwittingly launched a colonial rebellion to which their only response was to pour in more troops. A French journalist, in a report published by *Le Monde,* wrote that "the condition of Morocco is declining into an epilepsy of violence and brutality."

Al-Alam, Istiqlal's underground newspaper, said, "A deep collective grief has fallen over the nation. Morocco has fallen into the hands of demons. Every Moroccan person must protest with any means possible to him. This is a holy war. Not only against the occupiers and other Europeans sucking the blood from the people. Against some Moslems as well. Particularly the pretender Moulay Arafa and all those who hang to his filthy djellabah. To eternal hell for all of them. Sending them there is blessed by the Prophet, who will provide rewards in heaven to those who die in this holy war against the infidels."

Pierre Didier advised me to stop eating in French restaurants because "the staff are serving stews composed of human flesh. I have a cousin, a medical student. He found . . . at the end of his fork . . . the tip of a human penis. . . . He and his companions took the evidence to the police, who thought the medical students had access to dead anatomical parts, so the officers at first treated the whole thing as a hoax. When the students finally convinced the officers to look into this matter and the officers investigated the restaurant, they found that no attempt had been made to hide anything. All the stew pots remained filled with human remains. An Arab wit submitted to me today a piece in which he says that no doubt the restaurant staff were executed, perhaps eaten too."

Morocco was descending deeper and deeper into a Hobbesian state of nature, where life is poor, nasty, brutal, and short. At best, things could only get a little bit worse rather than better. The policemen always wore their rounded metal helmets rather than soft caps. There were more than 200,000 French soldiers in Morocco, the most ever, including elite SAS paratroopers, armored cars, light tanks, and the Camel Corps.

Though they faced an overwhelming military juggernaut, the natives would not be brought to their knees. When buildings were shattered by cannon fire, protestors attacked the French with bricks torn from the walls of the buildings. Central authorities at the Quai d'Orsay were not pleased, perhaps regretting they had told Guillaume he could depose Mohammed V if necessary.

Aid el Kebir is Islam's greatest feast day. The slaughter of a ram determines whether the year to come is to be peaceful and prosperous or disastrous. The ceremony commemorates the day when, by divine order, Abraham prepared to sacrifice his son Ismail. Before he did so Allah interceded by providing a ram in place of the child.

In Morocco *Aid el Kebir* was always celebrated in Rabat. Fulan asked me to attend the feast because he knew the French were planning to avenge an attack a week ago by an Arab mob against a group of Europeans in Port Lyautey, which is a few miles north of Rabat. The attack was covered by the Western press in full gory detail. *The New York Times* described how Arabs carved European womens' breasts and stomachs inside-out. Fulan was told that the French revenge would take place the night of *Aid el Kebir*. "If you are there at Port Lyautey and report first-hand what you see, the impact on the Western press will be very helpful to our cause."

The custom of *Aid el Kebir* is for the Sultan to ride outside the palace walls to cut the ram's throat. However, because of increasing assassination attempts, some of which Moulay Arafa had narrowly escaped, he refused to leave the palace that day.

According to a report by a *New York Times'* reporter, the Sultan thrust his knife into the ram's throat on the palace grounds, then stood back while the carcass was placed in a jeep and rushed off to the palace. The lore is that if the sacrificial ram arrives at the palace alive, the land will be blessed. A few minutes later came word from the palace: "The animal arrived still breathing."

The omen was favorable, but few Arabs believed in it. Behind locked doors, many Moroccans celebrated the day in the name of the exiled Mohammed V. That night, as Fulan said they would, the French retaliated for the killings in Port Lyautey with a brutal display of force. They cut off the medina with three cordons of troops and police. Inside the medina were detachments of Legionnaires, French infantry with tanks, Berber *Goumiers*, and police from whose wrists swung weighted truncheons. The medina had been divided on a police map into six sectors. One by one the sectors were attacked.

First, Legionnaires began breaking down house doors. When the doors were down, *Goumiers* stormed in and forced every male, except small boys, outside by pulling hair and kicking backs. Screaming women were beaten back with clubs and gun butts.

Outside, police formed a gauntlet. Legionnaires shoved the men through the gauntlet at rifle point while policemen slugged them with their truncheons. The destination was a sheep market, where the Arabs were herded together under the deadly gaze of a Patton tank muzzle. At the sheep market police thrashed the Arabs with their truncheons while *Goumiers* beat on them with rifle butts and thick tree branches. It was estimated that 30,000 Arabs suffered through the gauntlet that day.

Beating another person is fatiguing. French leaders, mindful of this, used a humanitarian tactic to minimize suffering of the enforcers. Those who had attacked a sector rested while the next sector was herded and beaten, then went back into action on the following sector.

Nouasseur

General Jackman ordered all American military families living off-base to move on base. The straight road from Casablanca to Nouasseur was a ribbon covered by cars, jeeps, trucks, and vans spilling over with furniture, toasters, radios, childrens' books and games, and dogs trying to get their heads as far out of a window as possible. The order had been clear: *Bring little more than the clothes on your back.* But Americans usually interpret rules to concur with what they think should be done. A corporal told me his son asked him if this meant that the Nazis had won after all.

At Nouasseur tents were pitched between Dallas huts. Many of us moved out of our Dallas huts and into the tents so that families could occupy the Dallas huts. There was a food and furniture shortage. Most of the Americans who had tried to haul food and furniture ditched it because it created traffic problems. General Jackman had anticipated the problem. Hours before the evacuation of Casablanca, he positioned earth-moving equipment vehicles along the road. The drivers had simple orders, push off the road anything that was delaying traffic.

There was a lot of food and furniture warehoused in Germany, designed to be used at moments like this. But the only way to get it to Nouasseur in a reasonable amount of time was to fly it in, which we could not do without compromising the secret protocols established for the Q Area.

The aircraft controllers did not have "Q" clearances, so they did not know that the schedules of B47s and B36s were meticulously and secretively managed by an elaborate code system. The strategy was to have a certain number of B47s and B36s in the air on a twenty-four hour basis, some of which would be "hot," while other "hot" ones were on air strips prepared to take off. Scheduling was done in frames of seconds, or at the most a minute. Aircraft Controllers were given instructions on protocol for traffic with no idea of why it was the way it was. It was impossible to just slip into the schedule some food and furniture runs. The main runways were always in or about to be in use. Landing an aircraft not on the schedule required days of preparation and could be done no more than three or four times a week.

At night the base was guarded by a circle of nervous rifle-bearing guards. The base perimeter was too long for the air police to guard in an emergency situation, so all of us became night guards two or three nights a week. The best military policemen guarded the Q area and the Medouna Hill Reservoir, our water source, a few miles from Nouasseur.

Providing perimeter security for a base the size of Nouas-seur was overwhelming. B-36 runways were over forty football fields long. And the Air Force was not the Marine Corps. A dozen German Shepherd guard dogs arrived on a C-130 from the Air Force guard dog school in Wiesbaden. The dogs had been trained to do a lot of things. Flying was not one of them. They were sick and useless the first few days after they arrived.

There were a dozen permanent-duty guard dogs at Nouas-seur to patrol planes and the birdcage. They were now roaming the perimeters of Nouasseur and Medouna Hill at night. I felt more comfortable when I was close to one. It was not that I lacked courage. I think I had the average amount of that. What I lacked was skill sufficient to survive an attack by more than one skillful armed opponent. And I knew it.

At Nouasseur we had the weapons and delivery systems to demolish large cities, and more. We had devastation at our fingertips, but we were almost helpless facing a few hundred men carrying obsolete, yet still deadly, rifles and swords. The General tried to get additional resources, especially attack heli-copters and trained ground combatants. He was overruled by the argument that "we do not want to get people thinking about what is there at Nouasseur that is so important to protect. Do what you can with what you have."

What a quandary, I thought. If we designate Nouasseur a highest priority site for defense—pouring in experienced combat troops and heavy artillery—we admit that there is more there than we have claimed. If we don't keep Arabs from taking over the base and "looking around," we face the problem of having an Arab leader boasting that he now has the atomic weaponry to wipe out any part of the country he wishes.

I was working on a piece about the brutality that had besieged Morocco when Jilly came into the Minaret office, dressed and armed for guard duty in fatigues and an oversized helmet tilted back so that all the freckles on her forehead were clear to see. She closed the door quickly because the base was on a "minimum light alert." I thought it was an exaggerated caution; I was working by candlelight on my typewriter.

"Here tis, *mon* editor," she said, handing me some copy, "my award-winning report on being in the mountains with Chereef Kittani." She smiled awkwardly while readjusting the rifle strap that had slipped to her forearm when she handed me the report.

"Where are you off to," I said, "perhaps a . . . what is it you Brits hunt . . . foxes? Is your horse outside? Bet it's a black stallion."

She laughed uncomfortably. "I'm buggered and you want to play the straight man!"

"Sorry, warrior. I just thought you might be breaking the rules, hunting a little fox with that monster rifle."

She sat on my desk. "Guv, this is my third night out. It gets bloody scary. Everything is pitch black out there. I keep thinking a horde of wild-eyed Arab warriors will come down on me. You go out. Don't you feel it?"

"In every bone in my body," I said. "And I'm sorry about the lousy attempt to be funny. Actually I'm worried for you. You're such a great colleague and a good friend, too. I'll never forget the fun I had when we went into Berber land . . . you were such a lively spirit."

She took off her helmet. Scratched her head. "You're a funny bloke. I think I know you, then I know I don't. There's something about you that is so puzzling. I like you a lot. But why is it that things don't add up when I think about you?"

"Like?" I said.

"That's it," she said. "You answer questions with questions. Thank you very much. I finally figured it out. I will never figure you out."

"So how do you position yourself as the writer and what's the theme of your piece," I said.

"Well, I couldn't find a way to explain what I was doing there without telling it like it was," she said, "and you nixed that so I wrote a story in the third person about Chereef Kittani and his followers. Simcha helped me a lot, and there was a bit of stuff about him in the base library."

"I'll read it the moment you walk out that door," I said. "I hope I don't get to reading it for awhile."

She giggled nervously as she struggled getting the helmet back on her head. "I'd give a bloody good part of England to believe you really mean that." She said it so seriously, without the "guv" or "*mon* editor" tags. I had the feeling she was trying to talk directly to me, whoever I was. It felt good.

She stood up and sighed. "Hope ya like what I wrote. Ta-ta, mister piano player."

She fumbled with the door latch because she wore the rifle on her right shoulder and it slid down, banging against the door when she tried to turn the latch.

I walked to her, unlatched the door and saw light tears in her eyes. I've never known why tears in a woman's eye hold so long in a bubble before they run, whereas men's tears run like streams from the eyes. "Everything all right?" I said.

"Tell the bloody bad guys to beware dead-eye Jilly," she said. She banged the barrel of her gun against her helmet, an expression of defiance I suppose. And off she went into a nighttime she feared.

That night the wild boar on exhibit that week escaped from his pen at the *Petits USA* village. Probably a child let the loose nail off the hinge just for the fun of it. It was a very beefy specimen, over five feet tall, prized by its captor as a gigantic three-hundred-pound feast. It wobbled toward the air base, grunting and snorting. It was mating season so perhaps there was something about the smell of the guard dogs that drew him. Or, perhaps it had nothing to with mating. Feral boars from the Atlas like to kill and chew. Berbers say it is because they are jinns fighting to find their way out of their bodies. The smell of something to eat, dogs or people, might have been the attraction. There were a lot of different body odors out there. Boars, more so than many other animals, are attracted to smells, especially bad smells.

During his meander the boar came upon two guard dogs who went into a frenzy, barking harshly while quickly backing off from the boar. The boar gnawed his lower two tusks against the upper two, making a frightening sound in the pitch dark. Boars do that both for the intimidating effect and because it sharpens their tusks for the kill.

Except for the two frightened air policemen holding the dogs' leashes no one knew what set the dogs off. Some of the makeshift guards started shooting in the direction of the sounds. Then guards at other posts on the outskirts of the base fired randomly at where they thought the shots came from. A chaotic crossfire followed. Everyone was shooting at everyone else and at no one in particular.

The next morning there was relief in the news that only one of the guards was killed and one badly wounded from gunfire from other guards. Both dogs were mutilated by the boar, who was subdued with bursts of rifle and revolver bullets. Jilly was the guard who was badly wounded.

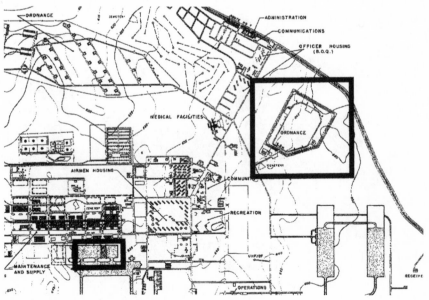

Nauasseur Air Base showing Q area in upper square.

Moroccan natives at the Petits USA village.

Souk at El Kelda Des M' Gouna.

Chapter Fifteen

General Jackman's Office

We were listening to one of the rare exceptions in General Jackman's jazz collection. His discs focused on American big band jazz and American WWII military jazz bands. Here and there the General allowed something else, like this currently playing Reinhardt-Grappelli recording of "Are You In The Mood." He always had an explanation for such exceptions, and always gave you the explanation.

In the case of Reinhardt and Grappelli, said the General, "we have two Frenchmen, well, a gypsy guitarist and a French violin player, who perform some aspects of jazz better than any American can. There are probably not two other Europeans who can do that. It deserves respect, or at least to be listened to."

"Where did people like that go when the Nazis took over," I said.

"Grappelli went to London," he said. "Reinhardt stayed in Paris playing back alley clubs on the Left Bank. The Nazis were picking up anyone playing what they called American nigger music. Reinhardt would have been a prize catch because in addition to playing the music he was a gypsy. The Nazis wanted the gypsies in work camps, but he managed to stay one step ahead of them.

He put down his vodka with a signal that we were back to business. "We need you in Cyprus to do two things. The first has to do with a conference. Things are getting dicier on Aphrodite's

Island. You've been there, so you know how serious the Greek-Cypriots are about independence from the British and union with Greece. A Greek UN representative made a formal request in New York that self-determination for Cyprus be included on the agenda of the General Assembly's next session."

He shook his head as though frustrated. "In a stroke of pure Gilbert and Sullivan madness," said the General, "the British Minister of State for the Colonies, speaking in the British House of Commons, announced the withdrawal of constitutional proposals for Cyprus."

The General filled his vodka glass. "How can people be so . . . and the Minister didn't even leave it at that . . . at that level of foolishness." The General picked up a sheet of paper, it looked like TWIX. "Here is his rationale. The Minister says, 'There are certain territories in the Commonwealth which, owing to their peculiar circumstances, can never expect to be fully independent.'"

"Did he add the phrase 'during wartime?'" I asked.

"No, no . . . this man is the devil's favorite idiot. He seems to completely forget that he has fired up the Cypriot guerrillas just when the Brits are short of troops to put them down."

"And" I said, "it's not just land we're talking about. Cyprus is a critical piece in our intelligence-gathering system. Lose it? We can't let it happen."

"So . . . " said the General. "Your official job is to attend a conference in Nicosia set up by the U.N. to smooth ruffled feathers caused by the British Minister of State's incautious comments. They'll assemble the usual bunch, that is, all the interested parties. The Conference Title is "Solutions to the Cyprus Problem."

"Catchy," I said. "Better title would be Problems in the Cyprus Solutions."

"When you're a diplomat you might try that," the General replied.

"Thinking of the diplomatic approach," I said, "what does the phrase 'all the interested parties' mean? Should the United States be included because we fly highly-classified, top-secret

U2 stealth-surveillance flights out of Akrotiri? Should the Turkish government be invited? Turks are a substantial minority in Cyprus, and the British control Cyprus because the Turks gave it to them as part of the 1923 Treaty of Lausanne. Should General Grivas be invited? And what about the threat to the Turkish mainland posed by a new Greek island within two stones' throws of Turkey's underbelly?"

"OK, let's leave that to the boys in Foggy Bottom," he said. "You go to the conference as a military journalist. But that's not the real reason you're going to Cyprus."

He walked from behind his father's desk and sat down beside me. "Let's up 'em," he said. He swung his shiny combat boots on to the desk top; I did the same with my dust-caked black oxfords. He had made sure that both of our vodka glasses were full.

"Son," he said, " a lot of us are asked to do things we hate to do, for the sake of victory. I broke a young girl's neck with one awful twist because if she lived our mission was periled. We're now going to ask you to do something disgusting for the sake of victory."

I thought about the word. He was pretty good with words. Usually found the appropriate one. What is disgusting? Peeing in your father's shoes? There are so many possibilities. Telling me I would do something disgusting was clueless, very vague.

"You remember Alain, of course," he said; and then deliberately waited for my response. Strange, I thought. I told him I remembered Alain.

"He is in The Nicosia Central Prison. The only thing we want to know is if he found out about the birdcages, and if he did, did he tell anyone about them."

"Why do you think he'll tell me?"

"I have the feeling, so does Major Courchene, that he developed a true friendship with you. According to her, and at this point the major doesn't dare lie to us, he took you for how you're presented, the editor of the newspaper. I meant to compliment you on that. Good going, especially for a novice."

"So he'll tell me out of . . . friendship?"

"There's a little more to it than that," said the General. "What do you know about truth drugs?"

"They're a myth concocted by the chemistry creeps in CIA," I said. "Those ghouls claim to have a cannabis complex that can be administered safely to induce from a conscious prisoner honest answers to questions about top secret material. I've heard enough about the tests to know it's bullshit. It's the LSD bullshit."

"So you would dismiss it all," he said, "because it's so disgusting you don't want to believe it could work, or because if it could work, you want to discredit it before it has a chance. Why is innocence so arrogant at times? People way ahead of you have discovered the shortcomings of cannibis compounds. Because they are way ahead of you, they have come up with some imaginative alternatives. They found out that if we addicted a prisoner to it and created the right conditions, we could get the truth out of him with a promise of more of the dope. Now we know that if we give it to a prisoner until he is addicted, he will, under the right conditions, give us the information we want in exchange for cannabis and trust."

I thought I caught on to what he was saying. Alain might reveal to me if—in addition to the cannabis I would give him to feed his new habit—he trusted me in some way that was important to his maintaining a scrap of self-dignity. And I didn't miss the point that I had to persuade Alain, putting aside my own personal feelings about rightness or wrongness.

As though he sensed I was thinking about my own feelings, the General said, "try to prepare yourself for an ugly sight. Alain is not the man you knew. I am sorry about that. You'll see him the day after the conference."

Later that night I went to the hospital to see Jilly. Though she had been shot in her left arm and hip she was doing well after two operations. "Does this mean," she said, "that I don't have to do any more bloody guard duty?"

Cyprus

This time I was met at Akrotiri by a British sergeant who waved me down to an armored car that looked like an armadillo on over-sized tires. The body was one piece of welded steel with a machine-gun turret. Six smoke grenade launchers were fitted to the hull, three on each side.

The sergeant, holding a Sten gun, welcomed me with a brief courtesy and pointed me to a seat behind the driver. It was cramped space, barely enough for a shorter person, and no room for the sergeant, so the driver and I went away together. Just before we did, the sergeant asked me if I knew how to use the machine gun. I said I didn't and he said, "if necessary, the driver will tell you what to do. He'll be in charge of the smoke grenades."

There were none of Drive's and the two Brens' nonchalant humor that greeted and entertained me on my first visit to Cyprus. Our exit from Akrotiri was uneventful, no fun and games with the gate guards. It was extremely noisy inside the vehicle. I found out later that all the running gear was within the enclosed body along with the crew. It was a sweat box. We drank a lot of water.

I was taken to the Ledra Palace, which looked about the same as it had on my Christmas visit. All that was left of the decorations were scraps of colored paper fastened by thumbtacks. The biggest change was the military presence. Battle-helmeted British and slouch-hat Gurkha troops were everywhere and well-armed. Outside, behind the Venetian walls, a minaret poked into a tawny-purple sky. A muezzin was calling the Nicosian Turkish population to prayer.

The meeting, titled by the U.N. as "Solutions to the Cyprus Problem," was held in a Ledra Palace conference room. It was chaired by Sir Percy Spender, an Australian who was vice-president of the U.N. General Assembly. I'd read in the *London*

Times about his confrontation with a Soviet U.N. colleague. The
Soviet said on the General Assembly floor that his country
would back self-determination in Cyprus in accordance with its
practice of upholding all appeals for self-determination. Sir
Percy asked whether there had been self-determination in Bul-
garia, Poland, or Czechoslovakia. The Soviet delegate replied
that Sir Percy was ignorant of the facts and obsessed by "cold
war propaganda." In those days there were respectable and
well-regarded statesmen and political figures in the West who
believed more in the Russian view than in Sir Percy's.

Seated at the table were representatives from the United
Kingdom, the Greek-Cypriot community, the Turkish-Cypriot
community, Greece, and Turkey. Each had two or three
assistants sitting behind him. I was in one of the uncomfortable
card table chairs lining the walls, along with other reporters
from Cypriot, Greek, Turkish, and British newspapers and
radio stations. Sir Percy, dressed in a gray pin-stripe suit with a
gold and black repp tie on a white shirt, opened the meeting by
reading the U.N. document that established the time, place and
purview of the meeting. He emphasized the final sentence: *"The
committee's charge is to gather information on views held by the
countries represented at the meeting regarding the Cyprus
question."* In other words, what people said at the meeting was
to be seen as intentionally self-serving and there would be no
decisions made.

Sir Percy put the document down on the table, in between
an espresso cup of coffee and a glass of water, scratched his thin
moustache, and said, "Gentlemen, this is not a debate and certainly not a deliberating process. With your indulgence we will
go around the table. Each representative will have an opportunity to state, in less than a half hour, if you please, his
position on the question of whether or not the United Nations
should call for Cypriot self-determination."

With the exception of the Turkish representative and the
Greek-Cypriot representative, the statements were fairly predictable. The representative from Greece, who spoke precise

English in high-pitched tones said . . . following a simplistic Socratic logic . . . that Cyprus is de facto a Greek island.

The British spokesman said that Cyprus was an internal matter of national security and, therefore, not legally under the scope of the United Nations Charter. His presentation appeared to be a sophisticated counterbalance to the simple-mindedness of the Greek's argument. Cyprus, he said, is a vital listening post for NATO in the Cold War, to which both Greece and Turkey now belong. Unless Greece were prepared, which it is not, to maintain the island's significance as a major contributor to the Allies against the Soviet bloc, it would be a Cold War catastrophe to declare Cyprus part of Greece. In addition, he said, the Americans have invested heavily in military bases for defense of Turkey's south-eastern coasts. Could the Greeks provide enough strength for defense of Cyprus? Once in possession of Cyprus, the enemy would have a short, open shot at the new American bases.

The Turkish-Cypriot representative yielded his time to the representative from Turkey—a small round man wearing a western-style plain brown suit with a tug-of-war going on between the buttons and the button holes of his jacket. He said things I had not heard before.

Turkey, he declared, pounding his fist on the table, had been tricked by the British Prime Minister, Disraeli, in 1878, into relinquishing Cyprus to the British. The Turks believed they were leasing Cyprus to Great Britain in exchange for protection against a Russian invasion of Turkey. It was the understanding that when that war was settled, the British would leave Cyprus, and it would revert back to Turkey. In 1914, after Turkey joined the Axis powers, the British annexed Cyprus outright.

Not then, and never since then, has this been accepted by the Turks, said the Turkish representative. "We went along with it," he said, "because it was not worth a war so long as the Turkish Cypriots were safe and able to maintain agricultural livelihoods. If the Greeks take over this island, Turkish

Cypriots will be in grave danger. The Turkish government could not allow this to happen."

"And," he said, "the Cyprus question goes far beyond the confines of international law. We can see Cyprus from our southern shore. Every Turkish schoolchild knows the legend about how what is now Cyprus was once attached to the Turkish mainland. Look . . ."

One of his assistants pinned a map of Turkey with another one of Cyprus below it on a corkboard. The Turkish representative removed the map of Cyprus and placed it contingent to the map of Turkey. The Cypriot panhandle in the northeast fit almost precisely into a space between the Turkish and Syrian borders, and the rest of northern Cyprus ran almost smoothly along the Turkish southern coast.

"According to the legend," he said, "Allah willed this at some far distant point in the history of Anatolia. Our Muslim scholars have three or four interpretations for this phenomenon. Our people believe in the legend."

"All of us can see," he said, "why the U.N. should not immediately attempt to deal with the Cyprus question. It is too complex, too delicate, too inflammatory for an international body to intervene with a simplistic solution.

"What," he went on, "would be the first vote of a sovereign Cypriot parliament? Union with Greece, which would pass because the Greek-Cypriots far outnumber the Turkish Cypriots. The Greek military would then come here and slaughter the Turks. Do you think for a moment that Turkey would sit still. You would have a war between two NATO allies. The Russians would surely enjoy that."

The spokesman for the Greek-Cypriot community was the Cypriot Orthodox Archbishop, Makarios III. The Cypriot Archbishop was also the de facto national leader of the Greek-Cypriot community because the Cypriot Orthodox Church is autoce-phalous, independent of any Orthodox Church hierarchy. He was a medium-sized man with the long beard, black robe, and pipe hat of an orthodox bishop. His heavy-lidded eyes were both suspicious and optimistic.

He spoke very slowly and deliberately, as though English was a challenge to him. I found out later that he had a masters degree from Boston University.

Some years after this conference, when Makarios was the elected President of the new Cypriot republic, he told me he spoke as he did for two reasons. One was he wanted people to believe he had trouble with English so that they would be encouraged to say things in English to one another they didn't want him to understand. I worked closely with Makarios as he attempted to establish the first university on the island. Both Turkish and Greek Cypriots were eager to participate, except for one thing, Makarios was adamant the university be English-speaking. The Greek-Cypriots saw their future in union with Greece. For them the university must be essentially based on Greek, though it would be acceptable to have English and Turkish as secondary languages for specific purposes, but never in classroom instruction, unless the course was on English or Turkish language.

For Makarios English had replaced German as the world's primary language of research and publication. Also, now that he was President he preferred an independent Cyprus. His original very strong backing for enosis had faded over the years. He often said, "I am the only Cypriot on this island. My mission is to improve that statistic."

"May I observe," said the Archbishop when it was his turn to speak to the conference, "that everything I have heard thus far is both true and false." Then he was silent for a moment. He knew how to get audience attention.

"It is true," he went on, "that the British wish to be here because all of NATO needs Cyprus to pursue the Cold War with the Soviet Union."

He put his hands, palms down, slowly on the table looked around and said, it is false that they must have control over Cyprus to do what they do here, he said. Arrangements could be made between the British and an independent Cypriot government. An independent Cypriot government could declare that the British military installations would have a status of British sovereign territory. This arrangement could be part of the agreement between the British and the Cypriots about how the British would give sovereignty to the Cypriots.

The Turkish representative, said Makarios, is correct in presenting the possibility that Cypriot self-determination could lead to a vote to make Cyprus part of the Greek government. But the agreement to give self-determination to Cypriots could include a provision that prevented this from happening. And Turkish people on this island could be protected by a United Nations military presence with orders to protect the Turkish people. The appearance of Greek military in Cyprus could be prevented by the strength and will of the United Nations.

The Turk exploded, saying, "this from the man who organized EOKA, who will probably be President of Cyprus if the Cypriots have self-determination, who is a close confidant of that Greek Colonel Grivas who, as we speak, is already on the island training, preparing Greek-Cypriot guerrillas to force the British out in order to install a Greek government here. This priest helps them sharpen their knives for Turkish throats."

Sir Percy scratched his moustache with one hand while raising the other. "Gentlemen. May I ask that we avoid personal charges and, of course, insults. We are here to talk amicably about the situation. To present our view without disparaging the views of others."

He looked at Archbishop Makarios and said, "Your excellency, would you care to respond?"

Makarios sat stiffly, his back ramrod straight. "I believe," he said, again slowly and deliberately, each syllable clearly sounded, "that we negotiate now for Cypriot independence or suffer a war of guerilla terror. The sound of knives sharpening is a minor fear. More deadly are the schools where young members of EOKA are learning to make bombs by mixing fertilizer, sulfur, nitrogen, and gunpowder."

"That sounds like a threat," said the British spokesman.

Makarios waved his hand dismissively and continued. "Yes, I know General Grivas. No, I am not allied with him. In fact, he has all but disowned me for wanting to bring about Cypriot independence through compromise rather than force of arms. I do believe that work stoppages and acts of sabotage would be necessary if there were to be a rebellion. But violence against fellow human beings is wrong and must be avoided. I cannot avoid this violence; but I tell you that if you do not, you will see murder at night and Greek-Cypriot children going wild in the streets. Do not try to deal with this in a cold rational way. It is something entirely else. Grivas is a ruthless patriot who possesses extraordinary skills at guerrilla warfare. He will do anything to achieve his goals. And he has no fear of death because he believes he is immortal."

The relationship between Makarios and Grivas had always been complicated. They needed one another but could never decide who should be boss. Grivas was born in 1898 about thirty miles northeast of Nicosia, the son of a grain merchant. He was a good student at the village school, went on to the Pancyprian Gymnasium and from there, at age seventeen, he entered the Greek Military Academy. As a young officer in the Greek army, he served during the Greco-Turkish War of 1920-1922. He learned about guerrilla warfare when his unit almost reached Ankara during the Anatolian campaign. He was wounded and cited for bravery.

He learned even more about guerrilla warfare when Italy invaded Greece in 1940, and he was a lieutenant colonel in the infantry. But his finishing school was during the Nazi occupation of Greece when he led a right-wing extremist organization known by the Greek letter X, Chi, which was described by some as a band of terrorists labeling itself a resistance group. In his writings on guerrilla warfare, he said that British propaganda blackened the good name of X. Whatever was the truth, even after his group was banned by the Greek government, everyone agreed that as a terrorist or resistance fighter, he was a courageous military leader and fierce in battle.

In the late 1940s he turned his attention to his original home, Cyprus, and became devoted to freeing Cyprus from the British and uniting it with Greece. In 1951 he visited Cyprus to plan an armed uprising. By that time Makarios was Archbishop and the de facto leader of Greek-Cypriots. Grivas was disappointed after his first meeting with him. Makarios preferred diplomatic approaches, especially in the United Nations, rather than armed rebellion. Grivas resented sharing leadership of the Enosis movement with anyone else, particularly with a man who rejected armed rebellion. These feelings were papered over from time to time, but eventually the soldier and the cleric became bitter enemies and everyone knew it.

That evening a tall man wearing the traditional attire of American diplomats in the Middle East approached my dinner table in the Ledra Palace. "Philip Barker," he said, "from Washington. I'm Gil Tompkins' replacement. May I join you?'" Actually I welcomed any distraction from the "live" music. A piano player who looked Italian surrounded himself with gadgets. In addition to the piano, he had an electrified keyboard, a sound box to imitate drum and castanets' rhythms, and a red candle on top of the piano. He wore black trousers, a white jacket, and a ruffly red shirt opened boldly to showcase his curly chest hair. The boom-thump-click sounds of his automated rhythm section almost drowned out the piano, which could have been the right thing to do.

I nodded and pointed to an empty chair at the table. He was different from Gil Tompkins. He looked establishment: poplin suit, blue button-down oxford shirt, brown tie, pipe in hand. But he didn't look silly as Tompkins did in his Safari suit.

We both had stuffed vine leaves, *taramosalata* with fried shrimp, followed by chicken *souvlaki*, with Cypriot wines. "Your reports," he said, over the *souvlaki*—he had made small talk and dropped a lot of names during the appetizer—"are useful but very brief. We need more names and backgrounds."

"Why?" I said. One of the positive effects Hedgeworth had on me was that it was difficult for anyone else to intimidate me. Even General Jackman paled in the shadow of Hedgeworth's bullying. And Hedgeworth taught me something else: when caught off guard answer questions with questions.

"Because we are in the intelligence-gathering business," said Barker, patronizingly, keeping his eyes on the pita bread stuffed with chicken he was cutting into. "Surely you've grasped that much, young man. You're the closest person we have to the Moroccan rebels. We need the intelligence you're gathering about them, and we need everything you can get."

"Excuse me," I said, "I don't know who this 'we' is. I'm sure 'we' is what you do. I thought my job was to make Moroccan nationalists feel friendly toward Americans. That I was to do that by gathering information for them. No one ever told me about gathering information about them for this 'we.'"

He looked at me as though he had just stepped off a spaceship on Mars and encountered a green-skinned, four-eared native. I wondered if he even saw the difference I tried to draw. Many years after this meeting and after considerable experience with this type of Washington denizen, I realized that Barker and Tompkins were representations of two old adages. The first is: If you dress well and look good, you don't need a real purpose in life. The second: If you can fake sincerity you've got it made. They were political appointments. Men who lived by their connections. Because they did something during a campaign for federal office, or were related to someone who did, or someone who made a large contribution to the campaign, they were given posts by the electoral winners. Other qualifications for these posts such as education and experience were inconsequential. A certain type, like Tompkins and Barker, were drawn to State Department and foreign intelligence positions.

We skipped dessert. Ordered more wine. He went on about how we had just stepped off on the wrong foot, how we would meet again soon and set things "right side up," is the way I remember him saying it.

"In the meantime," I said, "should I just continue doing my job as I've been doing it?"

"Absolutely," he said.

I thought I'd try again. "I really don't like what you suggested. Nothing personal. I've never thought of myself as being here to gather intelligence about *Istiqlal* to pass on to someone in Washington to do with what they might want. I'm a naïve idealistic Catholic who believes in right and wrong, that the Soviet Union is a military and an ideological enemy that must be defeated. I understand at a simplistic level what I've been doing here, helping ensure that our capability to strike the Soviets from here is maintained. Until someone explains to me how intelligence about *Istiqlal* helps Washington win the Cold War, I can't deliver. I'm not built that way."

He smiled thinly and said, "I'll talk to General Jackman about this. You do trust his integrity and commitments, I would hope."

"Yes," I said, "I'll not hesitate to follow an order from him, but there are a few things you should tell him and anyone who listens to you in Washington before you have someone order me to report on *Istiqlal*."

I told him that what I had just seen and heard at the U.N. meeting convinced me that what Makarios envisioned for Cyprus made the most sense for all parties involved except the radical Enosists like Grivas, who, as I now saw it, were of importance only to the Greeks. Too much was at stake, like a Greek-Turkish war, for enosis to have much standing on the international stage. American strategy should now focus on helping the Makarios view, which did not include enosis but did include the British being able to keep their military positions on Cyprus. Along with this we had to become more helpful to *Istiqlal* militarily in order to facilitate the overthrow of Moulay

Arafa. The best outcome for us in a swiftly-changing Mediterranean area was to keep our Moroccan bases and support Makarios. The advantages of reporting on *Istiqlal* to Washington were overwhelmed by the damage it could do to our maintaining the friend and helper role we had been playing.

I was having a *loukanika* sausage and scrambled eggs in the Ledra Palace breakfast room the next day when a stocky American in a Greek-style shirt sat down at my table by turning a chair around and sitting with his arms spread over the chair's back. He helped himself to an olive and said, "I'm Pittiker, your contact. I take you to see the subject. When you're ready, of course." He ate the olive and took a matchbook cover to pick his teeth. Pittikar was a special kind of CIA man. We called them "the goons." Usually they were hired on contract for a specific job and time period, say to take a trip to Latin America, buy some drugs and bring them to Washington. If they did well enough, there were some more contracts, and some of them eventually became irregular full-time CIA employees, taking on the odd jobs regular CIA agents tried to avoid.

"Ever seen any of this stuff at work?" asked Pittiker. We were in the back seat of a blue Chevrolet sedan, the standard car used by all medium-grade U.S. Consulate staff in European postings, on our way to seeing Alain at the Nicosia Central Prison. Pittikar was singing the praises of truth drugs.

"I've heard and read some things," I said. "As far as I know it's still not exactly legal for us to be using this stuff."

He lit a cigarette and gave me about the sternest look that I think he had in him. "Wise kid, huh. Aren't you a bit wet behind the ears to be a 'last chancer?'"

"Last chancer?" I asked.

"Aw, come on now. You pretend you don't know?"

"Nope," I said.

He looked a little elevated. I think he could smell my dislike for him, so any opportunity to teach me a few things was seized upon. "The last chancer," he said, "is the interrogator who is the end of the line for the prisoner. If nothing comes out of the interview, the prisoner is considered useless and . . . well, whatever."

I could believe that because if the prisoner were exclusively in CIA hands, especially if he were in the hands of "goons," there was little reason for CIA to keep him around.

The Chevy stopped a good distance from the prison, which was surrounded by tall walls. The British allowed only their own vehicles within forty yards of the walls at the corners of which heavy two-man Bren machine guns mounted on tripods kept aim on the Chevy and other non-British vehicles. It was raining heavily. Gusting winds pushed the rain in every which direction. Above the forty-yard zone, a helicopter bounced unpredictably in the erratic air currents, making irritating machine and wing noises. Guard dogs tied to posts within the forty-yards were filthy and irritable from the soft and muddy earth plus the constantly annoying helicopter sounds. They squealed and twisted on their collars and leashes.

A British jeep came out to meet us. The driver nodded to Pittikar and waved him and me into the jeep. I thought I must have been going through a foot of mud as I made my way from the Chevy to the jeep. When we got to the wall, I saw it was light yellow sandstone. It looked as though it had been there forever.

Before the Turks yielded Cyprus to the Brits, the building we were entering was a Turkish Inn, one of the hundreds built as the Ottoman Empire expanded. There were two essential requirements for each Inn. It must provide protection because it is in conquered, hostile land, and it must offer amenities suitable to those of high station in the Empire.

The exterior sandstone walls had small slanting windows, slits actually, discouraging unauthorized entry. Once past this defensive tactic, we were inside a very attractive campus. There were two stories with Gothic arches. The second-story rooms were built for wealthy merchants. Each had an octagonal fireplace for heat and cooking, a room for dining and another for sleeping. The first floor was for storage and appliances, with stores catering to merchants flanking the courtyard.

In the center of the courtyard was a lovely miniature mosque. There was a fountain, originally for ablutions and watering horses. This is what the Inn symbolized before the British turned it into a prison. Now, everything was a military presence. Most notably, perhaps, the mosque, which had been turned into a deep prison, a "dungeon" despite the British distaste for that word, except when they were referring to the Turks.

As we walked down the mosque's century-worn stairs of what was now a castle dungeon, Pittikar explained that I would interview Alain while he was under the influence of various drugs, and desperate for more. He was addicted. They had not given him any for three hours. "At that point," said Pittaker, "the subject is not violent. He still believes he can persuade someone to give him some drugs. He sees himself as conniving and very clever. He will tell you any lie you want to hear or confess to any crime."

The cold and musty smell increased as we descended. Pittikar decided I needed a lecture. It went like this.

During World War II, General William "Wild Bill" Donovan, chief of the OSS, the CIA's predecessor, held a lunch for some of America's most distinguished scientists at which he asked them to undertake a top-secret research project to develop a speech-inducing drug for use in intelligence interrogations.

What was needed, he said, is a substance that could break down the psychological defenses of enemy spies and prisoners of war, thereby causing an uninhibited disclosure of classified information.

Such a substance would also be useful for screening OSS personnel in order to identify German sympathizers, double agents, and potential misfits.

The scientists created a highly-potent extract of cannabis from which they could derive a viscous liquid that had no color, odor, or taste. The perfect substance. It would be impossible to detect when administered surreptitiously. It was called TD, for Truth Drug.

TD was tried upon witting and unwitting subjects. Lab technicians found it could be injected into almost any kind of food as well as candy. The lab techs were having lunch one day, reveling in these discoveries, when a junior lab tech raised a question. ""How," he said, "will we know how much to put in which food type. We'd need to know the eating habits of the people we targeted, or else they might overeat on what contained TD; and if that happened, they would pass out, useless to interrogation. This is very potent stuff."

Months more at the blackboard and in the lab led to the conclusion that a measured amount of TD in a hypodermic syringe that would be injected into a cigarette or cigar would work.

The report, written in "common English" for the policy guys in suits, said this: "After smoking such an item, the subject would get suitably stoned, at which point a skillful interrogator would move in and get him to spill the beans."

It was the typical thing that happens when experts, policy makers, and uncertain science come together to pretend that they were meant for one another. No one wants to disappoint anyone, so imperfections, unintended consequences, and, in general, any data suggesting the project is not really ready for use in the field are stuffed in untitled files and placed in the far rear of filing cabinets located in unvisited basement areas.

The confidence of the report was not born out in the tests. TD subjects reacted in a variety of ways, none of which were promising for a dependable TD. Some of the subjects talked endlessly about their perceptions of the worst things that ever happened to them. Usually it was something from childhood. They went on until their words melted together into gibberish. Other subjects became irritable and said they felt like two different people. Others fell into a stony silence. Their eyes bulged. Their hands shivered. Their knees cracked painfully into one another. Some of the subjects jumped out of windows five or more stories from the streets below, others ran through streets screaming about being chased by lions, tigers, and bandits with donkey ears.

Pittifar threw out all these admissions of failure as though he were initiating me into a world of dark secrets so that I would feel intimidated. We came to a bottom room of huge, damp stones. There was a scraggly gate squeaking in the corner. Pittifar wiggled a finger in the direction of the gate. "He's in there. Remember, you're his last chance."

I went through the gate, into a small stone-slab room with a floor that tilted slightly down to a drain that ran along the back wall into a small sewer cover in the corner. Alain was in that corner. It looked as though flooding surges from power hoses had settled him in a large puddle of his own excrement, unfinished food, and odd bits of paper that didn't make it into the sewer. The stench was powerful. He wore a brown T-shirt that stuck to his body. There was a mass of blood on his right eye rim, cuts and bruises on his face, black and blue marks on his head and neck. The most elegant man I had ever known was horribly disfigured, barely able to hold himself up in a sitting position in a cesspool.

I waded closer to him. He lifted his head, smiled slightly and said "It's good to have someone I can talk to."

"I'm glad you didn't say that in French," I said.

"I've been waiting for you," he said. He explained to me that he understood the way things go, that so long as he held out someone would eventually suggest that I be sent to interrogate him. He was not in as bad a condition as he looked, he said. He knew how to withstand electrical torture and truth drugs. The electrical torture was sustained, he told me, by biting on the right side of his tongue, if necessary until blood was drawn. Also, by mumbling what sounded like information: names, places, dates, events. The inquisitors must stop when this happens to figure out what the prisoner is saying, and to write it down if they can. Alain fooled them about the truth drugs by pretending to be reacting as they expected. He'd learned to do this in French Indochina where both sides often used drugs in interrogations.

Beyond these skills, what Alain had was will power so strong that he could outfox every fox he met. He told me he could outfox the CIA interrogators because he knew what they wanted, and they didn't know what he wanted. It was a trick he picked up as a boy dealing with his parents. "If you know what they want, you can manage the situation, particularly when they think they know what you want, but don't.

"What if they've got it right?" I said. "What if they know what you want?"

He smiled. "You start wanting something else."

"But it's all over now," I said. "We have you. You know what we want. If you don't give it to us we'll kill you. I can give you more drugs if you tell us. And you'll live. That might be hard to believe, but the General made a deal with Quai d'Orsay. If they're quiet while we interrogate you, we'll return you safely to them. I believe the General knows what he can and cannot do, and I also completely trust his word."

"You're such a naïve," said Alain. "Don't you know that you give me no incentive to tell you what you want to know? Offering me my life with no conditions about what that life would be like is empty. I am alive right here, right now, so I should give up something to keep this? I have my own shit stuck in my hair. But I am alive. What do you offer other than maybe to comb the shit out of my hair?"

He dipped his head into his own filth, came out with brown and red on his face with feces stuck to his lightly-bearded face. Then he said in a surprisingly strong voice, "You're going to get me signed up with CIA, and I am going to give answers to the questions all these people keep asking me."

"Why CIA?" I said.

"Because you don't have a foreign legion," he said, laughing hoarsely.

He lifted his upper body so that his back was more upright, coughed to clear his throat, and said, "The CIA is the only agency you have that tolerates rogues. When the right person tells them what a prize I am, they'll jump at the chance to bring me into their defiled nests."

He gave me a look that said, "You know what to do."

"Suppose," I said, "I were to suggest to General Jackman that he ask Bernard Hedgeworth to recommend you to CIA."

"Mon Dieu," he said, "you do catch on."

"This is what will happen," I told Pittaker in the backseat of the Chevrolet driving away from the prison. "Clean him up, do what you can for his wounds, put him in a bed, and tell all the guards that they'll get worse than anything they give him by way of torment."

"You don't have the clout to order me . . . " he said.

"Remember," I said, "you told me I was the last chancer. Why would the people a lot higher than you and me make me the last chancer. Why didn't they select you? I can promise the prisoner will answer our questions if what I demand is given. Stand in my way on this if you dare, Pittaker, but be prepared to pay the consequences. I don't like you. I'll hound anyone I can to make you suffer. What we're about to do with this prisoner is so far beyond your security clearance that we can't breathe a word of it to you. But I will tell you this, so you can know you've succeeded on this mission . . . oh, and I'll be sure to make a point of that . . . that you pulled off a really good mission. We're getting everything we wanted from this prisoner, and a lot more. Things are good. God Bless America, Pittikar!"

A month or so after that the Cyprus problem worsened. The colonial government threatened advocates of enosis with five years imprisonment and warned that all anti-sedition laws would be strictly enforced. Archbishop Makarios continued to support enosis, defying the law, but no formal action was taken against him. I think the British saw him, as I did, as the best horse to back, or at least keep in the race. But the volatility of the overall Mediterranean situation seemed to invoke more and more chaos in Cyprus. Greek-Cypriot anti-British sentiments bristled when Britain concluded an agreement with Egypt for the evacuation of forces from the Suez Canal zone and moved the headquarters of the British Middle East Land and Air Forces to Cyprus.

A few weeks later the UN General Assembly, after consideration of another attempt by the Greek government to get Cyprus on the agenda, adopted a New Zealand proposal, using typical diplomatic jargon. "We have reached the decision not to consider the problem further for the time being."

Greek Cypriot leaders called a general strike. Greek schoolchildren left their classrooms to demonstrate in the streets. Rioting was the worst ever seen. The predictions Makarios had made at the U.N. meeting in Cyprus were being fulfilled. I was betting that his views on Cypriot independence, with guarantees against enosis, protection for the Turks, and sovereign areas for the British military to continue Cold War surveillance would also be fulfilled.

Road to Todra Gorge.

Chapter Sixteen

Casablanca

I scanned the scene as I walked toward the *hammam*. French police, soldiers, SAS paratroopers, and Foreign Legion skirmish troops were everywhere, heavily armed, and spoiling for confrontation. I didn't want to leave the impression with any of them that I was reconnoitering. They were authorized to arrest and detain or to kill anyone they suspected of being a terrorist or a terrorist accomplice. Paris had spoken: Wipe out the terrorists and their supporters.

In front of the *hammam* the letter-writer, dressed as usual in a blue banded-collar shirt and a western suit, sat at his portable table under his threadbare umbrella, staring with droopy sad eyes at his pens and paper as though this was how he was supposed to look . . . forever?

The communal bakery traffic was the same. Many going in. No one coming out. The dried-fruit-and-vegetable store was busy, a swirl of djellabas reaching into bins to deposit pieces of fruit and vegetables in wicker baskets supported by cords of rope around the bearer's shoulders.

In the slit of space between the bakery and the *hammam*, where the first time I'd been at that place a young man worked on a wood lathe by jerking on a piece of string, a man in a loosely-fitting headdress smiled with his teeth while grinding coffee in a mill between his knees. The jerking movements of his shoulders caused a part of the headdress to flop down over his eyes when he cranked the mill. It was like a ritualistic dance.

He would crank twice quickly on the handle with his right hand, swiftly push the headdress back with his left hand, then repeat the routine. In jazz you would say . . . without missing a beat.

Though some of the meetings with Fulan had been canceled, we had had six meetings after the first one. The *mul-l-hammam* was accepting without welcoming me. He sat in his wicker chair puffing a kif pipe as though I was not there. It was, I suppose, his way of maintaining dignity. I don't think he yielded that first time I entered with Fulan because of the money Fulan handed him. It was something to do with who Fulan was and what he said. I didn't mind this face-saving behavior. In fact, I welcomed it because I didn't like the idea of humiliating another person, and, of course, I didn't want to make any enemies.

"It is our intention to turn this French mad violence against them." Si Fulan was clumsily seated in a wobbly stool on a steaming marble floor, rocking back and forth. The front legs clicked, the back legs clacked in search, I thought, of meaningful rhythm. He said something which I didn't hear because Aloutababa was pouring a bucket of very cold water on my head. Some of the water spilled generously on her wrap top. Her nipples erected. I was agog.

The next thing I heard was that Fulan wanted Mossad to increase shipment of Uzis. "Those submachine guns are perfect for us," he said.

I forced my eyes and thoughts to get away from Aloutababa, with moderate success. "Not surprising," I said. I remembered that the Uzi was invented by Israelis to work in nighttime guerrilla operations where there was a lot of confusion. One of the most important difficulties that the Uzi overcame is reloading magazines in the dark and in confusion. The Uzi magazine housing is inside the pistol grip. You reload by having the fist holding the magazine find the fist of the firing hand.

"Our people like it because it has a small number of parts, so it is less likely to jam from sand and dirt than are the submachine guns the French use, and even if it does jam, it is easy to strip and reassemble. They say it has soft recoil so they can fire it with one hand, even aim it over walls and around doors without exposing any part of their bodies except the hand holding the Uzi."

"The Israelis will be interested in those kinds of details," I said, "the Uzi is still in the experimental stage, so any reports on how it's working in Morocco will be useful for them in their dealings with the Algerian liberation movement. There could be a money problem. One of the reasons the Uzi is popular is because it's relatively inexpensive to produce. They make it with stamped metal. Still, I'm sure we could ensure getting more of them faster if we gave them more money."

Fulan shook his head. "Problem for us, also." Then, somewhat defensively, he added, "probably not easy for an American to understand."

"You must mean some American other than me," I said, "Maybe Moshe Menasha would chip in."

Fulan nodded modest approval.

"I can't go to him," I said. "I'm under orders to go no further with these arms shipments beyond telling you about them. If an American were tied into it . . . "

"Of course," he said, "we don't want to get any dust on the American flag."

I let it go. "Could you go to him?"

He stood up, threw open his hands and gestured forcefully with them. "Why would Menasha trust me?" he yelled. "If I were him, I would think it was a trick by the French to . . . how would you say, get him to say something that got him in trouble with the officials?"

"You're right," I said, "it was a stupid idea."

He nodded. His face returned to its normal fierceness. "Mina has a personal connection with him because of her mother," I said. "I don't know if you know how Mina's mother was brought to the attention of Menasha. It was Pierre Didier. After Mina began working for him, Pierre found out about her mother's situation. He went to Menasha to get her some help. Menasha hired her to move hashish around in the streets, serve as a lookout, and other things. It was a personal favor for his son-in-law."

"I see," said Fulan, "in case Menasha were to go to the French about your request for money to buy Israeli weapons, he would implicate his daughter's husband."

"It's an insurance policy," I said. "I have no reason to think Menasha would turn us in."

"*Bon*," he said. Then he yielded my attention to Aloutababa, who seemed to understand everything though hearing nothing. She put me on my back on pillows, then poured a heavy-odor oil on my body, from my neck to my ankles, then stroked it into my skin with firm fingers. I surprised myself by thinking of Simcha and Jilly, what it would feel like if they did that.

As we were about to leave, Fulan said, "I have something for you to give the Israelis. The Egyptians are now in control of the radar systems in their country. They always have been except for one thing. The rules and procedures were established and managed by British officers. The Egyptians . . . they not only think they are superior to all other Arabs, they now think they understand military things better than do the British. Do you see . . . ?"

I didn't, but guessed. "They're making mistakes?"

"Big mistakes," he said. "In Egypt everything is big. Especially their mistakes. They switch off the air defense radars each day at midday. Air attacks are always carried out at dawn or shortly after in the Middle East, they say. The British didn't know this so they wasted money and manpower running the air defense radars twenty four hours every day."

"Unbelievable," I said. "How . . . ?"

"The Egyptians have two curses when it comes to military wisdom. First, they think that they conquered everyone else throughout their history. Even the Romans. They had one vulnerability to which they admit and that was their helplessness in the face of Napoleon. However, they learned lessons from Napoleon that reinstated, in their version of history, their military supremacy."

"How," I said, "do they explain British rule over them?"

"Their King delivered them like lambs to a slaughter. Farouk grew fatter and richer standing on their backs. But now, the puppet King is gone and true Egyptians are in control. They think they are invincible."

"Si," I said. I realized it was the first time I had called him by his first name. "May I ask. The Egyptians are the most important champions of Arab nationalism in the world. Why do you give me information that the Israelis could use to inflict a deadly first air attack?"

"We like those Uzis," he said.

We drove past the Didier home, then the stone road took us upward to a semicircular concrete driveway bordered by cypress trees pruned into neat geometric forms. We stopped in front of a three-story brick-and-terracotta house. Hajji was there, probably because he would recognize me, beckoning us to follow him.

Jilly was driving, her first time out since her release from the hospital, her camera prominently displayed on the seat between her and me. Mina Halima was in the back seat. I had tried to stage it as a press interview. I told Jilly I wanted her to stay in the car until, if and when, Moshe Menasha agreed to allow us to take photographs of his home.

Mina and I followed Hajji into the house. The interior was resplendent with mosaic floors and walls, ornate wooden coving, sculptured plasterwork, molded stucco work, large cedar doors and windows with wrought iron designs that made me think of original Beethoven-penned scores. Hajji led us up three flights of curving staircases with marbled railings. There was an eight-branched Hanukkah candelabrum on a table at each landing.

Moshe Menasha greeted us on a large roof terrace of flowering shrubs, bougainvillea, hibiscus and jasmine. I could see the ocean very blue to the left, straight ahead I had a view of the medina, and to my right I looked down into a courtyard of intricately designed and colored tile work with a circular pool of clear flowing water refreshing a flock of small birds. Menasha wore a bright red silk robe that billowed opulently and a white skullcap. I sensed at that time I would never lose my fascination for Moroccan grandeur. I had come to buy guns. I was distracted by the view.

Menasha was obviously pleased to see Mina. She told me she had not seen him for well over a year. Now and then she went with her mother to one of Moshe's outdoor banquets held under tents between two of his sardine plants. There were dancers in vivid costumes, musicians with bizarre instruments, and wild animals barely kept under control. Mina remembered the banquets because they frightened her.

We followed Menasha to a ledge extending from one of the glistening white plaster walls where we sat on jewel-colored silk pillows. He casually lifted and rested his sandaled feet on one of the numerous ottomans scattered around the rooftop, along with brass trays, shining from the care of many hands over many years, supported by complexly-carved wooden stands.

As was the custom, I waited until after mint tea was served to speak with Menasha about my purpose for requesting this meeting.

I told him that I had two agendas. One was to create a reason for my visit. "I'll say you agreed to let me interview you for a story on your experiences in Brazil. My real purpose is to ask you to give *Istiqlal* money to buy Israeli arms."

Of course, I had cleared this with the General. He was not happy but also not unhappy. I had a feeling—it was a good feeling—that he was proud of me for daring to disobey his direct order to not get further involved in this after passing it on to Si Fulan. Also, he thought my recommendation that we give more military support to *Istiqlal* along with my idea to back Makarios made sense. Nonetheless he had questions. "Why do you trust Menasha?" he said.

"I have this gut reaction to him," I said. "He's honorable. I believe that if he doesn't want to do it, he'll just tell me so and that will be that. I think he's going to want to do it. All the right reasons are in front of him. The Israelis are doing the arms shipments in part because they want to make it easier for people like him to immigrate to Israel. If the situation here in Morocco doesn't change, the Jews will be even worse off than they were before."

The General held up his hand, stood, sipped his vodka, and said, "You're getting beyond me. Why will the Jews be worse off?"

"So long as Moulay Arafa is Sultan," I said, "he will need scapegoats for the deteriorating situation. He needs something to explain why even after he denounces *Istiqlal* the uprising continues. So, blame the communists and the Jews."

The General sat down and looked at me—was it reprovingly? "I think you have a helluva good . . . or bad game going here. Do you have any notion of the dynamics you might unleash by persuading Menasha to do this?"

"No," I said, "I haven't thought about that. I wouldn't know how to."

"I don't know what you might be setting off with this," he said, "but what the hell, you're providing a solution to a problem. Let's go with that. It's the best thing anyone can do, anytime."

"How do the Israelis get weapons into Morocco?" Moshe Menasha asked me as we were drinking mint tea from glasses in silver-plated Moorish-designed holders.

"For now, by helicopter," I answered.

"You have plucked the eyes from the radar machines?" he said. I suppose he was wondering what I the journalist was doing in these matters. "Where do the helicopters come from?" he asked, "Israel is too far . . . no?"

"I don't know for certain," I said. "We and the British can arrange refueling stops along the way."

"So, the American radar eyes are blinded," he said, "what about the French ones?"

"The Israeli helicopters are Hiller 360s. That's an American-made helicopter, and the Moroccan skies are open to American aircraft," I said.

Menasha said "Ohhhh," and I heard the praise in that simple statement. "You Americans," he said. "If I do this, how do I do it? To whom do I give the money? I will not leave it behind a loose brick in a wall or in a hole in a tree."

I was not surprised that Menasha would know about dead-letter boxes. American and Soviet spies had used them for years and the word got around. "I would like you to give it to Lalla Halima." Mina looked at me. It was a spontaneous thought, so I didn't know how to look back at her.

Moshe scratched his beard with four fingers on his jaw while pressing his thumb into the side of his nose. I thought it was not for an itch; rather, for inspiration. "Yes, I see," he said. I wondered what he was seeing. "She is entirely trustworthy," he went on, "and I could do this without bringing danger to any of my colleagues. What happens if gendarmes catch her with much money in her basket . . . ?" He was talking to himself. He scratched his beard some more. "Yes, I see . . . she says it is hashish payment. The ones making the arrest put the money in their pockets, send her away. What is hashish when a revolution is going on. Good, very good." He looked at me approvingly and stopped scratching his beard.

I had not thought it through as well as he had. Actually I hadn't thought it through at all. Nonetheless I was quite willing to be considered the father of a clever scheme.

Mina was not sharing our contentment. I saw it in her eyes. They were half concealed and suspicious.

"What happens next?" said Menasha. It sounded as though he had concluded another of many deals and wanted this to be over with, so that he could pass on the instructions to a subordinate.

"Mina will tell you," I said.

I went to the *Imprimerie Maroprint* building two days later to talk with Mina. Didier told me she called to say something unusual had come up, that she would remain at home and that if he had contact with me he should tell me to go to her home immediately.

Jilly drove me to the outskirts of that part of the medina where Mina and her mother lived. Two police guards at the medina gate entrance looked me over suspiciously, then let me go on. I was in uniform. The French had not quite decided how they would deal with American military on the streets.

Mina was crying when she opened the door. "I don't know what to do," she said.

We sat down on a lumpy divan. "Si Fulan told me not to go to work today," she said. "It was an order from *Istiqlal*."

"Perhaps," I said, "they want you to be available here for an instruction at sometime today."

"Or . . . ?" she said. "It has something to do with the building. You know *Istiqlal* is targeting pro-French newspapers and magazines."

"We have to warn Didier," I said. "Or would someone from his cell do that?"

"I'm in his cell," she said, "why wouldn't they tell me to tell him?"

"Maybe," I said, "the third person in his cell will be told to tell him to not be in the building."

"But," she said, "you said he was there half an hour ago. I am frustrated. Tortured. If I warn Pierre I break my *Istiqlal* oath to following orders without question, even if it means the death of a loved one or myself. And if I warn him I might put in danger some members of *Istiqlal*."

"I'll go to the *Imprimerie Maroprint*," I said. "I'll get him out of there, just in case." Suddenly I felt I should get there quickly.

It was unusually quiet on *Rue de Empreinte* that morning. The vendor wagons offering coffee, mint tea, and fried locusts were not there. The vans that delivered newspapers were parked on the street in front of *Imprimerie Maroprint*, but the loaders and drivers who usually hung around drinking coffee or tea while chatting and smoking were gone. It was a warm, languorous, seductive morning.

Jilly parked across the street from the *Imprimerie Maro-print* building. I said, "Wait here for me . . . " then a thundering blast overpowered my senses. The building's windows exploded. Pieces of glass stormed on the jeep's canvas roof, ripping parts of it to shreds. Jilly and I protected our faces and hands by doubling over forwards in the seats. Flames roared out of spaces in the building left by where the windows had been, followed by clouds of black smoke. Two typesetters covered with burning ashes came to a window on the third floor and jumped, probably to their death.

There was nothing Jilly and I could do other than remain doubled over. She slipped on a driver's glove and inched her shaking left hand towards me. I wrapped a handkerchief over my right hand and we found one another. I looked in her eyes and wished I could protect her from her fright. Jilly's eyes were almost always sparkling; but when they were in panic, I saw they could make me feel helpless and awful for feeling so.

Small, but deadly-sounding, explosions continued for a-while, perhaps caused by contents of inks and dyes popping open. There was no human sound, not even when the type-setters jumped out of the window.

Firefighting equipment in Casablanca was limited to six hand pumps and four Renault Fire Engines that carried the firemen, hoses, and ladders. There were no fire alarms. The *Imprimerie Maroprint* building ranked third on the Fire Department's priority list, so there was no rush to save the building when flames from *Rue de Empreinte* signaled trouble. Safety from fire was even less promising for Moroccan natives. Each year there was a provision in the Protectorate budget for fire protection in the medina. Each year it was voted down for lack of funds.

Eventually two Renault Fire Engines with two hand pumps arrived at the scene. As he wiped smoke and soot from his eyes, the *Chef des Pompiers* made a decision that the building could not be saved. Therefore, water should be hosed on everything close to it that might catch fire. Jilly and I held hands tightly throughout the ordeal.

Pierre Didier's body, charred to a black stick, was buried the next day. I watched the ceremony. First the rabbi took one of Pierre's black suit coats and, holding it in his hand, went to the left side of each male family mourner where he made a rip in the mourner's coat. As the casket was slowly lowered, the rabbi said a prayer, parts of which were chanted by the mourners. Each family member then shoveled a small clump of earth into the grave.

A dozen Arabs who had served under Pierre in the Fourth Moroccan Mountain Division in Italy were there, stony-faced silent, perhaps confused. It was known throughout Casablanca that *Istiqlal* destroyed the building because it symbolized co-operation with the French Protectorate. I imagined that though they didn't know Pierre was a member of *Istiqlal,* they couldn't believe he truly supported the Protectorate.

Back at the Didier home we all, there were around thirty of us, stopped at a bowl of water with a cup at the entrance to pour water over each hand three times.

Inside, the mirrors were covered. Except for the shuffling sounds made by our bodies, all was silent. Mamouche, dressed in black as were all members of the Didier family, lit the large Shiva candle. No one said a word.

The candle would burn for seven days of mourning. On each day the family would go to services and recite the Kadish, an affirmation of life, faith in God, and trust in God's will. On the seventh day Mamouche would softly blow out the candle, the mirrors would be uncovered, and the family would walk around the block outside the compound to symbolize taking a first step back into the world.

Simcha had dutifully followed tradition. Her hair hung straight, she wore no makeup or jewelry, her dress was black and unflattering, her eyes were droopy. She looked even plainer than she had on our trip into the Atlas Mountains after she got into the baggy clothes I gave her, and Jilly gave her a very unbecoming haircut. I got her attention and signaled with my eyes and head that I would like to see her in the vestibule.

She found me on the first step of the circular staircase, sat down beside me and put her head on my arm.

"I have something to tell you about Pierre," I said. "I shouldn't, but he was such a good man and you are such a good friend."

She put her hand on my knee. I don't think I ever realized how small it was.

"Pierre's pro-French newspaper is a front," I said. He was actually a dedicated Moroccan nationalist working in an *Istiqlal* cell."

Her body tensed. I had the feeling that her eyes were now wide-open.

"He became a nationalist," I said, "when he saw how the men who served under him in the Moroccan Fourth Mountain Division were treated when they came home after the war. Any belief he had about the French *Mission Civilatrice* disappeared, and a belief in Moroccan independence replaced it. I see him as a man who lived his life to be part of a noble purpose."

Simcha stirred, then stood leaning her hands on my shoulders. I was hoping she would keep them there. She glanced around with quick blinks of her eyes, as though she were looking for something. Then she stared at me with a challenge, and said, "If what you are saying is true, why would *Istiqlal* kill him?"

"Only four other members of *Istiqlal* knew him as a member," I said. "It's the way *Istiqlal* does things. The cells responsible for picking targets for assassination probably didn't know he was a member. Nor did the cells that develop the plans for assassinations. Nor did whoever it was who planted the bomb in his building. This . . . maybe this is why God gave us the word *irony*."

She started walking absent-mindedly up the stairs, stopped, turned and said, "How do you know all this?"

"I don't want to explain. I can't, really. I've already said too much."

"I'm going with my father to Israel," she said before turning and going up the stairs. "All of us are."

"It's probably a good idea," I said, "I'll miss you."

She stopped walking up the stairs, turned her head to the side and said, "Perhaps you'll come to Israel some day."

"I'd like to," I said. "And perhaps you'll come to America."

She shrugged her shoulders, turned to me and said, "Do you ever think about that night in that little bed?"

"Actually," I said, "I've wondered what you thought of it."

"And not what you thought of it," she said. "You sound like a Frenchman. You need to know my feelings before you can express your own."

"OK," I said, "fair enough. From the first time I saw you. You are the most physically appealing woman I've ever been near. That night was like a dream."

"But you never took another step," she said.

"Did you really want me to?"

"No, I guess not. I felt guilty enough about that one night," she said.

"Guilty . . . ?"

"You and Jilly," she said, "are my best friends in Casablanca. Jilly is so much in love with you. I know it's been hard for her to find a way to get your attention. If she were to know about that one night, I think she would be too discouraged to try to stay in the game. And that would be very, very sad."

I knew that Jilly liked me, was fond of me, but Simcha's words came as a surprise. I sat down on a stair, wondering how to reply.

"Why did you not take that second step?" she asked.

"Two reasons, I think," I said. "First, you now know from what I could tell you about Pierre that I'm mixed up with things that can be dangerous. I've tried to keep you out of them as much as possible because I never knew how much longer you'd be here and who would find out what about my activities . . .

and how you would be associated with them. I thought of you in a dungeon and myself safe and comfortable in America."

She sat down on a stair above me. "Is that why," she said, "you made me stay at *Chez Dimitri* when you and Jilly interviewed the Commandant at the Legion Post?"

"Yes," I said. I moved up to where I could sit and hold her right hand in both of mine. "Before you think too highly of me," I said, "I want you to hear my second reason for stopping after that night. I am Catholic, not in a strongly religious sense anymore, but my values and sense of morality is still Catholic. If I have one night with a woman and leave it there, it shows a weakness but not a serious character flaw. If I follow up it is all right if I have romantic affections for this woman and could seriously consider marrying her. If I follow up with only sex as the purpose, I have a serious character flaw."

She looked at me as though she wondered where our relationship was among all this Catholic moral reasoning.

"Where you were in all of this?" I said.

She nodded.

"I was sent to Syracuse University by the Air Force," I said, "for a year. One of the girls I dated there was Jewish. She was in a Jewish sorority. Jews were not welcomed in sororities there, so the Jewish girls formed one of their own. Her name was Sally. I never tried to sleep with her because I knew it would be too big a blow to my family were I to get serious with a Jewish girl."

She removed her hand from mine. I felt that I was losing something. I thought of grabbing it back and saying something like, "No, no I didn't truly mean any of that. I need you more than I need to know that I'm keeping you safe or my family from being unhappy." But I didn't say anything or make a gesture to stop her from standing and going back up the stairs.

The first time I saw Simcha, she was descending that staircase in denims and a light blue diaphanous caftan buttoned in the front with only one button. Her navel was exposed as was much of the rest of her. She walked with a carefree casualness, her firm upraising breasts bouncing suggestively with each step. She wore her long dark hair parted in the middle so that it fell forward framing a small brown face with full lips and high cheekbones. She came down the stairs and entered the room with an air of easy nonchalance, as though she might just keep on going right past us.

This time she was an entirely different vision. There was despair in each heavy step upwards. Yet, when she got to the landing she turned, her playful spirit seemed aroused. She waved her right hand, palm upwards, in a dramatic flourish, and said, *"Au revoir, mon editor."*

It was the last time I saw Simcha, except for her appearances in my dreams where she is charming the Nouasseur gate guards, sprightly coming down a curving staircase, or bouncing with Jilly on a cot singing "Lover", or in some other way enchanting me. Any visit from her was entirely welcome.

Aloutababa was blowing through a lacy soaped cloth, covering me with white frothy bubbles while Si Fulan was telling me we had achieved a great victory as he click-clacked on his thinking stool in the *hammam*.

"Algeria has exploded," said Fulan. "There is no turning back. The French will need all of their military resources and political support in Paris to deal with Algeria. They will give up trying to hold on to Morocco and Tunisia. I hear this everywhere, especially from the French. Mohammed V is coming home."

"That's good," I said. "You're in reach of your goals, but I think the American goals, to keep their bases here, don't look very good right now. I heard about Mohammed V coming home and that he'd probably be the King of an independent Morocco soon. I also heard that he says he will send the Americans home."

"No, no, no,", he protested loudly, "Your goals will be fully realized."

I looked at him, suspiciously. Aloutababa sponged the froth from my face and body with a seductive counter-clockwise stroke.

"We," declared Fulan, "we *Istiqlal* have agreed with Mohammed V that when he returns—it's only a matter of months now—the Americans will be invited to maintain their bases here."

"I heard he would demand their removal," I said.

"You won't hear that anymore," said Fulan. "*Istiqlal* will have a big power position in the new Moroccan government. Without *Istiqlal* nothing Mohammed V wants to accomplish can be accomplished. We have told Mohammed V he will need the American forces to discourage any future French attempts to retake Morocco. Also," Fulan said sarcastically, "Mohammed number five had no idea of how much the Americans are willing to pay for the bases."

"Yes," I said, starting to share his enthusiasm. "Plus, an independent Morocco will qualify as an underdeveloped country and qualify for American development aid programs." Then I stopped and thought as Hedgeworth would, and asked him, "Why does *Istiqlal* take such a keen interest in keeping American forces in Morocco? Did we do that good a job helping you? Is this a sense of obligation? Gratitude?" I tried to say it with the tone of dubiousness that Hedgeworth might use.

Fulan said, "Yes, partially. But also because we want American backing when we revolt against Mohammed V."

He said it so casually that I thought I misunderstood. "Do you mean you want our support if there's any kind of rebellion against Mohammed V, as, say, by Berbers?"

"No, I said that *Istiqlal* will revolt against him. Him, his royal majesty, Mohammed V."

I was confused and probably showed it because he said, "You don't know much about Mohammed V and the Moroccans. You think that because the people were so aroused when the French abused him he was a popular leader. The people were aroused because their spiritual leader, their link with Allah, was taken away from them. This left them at the mercy of evil spirits. Allah would not be able to intervene because he had no earthly instrument through whom to act."

"So, you're telling me that he was not loved as the temporal leader?"

"He was not at all respected as a temporal leader," said Fulan. "He is a cruel, greedy man who had the eyes gouged out of anyone in the Palace who so much as looked at one of his concubines rather than stop at the quick glance necessary to do his job. No one knows how many he fed to his twenty lions for going further."

"What will be your justification for the rebellion," I said.

"Within a year or two," said Fulan, "everyone in Morocco will know what Mohammed V is. He will rule using the same techniques of violence that the French used. He will probably hire some of the current French policemen and bring in some ex-Nazis to run the dungeons, after putting them in Moroccan uniforms. He will put far more money into maintaining his and his regime's survival than into education and social programs. *Istiqlal* will find ways to make these decisions public. The people will be ready for a change."

"But," I said, "that's all temporal leader stuff. Won't the people feel that no matter how bad it is, things would be worse if they lost their link to Allah?"

"We have a plan for that," said Fulan. "After being treated as they were by the French in the declaration of Arafa as Sultan, the members of the *Oulema* will develop, over time, an alternative way to think about how and when it is consistent with their beliefs for a Sultan to be removed. For example, when El Glaoui and Abd el Hay Kittani approached the *Oulema* about replacing Mohammed V, the *Oulema* took the position that Kittani, though he is a descendent of the Prophet, cannot speak to this because the brotherhood he leads, the *zaouia,* are not recognized as a religious representation of Islam. Influential members of the *Oulema* now say there are sound Koranic reasons for accepting the *Zaouia* as a legitimate representation of Islam. This would provide Kittani with the credentials to be the intermediary between the Moroccan people and Allah."

Aloutababa rinsed my body with warm water flowing softly from a hose.

Nouasseur

I never really thought much about the rhythms and cycles of military life. The military is a schedule with rules. A military base is a place established and equipped to run the schedule and follow the rules. The schedule and rules are sometimes more important than the mission. I should have thought of that before the General told me my time was up, my contract with the Air Force was finished, so I could reenlist for another four years or go back to the States for discharge. I had thought that so long as a person doing well at his position was willing to stay on he could do so. I even imagined they would jump at the chance of extending me for . . . say another four months or so. I was not interested in signing up for another four years.

"Son," said the General, with Glenn Miller's *String of Pearls* in the background and freshly-refilled glasses of pepper vodka in front of us, "in the professional military, we never mistake a mission or a place as a permanent identity. We're just doing this mission at this place because that's the job we have been given for a specific period of time. I think you've made the mistake of thinking the mission, the place is your identity. You're young and you're very competent. We were lucky to have you here with us. Now move on. Get out of the Air Force, grow apple trees in Washington or sign up for another four years and be sent to another place with another mission."

"Is it," I asked him, "that the job I've been doing is being abolished, or have you found someone better than I am to do it."

"That's the second mistake," he said. "You've got your ego so wrapped up in this job that it kills you to think we'd find someone better."

I wanted to change the subject, so I asked him what, if anything, Alain had told us.

"Alain gave us a lot," he said, "and you did it. You brought him out. And the CIA is delighted to have him working for them. By the way, he said nothing about the birdcages to them. Doesn't appear to have caught on to them. At least that's what they told me."

"Funny," I said, "we wish there were no CIA, but because there is we have a place to leave Alain . . . alive and, who knows, maybe useful for our side. It worked out perfectly for me. I didn't want him dead, not even suffering, but I didn't want him loose in Paris ready to profit from his knowledge of what's here in the Q area."

"Do you know whether or not he has that knowledge?" asked the General. "It's all right to talk about it. You've done a good job here partly because you know there are some things you had to keep to yourself."

"No," I said. "What we do know is that he sensed we thought he had something we desperately didn't want him to have. Even if he didn't have it, he was too clever not to play us as though he did. God, do I admire him or Hedgeworth more."

"And we admire you, son," he said. "But that's it, my words of praise will go unrecorded in any way. I have a feeling that you've been with us long enough to know why it must be this way."

I remembered what Hedgeworth had told me, "If you do well, nothing you do will be recorded anyplace. Someone might remember and recommend you for an assignment. That's about as good as it gets for people like you. If you screw up, they'll either hide you or make an example of you, to show how alert they are to incompetence in the ranks. You might end up infamously in columns of investigative journalists or congressional oversight committee hearings. So why should you do it? Because once you're into it everything else is pure boredom."

When I left the General's office, I was confused and disappointed. I had only one idea about what I might do after I left the Air Force. It was to be a foreign correspondent, but I knew that would be a long shot, at best. There were a lot more people with real talent who wanted to be foreign correspondents than there were openings. I trusted and respected the General and Hedgeworth. Yet both of them told me to walk away from what had been my first real job without expectation of using it as a building block for a career.

I thought about Pierre, Simcha, and Jilly. Would I ever understand why Pierre died? He was a noble man with commitments to the Moroccan people that far exceeded those of the terrorists who exploded the fire that burned him to death. Simcha was probably gone forever. I didn't even have a job to jump back into when I returned to the states. How would I ever arrange something as elaborate as a trip to Israel. I hadn't even had the wits to get an address.

And Jilly. Why hadn't I asked her for a real date, two nights before I was to fly back to the states. I had seen her in *The Minaret* office that afternoon. She hugged me as she said "I hope this is not goodbye." I didn't know what to do. I was physically attracted to Jilly, but I didn't do anything about that during the time we had worked together. I feared it would expose my secret role at Nouasseur, that she, being a lot more clever and street-smart than I, would catch on to "strange things" I do and come to the wrong or the right conclusion. Either discovery would leave the General no choice but to get her out of town with a report in her personnel file. But, I said to myself, why not now. I knew I would really enjoy spending some time as good friends rather than as coworkers. I was never as good at answering questions I put to myself as I was at putting them.

I went to *The Minaret* office, opened the door and saw a beam of light coming from under the closed door to the sick room. I turned on the lights over my desk and heard Jilly say in a husky voice, "*Mon editor,* more subtlety, please."

"Are you there in the sick room," I said.

"Right now I have a different name for it," she said. "Come see."

I turned off the lights over my desk, walked over and opened the sick room door. Jilly was sitting in the bed, with the khaki sheet just above the bottoms of her naked breasts. Her clothing and underwear were folded neatly on the floor.

"You'll be gone in a few days," she said. "I really and truly believe that there is something we've wanted to say to one another for a long time. If I'm wrong . . . I'll put my clothes on, crawl out of here, and be red-faced for the rest of my bloody life. . . . But I just had to take the chance."

"Jilly," I said, "this has been the worst day of my life." I sat down on the edge of the bed." "But as of this moment it's getting a lot better."

We spent most of the next day going through her boxes of photos, picking out those we thought would be appropriate for her book of pictures to go with Edith Wharton's essay on Morocco. She was curious about what I would be doing a few months from now in the States.

"So am I," I said. "I've not made any plans. I thought they'd ask me to stay on here for another six months or so. They're inflexible. Reenlist for another four years and wait for an assignment which might be here doing what I'm doing or might be someplace else doing a different kind of job."

Jilly saw me off at the MAC Terminal the next morning. I was scheduled to leave in an hour for a one-day stopover in The Azores, en route to the States. We were standing on the tarmac in front of the Operations Office, my duffle bag flopped between us, when she said, "Oh, c'mon guv, what *is* that over there." She was pointing at the Q Area. In the morning sun, from that spot, the Q area emerged from the pre-dawn as a block of pure white, placid buildings.

"Could I just give you a farewell hug instead?" I said. I thought I sensed her meaning. There was something about the Q Area that affected everyone, though in different ways. Jilly knew that . . . that if people like myself who knew something about it strained to keep it secret, it must be something of importance, at least to them. She also knew that people like myself would never tell her why it was important. So, when she said "What *is* that over there?" she meant what is there between us that you won't explain for just the two of us.

"This may be your last chance," she added.

My last chance at what, I wondered.

She read my mind and followed up. "Your last chance at seeing that if you want to have a decent relationship with anyone you can't keep a secret from that person when they know the secret exists, know they look at its disguise just about every day, and know that the secret affects their life, perhaps in a major way."

At first it seemed to me that Jilly was being short-sighted and selfish. She was saying that I couldn't keep her if I didn't blab away secrets. Then I thought back to Ralph Tennon, who had been the closest friend I made in the Air Force. Ralph was in the Security Service's class ahead of mine at Syracuse University. He was a decent jazz trumpet player whom I met at a jazz session in a local Syracuse bar. We started playing together with other Security Service musicians. We became very close and knew more about one another than we did about anyone else. He was tall and thin, had bright yellow hair always cut short, and spoke with a pronounced Bronx accent; yes, in Russian as well.

Ralph graduated. We had a farewell party with two Syracuse sorority girls, and he returned to Security Service Headquarters at Brooks Air Force Base. We had promised to stay in touch, but he did not answer my letters or return my phone calls.

About six weeks after Ralph left, it was my turn to graduate and fly down to Brooks. The first official message given me was by an Air Force Colonel. My class had been gathered in a dormitory, and he was the speaker.

He said that we would now enter a two months training program in use of technical equipment and encryption. That is all we would be told, he said. He stressed the demand for secrecy. "You talk to no one about your work other than the members of your team. Not other members of Security Service, not your wife, not your girlfriend, not your sister, or your parents. You can drop out of the program now. If you do not you will be subject to time in a Federal Prison if you talk about your work with anyone other than members of your team. Don't laugh this one off, airmen. This is the real thing."

I should have been heeding his warning, but I was relieved to hear it because this explained why Ralph had not responded to my attempts at communicating.

Though we were banned from talking about our work with anyone other than a member of our team, Security Service men at Brooks mingled in barracks and the chow hall, at base social events, and at clubs. I ran into Ralph, unsurprisingly, at an impromptu jazz session in the O Club. When the music stopped, I asked him to join me for a beer and chat about our days at Syracuse. We went to his room and drank *Lonestar* beer.

Once we'd exhausted talking memories I got into our futures. I knew that his class had been assigned, but where and to do what I didn't know. He looked at me as though I'd gone too far, as, in his mind, I had.

"You're getting into dangerous water," he said.

"Ralph," I said, "this is you and me. I gave up being a KGB agent after I saw the first paycheck. I'll probably be doing the same thing as you do in six weeks or so. I might even be where you are. I know what the secret is, Ralph, though I might not know the details. We're going to be spread around the world spying electronically on the Russkies. Nothing much more dramatic than that, really."

"You are trying to get me to tell you what is secret," said Ralph. "I think our friendship is over."

Remembering Ralph helped me understand Jilly's concern about secrets and how they could affect our relationship. Keeping secrets can change a person, and sever the bonds on which friendships are intertwined.

The bus arrived. I threw my duffel bag in the baggage hold. Jilly was there in the waiting circle. I kissed her. She gave me her address. "However you feel about me after you're there," she said, "please tell me."

Chapter Sixteen

A bucket seat on a C-130 is not luxury travel. I heard clatter from every nut and bolt of the fuselage, the seat jerked every which way, and the engines sounded ready to cough out at any time. Nonetheless I had good thoughts. Maybe, someday, I'd visit Simcha in Israel. Maybe I'd get together with Jilly in America. I had never made such truly good friendships as I did with both of them. And I found both of them so physically attractive. Maybe I loved Jilly a little more than Simcha. What a nice position to be in, despite the bucket seat. We were climbing, not yet at our level-off position. And then it hit me. I didn't know where I was going. I knew what I was leaving. There was no way I could be returning to that. That didn't exist except back there.

Epilogue

And so it was a fairy tale ending. The Moroccan people achieved independence and the Americans kept the military bases to protect themselves and the Free World safe from the Red Menace.

Well, not exactly. At least not for the Moroccan people.

As Si Fulan predicted, Mohammed V, who became ruler of the independent state of Morocco in 1956, was not a benevolent king who promoted alleviation of the peoples' needs, reduced the mistreatment of prisoners, and gave up a few of the traditional expensive privileges of his position. In 1960 *The New York Times* ran a dispatch from Marvine Howe, who had reported from Morocco since 1956. One sentence revealed the bitter truth: "The arrests and police intimidation are more brutal and lawless than the action of the old colonial regime."

This was not a personality issue. It was built into the culture. In 1961 Mohammed V died and his son, Hassan II was crowned. Hassan preached dedication to the needs of poor Moroccans, but his actions were not consistent with his words. Amid his county's backwardness, Hassan enjoyed a royal life until his death in 1999. He was often seen with the international jet-setters.

It was said that Hassan ran Morocco almost as ruthlessly as Mobutu Seke Soto governed Zaire. Like Mobutu, Hassan crushed independence movements, eliminated political rivals with the help of Western Intelligence services, and lived a life of luxury. According to the French newspaper, *Le Monde*, Hassan's wealth was estimated at $1.6 billion. He owned around twenty palaces and villas in Morocco, and had bulging stock portfolios in the U.S. and Europe. He took in princely sums of money derived from transiting cocaine through Morocco and sales of homegrown cannabis. As for Morocco's 29 million other people, their lives did not go as well. One-third lived in poverty. One-quarter were unemployed. Half could not read or write.

Possibly the culture is changing. Mohammed VI, who succeeded his father, Hassan, as King in 1999, is known as a reformist, has questioned the ideology that Islam is the only basis for justice, and has introduced some progressive changes in public policy. Some call him "the Gorbachev of the Arab world." However, he has not yielded any of his sweeping powers. We will have to wait to see.

Though Si Fulan accurately predicted the corrupt behavior of Mohammed V and Hassan II, he underestimated their survival skills and overestimated the appeal of *Istiqlal's* ideology. *Istiqlal* was not inept. They knew that attacking Allah's spokesman in Morocco would be futile, so they declared opposition to the concept of a royal monarchy as the temporal ruler in Morocco. But their ideology was too Western for the traditional Arab. Consequently, not only did *Istiqlal* fail to take power away from the Moroccan throne, it watched Mohammed V and Hassan II expand both their power and their ability to use that power as they wished.

Violence continued in Morocco after I left. Nouasseur was on constant alert requiring continuing guard duty, especially for Jilly.

She became one of the best planners and managers of guard details at Nouasseur. Her experience driving around the base and her photographer's eye gave her a unique talent for assigning and directing the operations of securing Nouasseur after dark. Even the elite military/civilian police unit that guarded the Q Area worked with her. Periodically she drove to the Q Area gate and discussed with the person in charge of Q guards where she had her guards deployed and what if anything unusual was going on.

One night close to midnight when she was driving to the Q gate a hand grenade was thrown into her jeep causing an explosion that blew her body to pieces. The Q guards were very good at their job and they were close enough to the incident to capture four French enlisted men in blackened faces and camouflage clothing.

Though no one expected this to happen, it did not come as a complete surprise. Young French airmen quartered in the French section at Nouasseur held deep-seated grudges against the American airmen. As they saw it, the Americans had all the luxuries of life while the French had to scrape from the bottom of the barrel. Worse than that was the French military man's feeling of having completely lost face after the Nazis so easily put them to heel. Contrast that with the heroic and gallant characterization of American troops, even in France, and what you had was a situation in which a French airman would have to be a saint to avoid hating an American airman.

The name Si Fulan is a pseudonym for a man who stayed active with *Istiqlal* after independence was granted to Morocco. He was invited to Algeria by the *Front de Libération National* to help them drive the French out. Though he was thoroughly familiar with the French police and military in Morocco, and was a man of rare survival skills, he was killed by French Special Service paratroopers when caught making a bomb in a bathhouse.

T'hami El Glaoui used everything within his considerable grasp to save face when Mohammed V not only returned to Morocco but, the final insult, was named King of the newly independent Kingdom of Morocco. Banquets at his castle had been fabled for years, and they became even more so, attended by European dignitaries such as Winston Churchill, Scott of the Antarctic, and members of the British Royal Family, many of whom went home in awe of the hordes of tribesmen armed with long knives and scimitars, mesmerizing Berber dancing girls, and T'hami's stories of the past and announcements of future events. He told one group that he had personally engineered the return of Mohammed V to Morocco so that he, T'hami, with a jeweled dagger in hand, could slit the King of Morocco's throat in front of the King's favorite concubines.

In between his banquet moments, T'hami invited some French and Swiss doctors to diagnose his increasingly debilitating ailments. It was said that Winston Churchill persuaded him to do this. When he decided to follow Churchill's advice, he had all the medicine men at his castle transported to Marrakech where, he thought, they would be too far away to cast a spell on him.

Two French and three Swiss doctors came to the same conclusion: terminal cancer.

Anwar Sadat became President of Egypt in 1970, received the Nobel Peace Prize in 1978 for reaching a peace agreement with Israel, and was assassinated in 1981 by Muslim fundamentalists for doing that.

When I talked with Sadat in the early 1950s, I did not grasp the full significance of what he said about Sayyid Qutb. Sadat wanted me to understand that Qutb was a formidable enemy to the Western way of life because he denounced the nation-state and rule-of-secular-law as obscenities in Allah's eyes. Attempts to impose these Western forms of government in the Muslim world must be opposed with all forms of violence and sacrifice of holy lives available to the muslims. Qutb accepted only sharia-based communities without government if government meant competition with muslim-based law.

The Egyptian government hung Qutb in 1966. His books and teachings survived, particularly in Riyadh and Kabul where a few schools that attracted elite students emphasized the Qutb Doctrines. Osama Bin Laden attended such a school in Riyadh. When he founded Al Qaeda, he based its doctrine on Qutb's teachings. The faculty of religious law in Kabul regarded itself as a guardian of Qutb's thoughts. The Taliban used Qutb's ideas to form their doctrine.

The last I heard about Simcha was from a professor at an Israeli University who was in the Israeli Army Intelligence reserve. In the 1970s we both were working on a U.S. Agency for International Development political institutions project in the Middle East. He said the woman I described was a Mossad agent working in Lebanon.

Mina Halima is a pseudonym. After the death of Pierre Didier, she left *Le Petite Marocain* to work full time for *Istiqlal*. In the early 1970s I was approached at an international conference in Geneva by a Moroccan who said he was her colleague at a university in Fez. She asked him to say hello to me and wish me well.

Index